MAURIZIO LA CAVA

LEAN PRESENTATION DESIGN

HOW TO CREATE PRESENTATIONS THAT EVERYBODY LOVES

LEAN PRESENTATION DESIGN

HOW TO CREATE PRESENTATIONS THAT EVERYBODY LOVES

Find me on the web at https://mauriziolacava.com
To report errors, please send a note to maurizio@mauriziolacava.com

Editor & Proofreader: Adela Nistor

Book Layout & Cover Designer: Anna Magmel

Notice of Rights

All rights reserved. This book was self-published by the author Maurizio La Cava. No part of this book may be reproduced in any form by any means without the express permission of the author. This includes reprints, excerpts, photocopying, recording, or any future means of reproducing text

Notice of Liability

The information in this book is distributed on an "As Is" basis without warranty. While every precaution has been taken in the preparation of the book, the author shall have any liability to any person or entity with respect to any loss or damage caused or alleged to be caused directly or indirectly by the instructions contained in this book or by the computer software and hardware product described in it

CONTENTS

PREFACE 8

1. PRESENTATIONS ARE EVERYWHERE, AND THEY DON'T WORK — 12
1.1 Presentations: the job of everyone and no one 15
1.2 Why do presentations fail? 20
1.3 In summary 27

2. PRESENTATION DELIVERY – THE ART OF PRESENTING — 28
2.1 The dynamics of a presentation 31
2.2 PowerPoint presenter Mode 34
2.3 The social power of presentations 38
2.4 In summary 41

3. NOT ALL PRESENTATIONS ARE MADE TO BE PRESENTED — 42
3.1 Full vs Slim 47
3.2 Handout – the right compromise 48
3.3 Presentations that do not require a presenter *[case study]* 51
3.4 Audio presentations 54
3.5 In summary 55

4. THE STRUCTURE OF A SUCCESSFUL PRESENTATION — 56
4.1 The three main pillars of a presentation 61
    4.1.1 Fear of public speaking 62
    4.1.2 Ineffective slides 62
    4.1.3 Disconnected information flow 64
4.2 A Canvas to verify that your presentation works 65
4.3 In summary 67

5. A LEAN APPROACH TO PRESENTATIONS — 68
5.1 The tradeoff of presentations: effectiveness vs. efficiency — 70
5.2 A Lean process for presentations — 73
5.3 In summary — 75

6. UNDERSTAND THE AUDIENCE — 76
6.1 In summary — 83

7. WRITE THE STORY — 84
7.1 Storytelling for presentations — 87
    7.1.1 Did you know you had three brains? — 90
    7.1.2 Introduce the problem to catch your audience's attention — 91
    7.1.3 Overcome resistance and build your credibility — 93
    7.1.4 If you want them to do it, you must ask them — 95
7.2 In summary — 99

8. PRINCIPLES OF PERSUASION — 100
8.1 Reciprocity — 102
8.2 Authority — 104
8.3 Consistency — 105
8.4 Appreciation — 106
8.5 Social confirmation — 107
8.6 Scarcity — 109
8.7 Urgency — 111
8.8. Trust — 114
8.9 In summary — 115

9. A STRATEGIC CANVAS TO STRUCTURE THE CONTENT OF PRESENTATIONS — 116
9.1 How to structure a sales presentation — 120
9.2 In summary — 127

10. HOOKING – THE INITIAL HOOKING STRATEGY 128

10.1 Initial hooking strategies, where do we start? 131
       10.1.1 Tell a story 131
       10.1.2 Questions and interaction with the audience 133
       10.1.3 Share a shocking fact 134
       10.1.4 Use famous quotes 135
       10.1.5 Debunk a common belief and provoke the audience 136
       10.1.6 Give life to your message 137
       10.1.7 Exploit historical events 138
       10.1.8 Turn on the audience's imagination 138
       10.1.9 Go straight to the problem 139
       10.1.10 Align expectations 141
       10.1.11 Use a surprising metaphor 142
10.2 Combine multiple strategies 143
10.3 In summary 145

11. VIEW MESSAGES 146

11.1 Forget PowerPoint 149
11.2 The logical flow of messages 150
11.3 The Minimum Viable Product 151
11.4 Sketching 153
11.5 In summary 155

12. CREATE THE PRESENTATION 156

12.1 Noise in presentations 159
12.2 The importance of empty spaces 161
12.3 In summary 163

13. MASTER THE USE OF FONTS 164

13.1 Character architecture 167
13.2 Choosing the right character 170
13.3 How many fonts should you use for a presentation? 171
13.4 In summary 173

14. WORKING WITH IMAGES — 174
14.1 Images in presentations 182
14.2 Combining images and text in slides 185
14.3 The Semantic Resonance of images 190
14.4 In summary 193

15. VECTOR GRAPHICS - ICONS — 194
15.1 Icons in presentations 197
15.2 Where to find icons 199
15.3 Icon formats 204
15.4 In summary 207

16. GIVE COLOR TO YOUR PRESENTATION — 208
16.1 The color wheel 210
16.2 Lights and shadows 212
16.3 Saturation 213
16.4 Focus effect 214
16.5 Temperature 217
16.6 The meaning of colors 218
16.7 The semantic resonance effect. *[Case study]* 222
16.8 Ready-to-use color combinations 226
16.9 Importing colors into PowerPoint 228
16.10 Color combinations - *[Practical case study]* 232
16.11 In summary 233

17. NEURO PRESENTATION DESIGN — 234
17.1 Learn to analyze the context 237
17.2 Reading patterns 239
    17.2.1 Gutenberg Pattern 239
    17.2.3 Z-Pattern 241
    17.2.3 F-Pattern 242
17.3 Reading patterns do not work 243
17.4 In summary 247

18. DESIGN THE EXPERIENCE — 248
18.1 Proximity — 251
18.2 Alignment — 252
18.3 Contrast — 254
18.4 Repetition — 257
18.5 Controls people's eyes — 259
    18.5.1 Look where others look — 259
    18.5.2 Directional objects — 260
18.6 The golden rule of graphic design — 261
18.7 Practical case - the defeat of the bullet point list. *[Case study]* — 264
18.8 In summary — 269

MLC PowerPoint Addin — 270

+ GET YOUR FREE BONUSES! — 272

Bibliography — 274
Sitography — 275
University papers and articles — 276

CHAPTER

PREFACE

A mediocre idea communicated in an effective way could rewrite the future, while a very good idea communicated in a mediocre way would only be another failed and forgotten project.

In our everyday lives we often find ourselves talking about our projects in order to obtain an approval, a financing, a new customer or a new sale.

Whatever the circumstances, we try to influence someone in order to persuade them to act in favor of our idea, using our ability to communicate to change the world around us.

A pitch for a fundraising campaign for a startup, the presentation of a new product launch, an internal corporate conference for the CEO's approval of a cross-functional project on which the team has worked throughout the year, a sales presentation to our customers, presentations for our training activities... These are all common examples.

In today's professional reality, these communications are all too often translated into a presentation with a speaker who talks to an audience. The result (see image)?

Image 1 - Audience affected by death from PowerPoint

It is difficult for an audience like the one represented in the image to adopt and spread your idea to the point of supporting you to have a real impact.

The truth is that in most cases, even if the projects are excellent and the results promising, we end up neglecting the last 100 meters of the marathon of each project, those that separate us from the finish line: communication!

WHAT YOU WILL LEARN IN THIS BOOK

Forget the slides for a second. The goal of a speaker is to convince an audience to adopt his or her idea and trigger a change that leads to action. After all, if everyone was already in agreement, there would be no need to make a presentation. In most cases it would be enough to just print and send a report.

However, a report does not allow to create that emotional connection that a skilled speaker establishes with his or her audience. The ability to create and manage this connection is what allows you to resonate with people and effectively convey your ideas.

Creating the connection is simple: show a slide with an image that can trigger an emotion in the audience. At this point, everyone will be waiting to know how your comment relates to the slide. Now comment and print the message in your audience's memory. If you do it correctly, from that moment on, every time they will think about what you said they will see that image and feel that emotion.

A presentation allows you to enhance communication by combining the cognitive power of images with the disruptive power of human emotions.

In your opinion, what remains most impressed in human memory: images or text? I think we all agree that human beings tend to remember images much better than any other textual content. The brain processes visual content 60,000 times faster than text content. Human beings are naturally predisposed to process images.

According to the "picture superiority effect"[1] phenomenon, visually presented concepts are more likely to be remembered than concepts presented with words in text form.

---

[1] Defeyter, Margaret & Russo, Riccardo & Graham, Pamela. (2009). The picture superiority effect in recognition memory: A developmental study using the response signal procedure. Cognitive Development - COGNITIVE DEVELOP. 24. 265-273. 10.1016/j.cogdev.2009.05.002.

Specifically, the PSE states that when information is presented orally it has a 10% probability of being remembered for the next 3 days; however, if the communication is accompanied by visual content, the probability rises to 65%. The human brain naturally translates words into images so that they are remembered, so if you spare it a few steps, the result of the memorization process will be benefited.

Presentation Design is the discipline that explains how to combine images and text to achieve incisive communication with a real impact on the audience. It is a rich set of guidelines that, if combined in the right way, improve the effectiveness of communication. However, giving a presentation does not necessarily mean preparing slides: in fact, slides are one of the possible supports, as well as documents, slidedocs, press releases or even drawings and sketches. Drawing with a pencil, for example, can be a very effective way to communicate.

> *"There is no more powerful way to prove that we know something well than to draw a simple picture of it. And there is no more powerful way to see hidden solutions than to pick up a pen and draw out the pieces of our problem."*
> **DAN ROAM**

Freehand drawing is often part of everyday life: think of office blackboards with their colored markers and erasers. On many occasions they are useful to simplify complex concepts, to summarize a meeting and make it easier for the audience to remember the highlights of the day or even to visualize a concept or a scheme and trigger an interaction, or debate with those present in order to contribute to the development of an idea or the resolution of a problem.

The speaker has the task of choosing the best way to support his or her communication according to the specific needs: goal, topic, audience, duration of the presentation, etc.

Mastery in the use of presentation techniques affects the success or failure of your projects. Dexterity is not easy, and it requires experience.

In this book I will show you a rich set of tips from the world of communication, marketing and design with the goal of enhancing your ability to create presentations that influence the audience.

It is often thought that a beautiful presentation is necessarily the work of the long and wise work of a designer. You will learn how to achieve extraordinary and graphically flawless results in the shortest possible time without the need for any creative skills.

Preparing a presentation is a long process that takes time and energy; if not approached correctly even the most trivial choice of a color scheme or a simple layout can result in a huge waste of time and a mediocre result.

However, presenting a mediocre result to an audience means losing every possibility to create the human and emotional connection that is fundamental for the audience to listen to you and receive your message.

As a result, the audience will waste their time trying to follow an unintuitive presentation, which will cause an additional waste of time and energy. In short, a badly designed presentation takes a long time to be realized and processed and does not achieve the desired result.

In this book you will learn that you don't need to be a designer to create graphically exceptional presentations, you only need to apply the right techniques.

In other words, in this book you won't find a list of rules to follow closely to achieve the ultimate presentation, but you will discover, step by step, Lean Presentation Design by learning to combine innovative techniques in order to solve complex layouts and obtain brilliant presentations according to a logical and non-creative approach.

HOW TO MAKE THE MOST OF THIS BOOK

To create an effective presentation, you will need to become skilled both in the communication strategy and in the efficient creation of your slides.

The set of strategic aspects related to the Lean methodologies applied to presentations and all the techniques of rapid slide creation will allow you to make a significant leap in quality in creating effective presentations quickly.

In this book you will find all the strategic aspects of a structured approach to presentations.

So where can you find all the tricks and techniques to become super-fast?

In parallel to the book, I have created the official technical guide to Lean Presentation Design, available online on my website - https://mauriziolacava.com/the-official-guide-to-lean-presentation-design/.

As I take you on this journey, I will refer to specific chapters of the online technical guide to show you advanced techniques not presented in the book.

In short, you can consider the online technical guide as a practical complement to this book.

In addition, the online guide is constantly being updated and expanded.

So, what you are embarking on is a real journey of constant learning and improvement in the way you share your ideas with others through effective presentations created in the blink of an eye!

USEFUL TOOLS

Over the years, designing many presentations and having a dedication to efficiency, I have monitored the way I work and found that some activities were recurring and required long working times on PowerPoint.

I focused on recurring tasks that took longer and invented PowerPoint features that automate these steps and improve their accuracy.

That's how MLC PowerPoint Add-in was born, a PowerPoint extension developed by speakers for speakers.

To this day, the Add-in offers more than 20 exclusive features that I can't do without when I create presentations.

You can try the Add-in for free through this link https:// mauriziolacava.com/my-addin.

CHAPTER

PRESENTATIONS ARE EVERYWHERE, AND THEY DON'T WORK

« DESIGN IS NOT JUST WHAT IT LOOKS LIKE AND FEELS LIKE.

DESIGN IS HOW IT WORKS »

STEVE JOBS

The world seems to have gone mad for presentations. There are presentations everywhere: in every meeting, in every small or big event, in every school or university class, literally in every occasion.

Have you noticed it too, have you been involved in this revolution?

Think about it for a moment and be honest with yourself.

How much time do you spend preparing presentations for your work or personal projects?

What's the last time you wanted to share your idea with others, convince them to embrace it and act on it?

It could be a pitch presentation for a brilliant business project, a sales presentation for a new business contract or even a summary presentation of a data analysis to support a strategic decision-making activity in the organization you work for.

The purpose of your presentation could be a recommendation to top management or the board so that you can direct the business in the right direction.

You may find yourself giving a presentation to motivate your team or to communicate the business objectives of the year.

In other circumstances, you may also have to give presentations for someone else and depend constantly on their feedback.

You may have the leadership to lead the presentation development process or simply do what you are asked to do.

You may be able to use PowerPoint or Keynote, but are you really able to create effective presentations?

1.1. PRESENTATIONS: THE JOB OF EVERYONE AND NO ONE

It's common to know how to use the tools, perhaps because leaving university you're used to work with them more often than an executive in a company who has had his presentations done for years.

You're quick to find an image, paste it onto the presentation, crop it and prepare the slide by choosing fonts, colors and layouts.

It feels like your passpartout to stand out and prove that you're skilled, but this ability has the potential to turn into a prison very quickly!

This is where all the dynamics in which you find yourself creating and redoing presentations for others come into being. Maybe you don't like a color, the position of a text or the font, so you must get your hands on it and change it all again.

You often ask yourself what impact the modifications that you are asked to make have from a communication effectiveness point of view but, in the end, your stakeholder is always right, so you let the questions pass and execute the requests as quickly as possible.

The real reason you're asked to create presentations is because you're the fastest with the tool and has nothing to do with your ability to create an effective presentation. If you could create effective presentations, you could direct your stakeholders to show them the best way to make their presentations succeed and make a good impression in front of their audience.

Many of us learn how to use software, but few of us really learn how to create effective communication and visualize it through a memorable presentation that remains etched in people's memories.

Last night, while I was thinking of starting to write this new edition of Lean Presentation Design, during a dinner with a friend, a professional in the world of corporate finance, a talk about presentations came up.

She told me about her frustrations every time that, after collecting all the necessary data and finally organizing the reports correctly, she had to prepare the presentation to update the top management.

In particular, she said something that struck me.

She told me that she spends much more time preparing the presentation of her work than producing the content.

Yet, her job is rather complicated: she must extrapolate, collect and merge data to identify relevant insights. The search may also not immediately yield relevant results and therefore take a long time.

So, although producing the content of the presentation is a complex task, preparing the presentation takes even longer.

Strange?

If you think about it, it is absolutely normal.

After all, creating presentations is an ability, like all others.

Would you ever get involved in a technical process of extrapolating data from a company management system in order to identify relevant insights to give recommendations to top management?

Let's face it, it's just an example, I might even ask you if you'd like to improvise as an analyst of the performance of the space shuttle fuel to ensure its safety during the next launch.

Once again, it's just an example, it obviously depends on your occupation.

Let's say that it would not be appropriate to take responsibility by improvising in the use of a skill that you do not have.

Yet, everyone creates presentations without really knowing the tool (trust me, there are few who really know PowerPoint) or what it really means to design an effective presentation.

The result?

An awful lot of ineffective presentations and brilliant ideas that go completely unnoticed.

Image 1 - Most presentations are ineffective

When was the last time you found yourself at a very boring presentation during which you had difficulty following the speaker?

Maybe you are at an event whose theme could even interest you, but you begin to feel a sensation of numbness, of fatigue in focusing on what they say, and you suddenly find yourself scrolling your Instagram feed.

You wonder how it is possible, since you are interested in the topic, so you go back to focusing on the words of the speaker.

Nothing: you lose him after a while, you can't follow, you ask yourself why he's making it so long when he could go straight to the point and tell you what you really want to know.

You look around and notice that a person, a few rows behind you, is literally sleeping, while many others have opted to use their smartphones to do something else.

Then you look at the speaker who, completely insensitive to the situation, proceeds undaunted in his speech, as if he were speaking to himself.

At that point you realize that he's actually talking to himself and you wish that something like this never happens to you when you're in his place.

But in your opinion, is the speaker really insensitive, isn't he doing his best to give that presentation?

Perhaps his best is not enough, and he has created yet another ineffective presentation that will end up being forgotten by the audience.

What will you remember of that speaker?
Probably not a lot!

So, the next time he gives a presentation, you won't be happy to attend. There are times when you can choose and times when you will be forced to participate.

In any case, a failed presentation will affect your expectations of that speaker forever.

Now try to imagine a brilliant speaker, who presents interesting ideas in an engaging way, interests you, makes you feel part of the presentation and gets his key messages imprinted on you.

Sometimes, the messages of a presentation can remain imprinted for a long time and perhaps bear fruit even after a few years.

Have you ever thought that presentations could have a long-term resonance?

A few days ago, while I was walking around the Termini station in Rome, I got an interesting phone call.

A young film maker who launched a fascinating video-podcast program explained to me that he would like to interview me to give a joint talk in his channel because the theme of the presentations is of interest to his audience.

Spontaneously, I asked him how he found me, expecting an answer related to the website or some book I wrote, but the answer was totally different!

In fact, the interviewer told me that more than a year ago he had attended my launch presentation of my latest book.

On that occasion, we had not been able to get to know each other but, recently, when he decided to create a discussion about presentations, I came to his mind.

The thing that struck me was that he really remembered the details of my presentation after more than a year, and that had prompted him to act and contact me.

Presentations leave their mark, both positively and negatively.

Creating presentations has become part of everyone's work. Creating an ineffective presentation is the same as doing a bad job.

How does it look if you do a bad job?

Let's imagine you oversee marketing; you have just carried out a competition analysis and calculated all the market shares to show in order to propose the introduction strategy of a new product on the market.

On the day of the presentation you introduce your work, start the presentation, show the context, introduce the new product and finally get to the interesting part: the market share analysis, the focus of the presentation.

While you are presenting the results of your calculations, you see that someone is twisting their nose revealing some uncertainty. You stop, and like a good speaker you immediately respond to the need for clarification that you sensed in your audience, asking if something was unclear.

In response, you are explained that the market shares shown are wrong for a trivial miscalculation.

That would be embarrassing!

From that moment on, you will be remembered as the one who miscalculated the market shares and the next time you face the audience on a similar topic, even if it was just an oversight, people will feel the need to verify.

Of course, oversights happen to everyone and with work and dedication you can make up for them, but you have to be careful. Your audience's trust is too precious an asset, and you can't risk losing it. It takes a lot of sacrifice to build it and a moment to lose it forever.

In short, if you do a bad job your personal brand will suffer the consequences, whether you work within an organization or directly on the market, in case you are self-employed. Have you ever thought that the same thing could happen with presentations?

In fact, it does happen, but it's even more serious.

If you fail to engage the audience and be persuasive when you present your ideas, the result will be poor, regardless of the value of your ideas.

Also, because of the "halo" effect, you will automatically be perceived as less capable than you might be.
Giving a poor presentation is like showing up at a wedding in a stained outfit!

Are you wondering what the "halo" effect is?

Halo effect (sometimes called the halo error) is the tendency for positive impressions of a person, company, brand or product in one area to positively influence one's opinion or feelings in other areas.[1]

I am telling you that, because of the halo effect, if you are not able to give an effective presentation of your work, your audience will think that you are not even able to do your work.

We both know that if you want to pursue a career in the company or if you want to make your way by acquiring new customers, you will need to be able to be appreciated for the value of your ideas.

But how can you be appreciated if you are not able to communicate them in an effective and engaging way?
How do you plan to make a difference if each presentation goes unnoticed?

But this is not just your problem.

Presentations are used by anyone, in any industry, to spread people's ideas and persuade others to act.

Unfortunately, presentations often fail, taking the ideas they were supposed to bring to life into the abyss.

Have you ever wondered what the cost of a failed presentation is?

Think about it for a moment.

———

[1] https://en.wikipedia.org/wiki/Halo_effect

Presentations are often the subject of important decisions that have a real impact on people, business and organizations.

How important are your presentations?

They may be important for the business or project you are presenting, and they may be important for you, for your career.

What is the cost of failing your presentation?

What happens if your message is not understood, your recommendations are not accepted, and your next presentation ends up in oblivion like all the others? What is the cost of failure of an investor pitch for a startup that urgently needs to raise finance to exist, what is the cost of a failed sale if you are the sales manager of a multinational food company and you want to acquire a new distributor as a channel to reach the final consumer?

The same goes for a team that is selling a consulting project, pitching with other consulting companies, to win the race and acquire the customer.

In such scenarios, among other things, your organization will have made a significant investment in advance to be able to better prepare a good pitch.

So, in addition to the opportunity cost of not acquiring the client, you must add the resources already invested for the preparation of the pitch.

The cost of a failed presentation depends on the impact your decisions have on the business and therefore on the importance of the messages you convey on behalf of your organization.

In turn, the impact of your decisions depends on your role and responsibilities.

An ineffective presentation can cost you a lot of money, negatively affecting your personal branding and your organization.

The ineffectiveness of presentations, however, is not the only problem facing the world of speakers.

In fact, creating presentations costs a lot of time, and you often end up working beyond office hours, on weekends or possibly on holidays.

When's the last time you agreed to finalize a presentation while traveling on a plane, train or even in the subway, rather than relax and read a good book?

Image 2 - Working beyond office hours to finish a presentation

Personally, I don't think anyone likes spending the weekend creating the presentation for the Monday morning meeting.

In short, these presentations generate a huge workload, they make you work beyond office hours, and despite all this dedication they are often ineffective.

And it doesn't end here!

In fact, not only you'll waste a lot of time preparing an ineffective presentation, but you will also waste the time of all those who have come to listen to you without understanding it.

If you are lucky and people are really interested, they will ask you for slides at the end of the event so they can read them on their own and understand them.

In that case, what was the point of investing all that time in preparing a presentation and attending a meeting if, in the end, it would have been enough to send the presentation by e-mail and be available for any questions?

This is just one of many examples of failed presentations, but there are many more.

1.2. WHY DO PRESENTATIONS FAIL?

We agree that presentations take a long time to produce and often do not work.

I'm sure that you too have experienced some really boring presentations from which you haven't been able to extract any value.

To understand how to design an effective presentation within a reasonable time frame, you need to understand why presentations fail.

What comes to mind when I say the word: presentation?

Think about it for a moment, try to visualize it.

There were probably slides in the image your brain just rebuilt.

When we talk about presentations, we are used to immediately think about slides, and when we think about slides, we often think about PowerPoint.

There are many different tools for creating presentations, but PowerPoint is certainly the most widely used one.

Today, 25 years after its birth, PowerPoint is part of the children's exams in primary schools since teachers believe that knowledge of this tool is vital to the lives of children at all levels of education and in their careers. Steve Pinker says scientists can no longer lecture without PowerPoint. Masses are made with PowerPoint in churches reconstructed by incorporating large screens. Diplomats use PowerPoint for UN presentations. Businesses and nonprofits of all sizes use PowerPoint.

Newspapers, magazines and books mention PowerPoint without even having to explain what it is. In a world of 7 billion people, Microsoft says PowerPoint is installed on more than a billion computers.[2]

PowerPoint is a very powerful tool, not always easy to use, but certainly accessible to everyone, perfect for most of the occasions in which it is used.

Thanks to this tool, now a dominant part of the Office Suite, it is possible to give life to complex, media-rich presentations, which can then be presented or distributed for reading.

However, it is reductive to think of presentations only as a set of slides.

Presentations are, first of all, a dialogue between people. Each presentation is a moment for sharing your ideas with a predefined objective.

"Ideas are the tool that gives, to every human being, the power to change the world".[3]

Think about it for a second.

Every great revolution that has changed the course of history or even every launch of new products and disruptive technologies that have changed the habits of mankind comes from the same seed: an idea.

They may have been brilliant ideas, but what really made the difference was the ability of the creator to communicate them to others so that they could understand, adopt and share them, thus triggering a change.

Because you can have the most brilliant idea of this world, but if you don't learn to communicate it effectively, it will die within you.

---

2 Sweating Bullets, Robert Gaskins, PowerPoint creator
3 Nancy Duarte, the secret of great talks

Yet, you focus more on having nice slides than effective communication.

When the time comes to create a presentation, the most common reaction is to launch PowerPoint and start drawing slides.

Usually we start from a collection of slides that can be recycled. Slides of other presentations that have already been made and which just need to be modified a bit to be reused.

At this point begins the work of adaptation and embellishment in which an indecipherable amount of time is lost.

Here's how you can get rid of alignments, distributions, object groups, fonts, font sizes, titles, slide schemes, colors and more with PowerPoint.

How much time do you spend embellishing your slides?

Every time you create a presentation, you take hundreds of decisions that affect the experience you're designing for your audience, slide after slide.

The problem is that you rarely design the experience for the end user (the audience) in a conscious way.

How much time do you waste choosing colors that don't work together, a font you like but don't really know how effective it is, adding transitions and animations that only guarantee a seasick effect to the audience thinking that your presentation is more attractive?

By doing so, you invest your time in embellishing presentations that are ultimately ineffective.

But creativity isn't for everyone, and often, the speaker isn't necessarily a designer with a creative background.

The presentations are created by managers, entrepreneurs, doctors, by you and me, by everybody!

How to quickly take communication and design decisions that ensure the effectiveness of the result?

The challenge is to choose the right font, color palette, object placement and layout for each type of content according to the target audience correctly, quickly and from the beginning.

We both know that these are the choices that require the greatest investment of time. The choices that lead to the display of your messages.

Often, you are faced with your own indecision, you do not know which font you like best, which is the best position for a text or a shape. You are not sure which image to use and then you opt to use several of them, but they do not fit on the slide and then you start shrinking them.

The shrunk images all have different sizes, and in resizing them, you make efforts to make them similar.

In the end, you look at the slide and you're not convinced, you don't like it.

Unfortunately, however, you've just spent 20 minutes of your time embellishing this slide, so you'll settle for it and move on.

Regardless of whether you find yourself in this way of proceeding, there is one thing I am certain of, and that is the rationale with which you normally make these decisions.

In fact, these are decisions taken in a purely creative way.

Think about it.

The positioning of an object in a specific part of the slide, the size of the text, the font, the colors and also the general layout of the slide are the result of a series of tests in order to understand if you would like the result.

Let's say you created a slide that you actually like.

Now, if I asked you if that slide was objectively effective for your audience, what would you tell me?

See, it doesn't mean that what you like is necessarily the most effective solution for your audience as well, and it doesn't mean that what someone likes in the audience is the most effective solution for everyone.

What am I suggesting?

That beauty is subjective.

You should design for people, not for yourself.

"Designers create solutions that improve people's quality of life" [4]

A presentation is effective if it works for the people you are communicating to.

The starting point for a good presentation should be the people who will receive it.

Pursuing beauty is an unnecessary waste of time, since it requires a huge investment of time to achieve a solution that is subjectively the best.

I have written subjectively the best.

This means that you are wasting your time creating slides that you think are beautiful, but you are not able to determine if they are objectively effective for your audience.

Let me give you an example to better explain myself.

Have you ever seen this image before?

Image 3 - An innovative packaging for pasta by N. Konkin

This is the rendering of an innovative packaging of pasta.

Do you like it?

People generally respond positively, but there's always someone who doesn't like it.

This is normal!

In fact, it's absolutely legitimate that they like it or don't like it, everyone has their own personal taste. However, the intent of this redesign was not to embellish an existing object, but to create a new packaging that would stand out on the shelf and attract attention before all the others.

Image 4 - A packaging designed to attract attention

---

4 Reynolds G., Presentation Zen: Simple Ideas on Presentation Design and Delivery (2nd Edition) (Voices That Matter), 2011

We can argue indefinitely that it is beautiful or ugly, but it is indisputable that it objectively attracts attention.

That's design!

It is commonly thought that in order to make a presentation effective it is necessary:

1. To embellish the presentation
2. To improve the photos of the slideshow
3. To rewrite and color the texts so that it looks more appealing

Do you find yourself there?

Nothing could be more wrong!

Here is the logical sequence of hypotheses that usually divert us from the objective of effectiveness:

1. I need slides to communicate
2. I need better slides to improve the effectiveness of communication
3. I need beautiful pictures to get the most beautiful slides, so I need a designer

Let's see together the definition of communication:

Communication is the process of transmitting a message to others [5]

I read the words "process" and "message", but I don't read the word "slide"! Now, follow me in my reasoning through the definition of design:

Design is a plan for arranging elements in such a way as best to accomplish a particular purpose [6]

So, design does not mean embellishing, but finding the right combination of elements to maximize a specific objective, such as effective communication.

Design is a project-based approach to finding a solution to achieve a goal. The definition of design in the Oxford Dictionary reads as follows:

Do or plan (something) with a specific purpose in mind [7]

With reference to other operating sectors, design is expressed in:

- **Graphic design:** creative research and design of books, advertising prints
- **Town design:** design aimed at giving order and shape to parts of a city, to collective equipment, to public parks
- **Visual design:** the design of images for visual information: signs, symbols, signals
- **Fashion design:** design in the fashion industry, activity of the designer.

The designer listens to the end user and works in a business environment to solve real problems with his or her product. The designer designs according to predefined restrictions and with a specific objective.

In short, the designer is to all intents and purposes a project planner.

You see, there is a huge difference between the world of art and the world of design.

Art pursues absolute beauty; design conceives communication in function of a predefined objective of change for its public.

---

5 dizionari.corriere.it
6 https://quotesondesign.com/charles-eames-2/
7 https://en.oxforddictionaries.com/definition/design

Image 5 - Art vs Design

Making art means having the ability to communicate a different message to everyone, while designing means having the ability to communicate the same message to everyone.

How does this affect the way you work?

Imagine that while you're drawing your next slide, I'm passing by and stop to ask you why you're putting a certain shape around a text.

If the answer is that you think it makes the slide more beautiful, then you're wasting your time.

In short: less is more!

Stop inserting colored boxes, ribbons, decorations, animations and transitions that don't add value to your communication and that you, and only you, think are cute.

To make the process of creating your next presentation more efficient, it is essential that every action you perform brings you closer to the real goal of the presentation itself.

Presentations often aim to achieve a business goal but, in general, it's about persuading an audience to do something they wouldn't have done without that presentation.

Do you understand the power of knowing how to create an effective presentation?

It means having the power to change people's behavior!

To have an impact on your audience and influence people's behavior you need a really effective presentation, and design alone is not enough to achieve this magic.

Of course, having a good design means knowing how to communicate more effectively in a visual way, but presentations are not only made of slides.

Presentations are made by people who exchange ideas during a moment of sharing.

People make a difference, not their slides.

That's why it would make much more sense to start with the people you're preparing the presentation for, and not the slides you already have ready that you can recycle.

Have you ever sailed before?

Imagine you are on the black boat shown in the picture. In your opinion, where does the wind come from in this image?

Image 6 - Creating a presentation is like sailing, you proceed in reverse

If you look closely, you will notice that the flag is flapping in the direction of the boat.

You can then deduce that the wind direction will be towards the boat.

If you are on board and want to reach the buoy with the flag, you can certainly not point the bow straight to the buoy, in the direction of the wind, and hope that the boat moves on.

In fact, it is well known that the sailboat does not sail against the wind.

For this reason, when drawing the course, you will have to identify on the map the point of arrival (the flag), draw a path of zigzag at 45° with respect to the wind to the point where you are.

In practice, you will have to reverse engineer the route according to data constraints.

So, even before you view your messages and launch yourself into adventures on PowerPoint, it's essential to understand the audience you're presenting to.

Based on the audience and the target, you can extrapolate the content to be presented.

You can understand that the ability to summarize and carefully select all the information you really need to get your audience to act is not easy. So, it's an indispensable phase that needs attention.

There's more!

In your opinion, does the order in which you present information in the communication flow have an impact on the effectiveness of communication?

I guess you're already shaking your head and saying yes. We can therefore agree that the order in which the information is presented makes the difference between an effective presentation and one that will not work.

Therefore, effective communication is made up of a wise choice of information that is really relevant to the objective and the order in which it is presented.

All this must then be combined with the ability to visualize the information through a presentation that remains imprinted in the minds of the audience.

A good design will not work in the absence of an effective communication flow, and a good communication flow will not strike attention if not enhanced by an effective design.

There is a world behind every presentation!

You think it's difficult?

I agree, it's not an easy job at all but I'm sure that, with the right approach and new techniques, if you'll ask yourself this question again at the end of this book, you will have changed your mind.

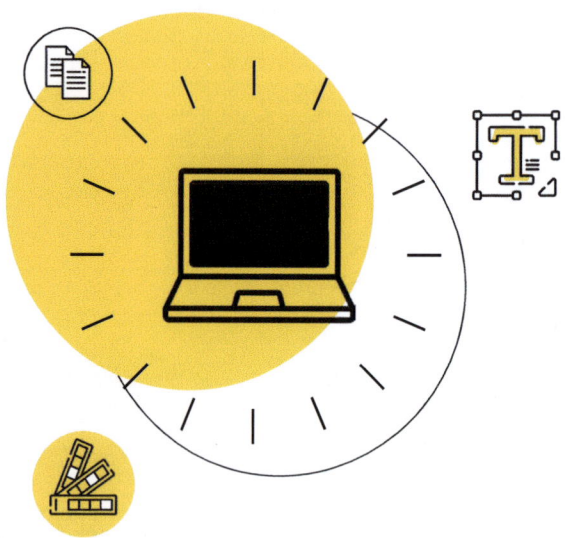

1.3. IN SUMMARY

The world is invaded by presentations, and they are now created for every occasion.

Many people learn the basics of using PowerPoint, but few really know how to create an effective presentation.

In fact, most presentations don't work.

Why?

Mainly because you lose time and concentration in embellishing your slides, rather than implementing a serious communication strategy.

Presentations often start from the slides and not from the identification and understanding of the audience.

You waste time choosing animations and transitions rather than really understanding what change the presentation wants to trigger in people.

Designing means planning according to a specific objective and in accordance with predefined limits.

Slide embellishment is art, not design, and as such an end in itself from the point of view of communicative effectiveness.

CHAPTER

**PRESENTATION DELIVERY –
THE ART OF PRESENTING**

« THE SUCCESS OF YOUR PRESENTATION WILL BE JUDGED NOT BY THE KNOWLEDGE YOU SEND BUT BY WHAT THE LISTENER RECEIVES »

LILLY WALTERS

During a presentation interact a speaker, his slides and an audience. In the previous chapter we said that a presentation is a dialogue between people.

So, the speaker will interact with the audience and, if he is capable and engaging, the audience will interact with him.

But there is more, so follow me.

In fact, the speaker will also interact with his slides.

How?

During the presentation, he will have to synergistically integrate himself in order to enrich his speech with the slides that he will show behind his back.

He will have to be careful so that the presentation never steals the scene and plays the supporting role for which it was designed.

2.1. THE DYNAMICS OF A PRESENTATION

You're preparing the presentation for an upcoming event.

You asked a colleague to give you a slide with details about her work to complete your presentation.

You've finished your part, now you're just missing her slide.

So, you go and ask her if the slide is ready.

She turns around, says it is, and she shows it to you:

Image 1 - Sharing an ineffective slide

I can imagine your expression at the sight of this slide!

But why did you twist your nose, you don't like it?

Yet, this kind of slide is constantly presented during events and corporate meetings.

Imagine being in front of the audience during your presentation and projecting this slide, what do you think will happen?

The first reaction of the audience will be to quickly move their eyes from you to the slide.

Instantly, by clicking the button to change the slide, you will have told all the people in the room to stop looking at you and look at the screen.

The problem is that, at a first glance, no message particularly stands out and then people's eyes will be forced to read the content of the slide, line by line, to find the message that matches what you said.

However, the slide takes a long time to be enjoyed and, while the audience is reading, you will be quickly commenting on the key messages it contains.

People will be disturbed by your voice during the reading because they will not be able to quickly find feedback on what you are saying in this magnum sea of information.

They will strive to keep reading and stop listening to you.

In the meantime, however, you will have finished commenting on the slide and will move on to the next slide. The audience will not be able to read the slide at the speed with which you comment on it and they will see the slide removed from under their noses just as they were making the effort to understand its content.

Let's summarize this experience:

* You showed a slide that completely diverted the attention of the people you were talking to and led them to read
* When you project text onto a slide, people will always try to read its content
* If the text to be read is abundant, it will take more time to read and while reading, people will stop listening to you.

During my company training or university lessons I often enjoy projecting a slide full of text, the content of which is not relevant to what I'm talking about; it is incredible to see how all the participants in the classroom remain hooked by the slide and lose themselves in the reading, despite the slide being about something else.

It doesn't matter what the content of the slide is, if you project text people will immerse themselves in the reading.

Now, let's go back to the moment before you clicked the button to show this terrible slide.

The little button to move the presentation forward generates a transition effect behind you and this naturally attracts people's attention.

This means that, thanks to that remote control, you have the power to tell people when to look at the screen.

Have you already guessed the problem?

You have a button to tell people to stop looking at you and look at the screen, but you don't have another button to let them come back to you.

So how do you get people's eyes back?

Simple, with the design of your slides!

So, if you have a slide that can be enjoyed at a glance and that really reflects what you just said, after your click, people will quickly look at the slide, will find themselves in your message and will return to look at you.

For this to happen, however, it is necessary that the slide never anticipates the content of the presentation but matches exactly what you just said.

The slides follow the speaker, they should never anticipate him.

In fact, if you project a slide, turn around, and read it to remind you of the message you need to communicate, you lose the leadership of the presentation.

What do I mean?

By doing so, you will be unconsciously telling your audience that you don't know the next message of the speech and that you have to watch a slide to continue.

So, people will understand that you are not the one leading the presentation, but your slides are, and you are just following and commenting.

For this reason, every time you show a slide, people will look at the slide and no longer pay attention to you.

If you want to maintain the leadership of your speech and keep people's attention high, you have to be the focus of the presentation.

You must be the one to introduce the next message, the slides will have to follow you and will have to allow the audience to see the key message that you have just communicated.

People should find in the slides what you have already said, never more.

This way you will be the leader of the presentation and you will have people's attention.

Remember, the first golden rule of Lean Presentation Design is:

If you say more than your slides say, you're doing well

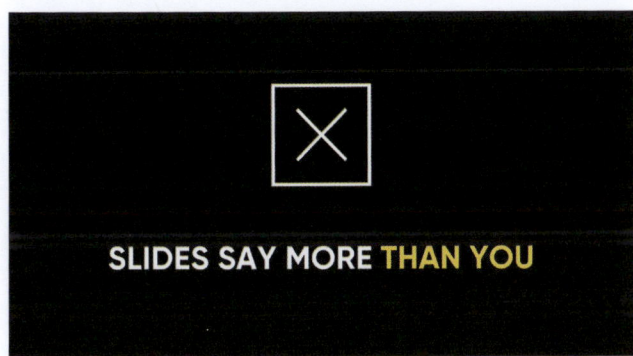

Image 2 - Always say more than your slides

If your slides say more than you do, you have a problem.

Image 3 - Never say less than your slides

You, the speaker, are the one who makes the difference in a presentation, not your slides.

Of course, slides can significantly enhance the effectiveness of your presentation, but they should never be the focus of your audience.

So, a good, well-designed presentation enhances your message, while a wrong presentation may make you lose people's attention and defeat all your communicative effort.

2.2. POWERPOINT PRESENTER MODE

In the previous paragraph I suggested that you present each slide in advance during your speech.

To anticipate each slide before it is projected, however, you must always know what the next slide is, and you must be able to anticipate it in your speech.

This implies the need to perfectly know the flow of the presentation, right?
Actually, that's not really the case.
In fact, if you often have to give various presentations, it would be impossible to memorize the flow of each one and remember it on the day of the event. I will tell you more, it would be a huge effort, and totally useless.

Presenting in public is not a simple matter.
Depending on the person, the context and the importance of the presentation, you may be subject to stress.

If you are making a presentation to the CEO of the organization you work for or if you are presenting your startup to an investor for a strategic financing round, without which you could close your doors, I can imagine that you could be a little stressed on the day of the presentation.

In my opinion, it is absolutely natural to feel stressed when you are giving a presentation in front of people.

In such a stressful situation, do you know what is the first ability that leaves you?
Come on, try to guess.
I'll tell you, your memory!

The typical darkness of "I can't remember what I should say next" that, under stress, can only make the situation worse.

For this reason, learning by heart is never a good idea.
How do you solve the problem?

The tool that I always use during my presentations is PowerPoint's presenter mode.

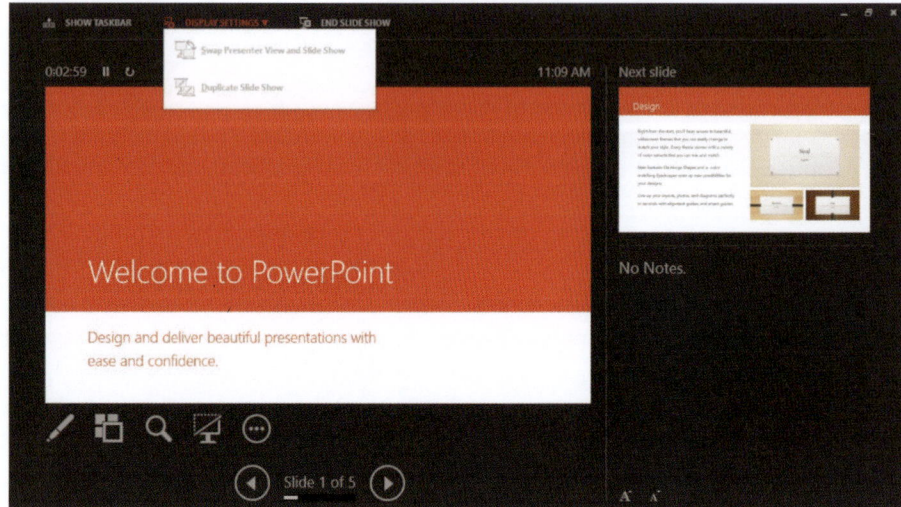

Image 4 PowerPoint presenter mode

PowerPoint's presenter mode allows you to always see the projected slide, which everyone sees, and the following slide (visible only to you).

Of course, it would be nice if you could also see a third slide, in case you want to make some jumps, but for the moment let's be satisfied with what Microsoft offers us, which is already a valuable help for our presentations.

When I give a lesson in a classroom, I often find myself having to make very long presentations, even over entire days.

It would be unthinkable to know by heart all my slides and it would be intolerable to keep turning around to know what I have to say.

For this reason, for me, the presenter mode of PowerPoint is indispensable.
When you start using it, you will also notice that you will be less stressed because you will always have control of the situation.

However, the use of presenter mode places an important constraint on the configuration of the room where you speak.

In fact, logically, the pc will always have to be between you and the audience, and you will be positioned between the PC and the screen.

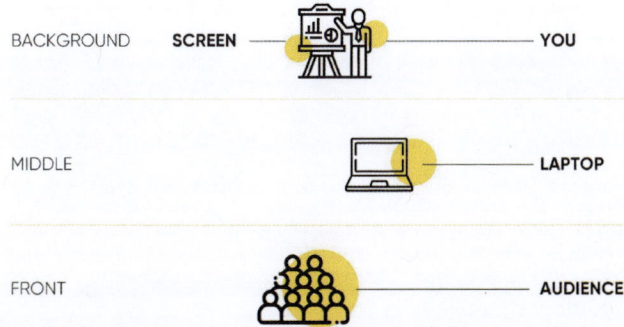

Image 5 - Optimum layout to use the presenter mode

Unfortunately, this configuration is not always possible.

You may have your PC on a podium moved sideways from the area where you are, which would force you to stay away from your audience.

You may have a short HDMI or VGA cable to connect your PC to the screen, as it could be the case when you project on a TV and therefore the cable is directly connected to the TV.

In this case the PC will necessarily have to be behind you and near the TV.

How to handle these situations?

Keep in mind that these are the famous last-minute problems, because you only notice them when you have the opportunity to evaluate the classroom or the room of the event, and it is not always possible to analyze the setup in advance.

Not always being able to know the room configuration, there are some precautions that I always take before giving a presentation in contexts that I do not know.

First of all, I always carry with me at least two wireless presenters to control the presentation remotely.

Why two?

I'll explain in a moment.

In particular, if you have to choose a wireless presenter, I recommend that you choose one that has a volume control button, because it allows you to adjust the audio level of the videos inserted in the presentation without having to reach your laptop every time you project one.

Consider that you may need to move around the room, and maybe the moment you're ready to launch the video you're away from your laptop.

It wouldn't be right to go back to your laptop to turn up the volume and then launch the video, or to launch the video and run to your laptop to adjust the volume because the video is not playing at the right volume.

Why not adjust the volume up first?

Not the best idea.

In fact, when you insert videos into your presentation, you'll find that each one of them has different volumes and that's why you should reserve the possibility to adjust via the wireless presenter.

So, usually I set the audio very low on my PC (e.g. 10%) and put the volume of the speakers in the room at maximum.

This way, I always can turn up the volume from the remote controller in case I have videos that do not sound good.

Returning to the video, since one of the main problems is that the HDMI cable is often short, I always carry with me a flat HDMI cable (for ease of transport in the backpack) at least 10 meters long.

Image 6 - 10m HDMI cable

That's a nice cable, isn't it?

It may be possible that even this is not enough.

At big events, you may have to work with a director. Usually, the director is placed at the back, behind the audience, because he should not be on sight.

In those circumstances the cable does not help, and your computer must be near the director - in the back of the room - behind the audience.

What can you do in these situations?

To ensure maximum flexibility, even in situations like this, I always carry with me a tablet with a screen sharing app installed.

When I get to the event, I connect the tablet to the Wi-Fi and launch Join.me or Blizz to share my laptop screen.

This way, my laptop will work in presenter mode with the projector, and the tablet will show me what's going on my laptop.

Being a small tablet, I can place it where I feel most comfortable in the room.

Usually I place it on sight, in my chair in the front row or on the floor at the sides of the stage (as in the following image).

Image 7 - Tablet placed on a chair in the front row with active presenter mode

That way I always have the presenter mode under my eyes, even if my laptop is away from me.

There are extreme cases in which you are not allowed to use your PC and you are therefore forced to deliver the presentation on a USB stick so that it can be inserted into a PC of the direction that will then be used to project.

In this case, you cannot install join.me on the PC of the director - so the tablet technique will no longer help you.

I think this is the most extreme case.

What can we do?

In these situations, you will have a remote presenter that controls the director's PC, which allows you to progress through the slide stream, but of course you can't see the next one. I place my pc on sight and use a second wireless presenter to scroll the presentation on my pc.

In this way, coordinating the flow, I always know which slide will follow.

Impossible?

Honestly it was not easy at first, but if you know your material well, with a little practice you will learn, and it will become natural.
I cannot deny that I feel like some sort of Jedi master with the double presenter; but it works, and on several occasions this technique has saved me from presenting without presenter mode.

Finally, there are those cases in which the classroom is equipped with Wi-Fi projection mechanisms such as Clickshare.

Image 8 Clickshare - Wi-Fi screen sharing

These diabolical tools prevent you, in most cases, from extending your desktop to the secondary screen and support, by default, only the duplication of the primary screen (that of your PC).

This means that the secondary screen, used for public projection, will be a perfect replica of the primary screen and therefore on the PC you will see the slide, full screen, projected to the audience, not the presenter mode.

There are several Wi-Fi screen sharing systems, but Clickshare is the one I've encountered most often.

For this reason, I did some research and I discovered that there is a solution.

What am I talking about?

I'm talking about a software configuration of the instrument through the download of official accessory drivers, available online for free.

If you're curious about how to configure Clickshare for extended screen sharing, see the guide on my blog: *presenter view – how to enable it using Clickshare*.[1]

In short, PowerPoint's presenter mode gives you the freedom to present without having to constantly turn around to watch the slide, allowing you to conquer and maintain the leadership of your presentation and to focus your attention on the audience.

---

[1] https://mauriziolacava.com/blog

2.3. THE SOCIAL POWER OF PRESENTATIONS

We have said that during a presentation interact a speaker, a slide and an audience. But nowadays, we cannot overlook the constant presence of social networks, even during a presentation.

It is important to know the dynamics of interaction with social networks in order to better control your performance and never lose people's attention.

Have you ever attended a presentation where the presenter begins by sharing his Twitter profile and asking to comment in real time? I also remember cases where someone from the audience photographed the slides just projected and tweeted adding a message that summarized the message of the speaker.

The purpose of this practice, which I often find in English-speaking countries, is to use social channels (in this case Twitter) to reach a much wider audience than the one in the classroom.

I personally disagree with this way of using social networks mainly for two reasons:

1. A person engaged in photographing, tweeting and commenting on your slides during your speech is not listening to you, he is distracted, and you are the one who gave him the opportunity to do so;

2. You can't respond in real time to all the tweets that are being posted, unless you have a dedicated person to take care of them.

Presentations can have a powerful viral effect, but you need to use social networks in the right way. Combining a presentation with social networks in the right way allows you to:

1. Collect e-mails from interested parties among those present.

How many times does it happen that the conference organizer asks you for slides so that they can be distributed to those attending after your presentation?

Or how many times are you asked if you will distribute the slides after your presentation?

If you have decided to distribute your deck, a smart way to do this is to ask the people present to ask for it by writing you an email.

I recently attended the presentation of a digital marketing agency held at an important trade show in Italy.

I remember that the CEO of the agency told in a very simple way all the business benefits that can be achieved by using digital marketing channels such as a good blog, a mailing list, a good combination of social networks, etc.

To give a concrete meaning to the message, he also explained in detail some techniques and showed the results sharing real case studies.

The presentation contained real step-by-step guides that were easy to follow independently in order to apply innovative web marketing techniques.

At the end of the presentation, he said he would send the presentation to anyone who would have requested it by e-mail.

This way, he would selectively collect all e-mails from clients potentially interested in his services, and they would start the dialogue with him by contacting him to request the presentation.

Whether you are selling a service or teaching your audience, this is a very powerful technique to selectively open a dialogue only with those who are really interested.

2. Improve your influence by increasing your number of contacts on LinkedIn, Twitter, Facebook, etc.

In the same way that you collect e-mails, you may ask your audience to connect with you on LinkedIn to request a presentation via message.

This will increase the number of connections/followers on a social network of your choice simply by exchanging the presentation.

Alternatively, you could ask to share a photo of a slide on LinkedIn or Twitter with a comment and tag yourself.

The tag is necessary to receive the notification and to be able to share or comment in order to open a dialogue and give visibility to the post.

This way you will gain followers and give visibility to your content through word of mouth triggered by others. In return, you can distribute the slides.

Be careful, however, that the audience does not lose your speech by spending time photographing your slides, otherwise you create confusion in the room and reduce the level of general attention.

When I use this technique, I usually prepare the audience before the presentation starts and then I ask everyone to interact on a specific slide.

3. Increase the life cycle of the presentation well beyond the day of the speech

If Facebook is the friendship social and LinkedIn is the one for professionals, SlideShare is the presentation social.

SlideShare, founded in 2006, was acquired by LinkedIn in 2012 and has been growing ever since. Today it has 18 million uploads in 40 different categories and is one of the 100 most visited websites in the world.

It is possible to access your presentations from SlideShare, so you could share the presentation on this website before the speech and then refer everyone to the SlideShare channel to see it.

You may also ask to leave a comment or any questions in the comments, and you may ask to share it if it was appreciated. With this technique, you will bring traffic to your SlideShare channel, gain followers and give visibility to your content.

If someone shares the presentation you will have expanded the audience of reference, that will go well beyond the number of people in the room. You will also give life to the presentation in the digital world, and this will increase the life cycle of the slides that otherwise would have died after the speech.

These are just three possible examples of how to take advantage of social channels in order to give your content greater resonance. Use them as a stimulus to create your own strategy or devise new ways to share your presentations online.

The choice of social strategy depends on both your goals and the type of presentation you share.

Although the strategy of sharing the presentation to reach a wider audience than the one in the room is interesting, you should bear in mind that a presentation made to be presented is unlikely to be self-speaking, and may not be interesting if shared on social media.

In this case you may need to develop an alternative solution. Which one?

There are several of them, follow me and I'll tell you about them in the next chapter.

2.4. IN SUMMARY

During a presentation, the speaker interacts with the audience and its slides. If the speaker is engaging, the audience will interact with him.

Slides can steal the leadership of the presentation from the speaker, if not properly designed. When you project text, people will naturally be inclined to read and if they read, they will stop listening to you.

Remember that slides should show the bare minimum and should always recall a message that you, as the speaker, have already launched, without ever anticipating you.

The first golden rule of Lean Presentation Design teaches us that we must always say more about our slides and avoid that they tell more than we do, otherwise they will steal the scene.

Anticipating slides requires preparation.

Learning by heart the flow of the presentation is never a good idea, especially when dealing with a stressful situation, like talking in public.

The PowerPoint presenter mode is therefore a powerful ally.

Always use presenter mode to reduce stress and anticipate messages in the flow of your presentation. Social networks have the power to increase the audience in the room by amplifying your message outside the context in which you presented, and often for longer periods of time.

3

CHAPTER

**NOT ALL PRESENTATIONS
ARE MADE TO BE PRESENTED**

« MAKE
THE PRESENTATION
YOUR AUDIENCE NEEDS »

MAURIZIO LA CAVA

The expression "Lean Presentation" refers to a structured methodology of approach to presentations.

We will deal with this topic in detail when I'll introduce you to the process that rationalizes our approach in graphic-communicative design.

Lean is also a way of visualizing content, minimizing waste and focusing on the essentials.

Creating a Lean presentation means creating clean slides that don't steal audience attention for more than a few seconds.

The result is very visual slides with large images and little text.

In fact, people prefer, by far, to listen to you talking rather than read the umpteenth deck of slides projected during the event.

Image 2 - People don't like to read slides

You can easily deduce a reformulation of the first golden rule of Lean Presentation Design:

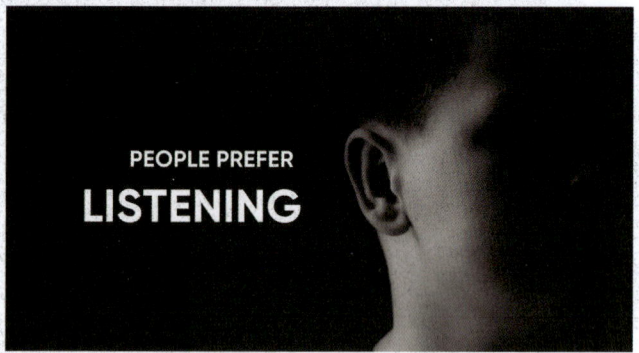

Image 1 - People prefer to listen

Image 3 - Write less and say more during a presentation

The speaker must always say something more than his slides.

Writing less seems to be the simplest solution but is often the most complex one.

Simplifying is not easy.

You know when you want to write a tweet and the limit of characters seems too restrictive, but after trying several times you can finally manage it?

It's the same with slides, only you don't have a character limit.

So, it's up to you!

For this reason, my advice is to try to write in big characters. Doing so will reduce the available space on the presentation, thus encouraging you to write less.

Having less text to read, people will only give a quick look at the slide and then they'll get back to you.

But there's more.

If there's very little content on the slide, you won't be able to read it and you'll be forced to know the speech.

Just as you don't want people to read as you speak, people don't want an unprepared speaker who turns his back on them to read what to say!

I'm advising you to create essential slides, with a few key words, straight to the point.

Easy?

Not at all!

Essential slides are an extreme condensate of often complex messages that require an explanation by the speaker, and the ability to visually synthesize an articulated theme is not to be taken for granted, especially if you are the leader of the project.

In fact, you will always feel as if you are losing essential information and you will always find it hard to exclude it.

During lessons I get asked by the students: "how can I create an all-images-and-key-messages presentation if I want to distribute it after the event, wouldn't it be impossible to understand?" or "how can I use text reduction and message display techniques if the presentation will not be presented but read by my interlocutor?".

Doubt is legitimate.

Often, in a company, presentations are used as real self-speaking documents that are sent by e-mail.

Sometimes, the presentation is just the delivery document of a project. Think, for example, of the consulting companies that, at the end of the project, give you a gigantic presentation that summarizes the work done.

You understand that, if you were to create lean, essential presentations, sending them by e-mail would be of no use, because they would not speak for themselves.

We are therefore talking about *self-standing* vs. not *self-standing* presentations.

Personally, I am not against the use of *self-standing* presentations, which are rich in content and designed to be distributed via e-mail.

I think they are a type of document that meets a real need of people.

So, as long as you reach your communication goal, in my opinion it is absolutely legitimate to present a not *self-standing* deck or send a *self-standing* deck.

N. Duarte clearly distinguishes between documents and presentations, arguing that documents support the reader, while presentations support the speaker.

Personally, I think both are good communication aids, as long as they allow you to achieve your goal - to share your ideas in an effective and engaging way.

After all, PowerPoint is constantly used to create documents that are distributed within the company.

So, it's just a matter of knowing how to optimize them to maximize the result of the recipient's reading experience.

DOCUMENT — Support readers
- Reading
- Informative
- Self standing

PRESENTATION — Support presenters
- Listening
- Disruptive
- Support

Image 4 - Documents vs Presentations [1]

The problem arises when you do not know which side to take, you have little time, and therefore you create a single presentation in an attempt to fulfill both purposes. Remember your grandmother's wise words: "Those who want too much get nothing".

David Rose argues that slides should never be distributed:

> *"Never, never distribute copies of the slides, and certainly not before the presentation. It would be the kiss of death. By definition, slides are supporting material for the presenter... YOU.*
>
> *As such, they should be completely incapable of communicating on their own and would therefore be useless to give to the public, as they would only be an element of distraction. On the other hand, if your slides also communicate on their own and you do not need to be heard, why the hell are you there in front of the audience?"* [2]
>
> **DAVID ROSE**

Slides are visual frames of the story you're going to tell. A story is full of surprises and twists that allow you to keep the attention of the public high. If everyone knows how the story ends, you will lose any chance to surprise and amaze the audience.

But let's keep our feet on the ground, surely the day will come when you will have to distribute a presentation so that the audience can enjoy the content even in your absence.

Usually, you end up creating self-standing presentations, rich in content that are then ineffectively delivered orally.

You find yourself stuck in the middle, between a document and a presentation, producing what we call: *slideument.*

---

3 componenti di una buona comunicazione

- **Condividi qualcosa di rilevante**
  Parlare non è abbastanza. Devi necessariamente avere qualcosa da dire che davvero interessi e ispiri la tua audience. Se sai già che cio che hai da dire non interessa il pubblico allora lascia stare.

- **Condividi nel modo giusto**
  Anche contenuti eccezionali possono finire per essere ignorati se non contestualizzati correttamente. Crea degli esempi, usa case studies e simula scenari vicini al tuo audience che permettano di intuire il messaggio. Sarà più facile per l'audience recepire la comunicazione.

- **Condividi di nuovo**
  Condividi qualcosa che le persone non sappiano già. Questo è il miglior modo per attirare la loro attenzione. Se condividi qualcosa di già sentito o noto finirai col perdere l'attenzione del pubblico.

Image 5 - Example of a slideument

Remember that every time you present a text you will instantly lose people's attention, and regaining it will become more and more difficult as the presentation progresses.

On the other hand, a presentation properly designed to support the speaker will be completely incomprehensible to the reader.

---

1 Slidedoc: https://www.duarte.com/powerpoint-presentations-vs-slidedocs/
2 David Rose, digital entrepreneur and Venture Capitalist.

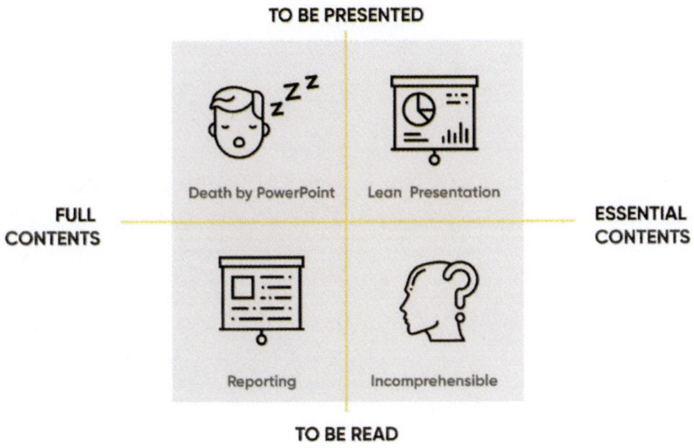

Image 6 - Lean Presentation Design Matrix

According to the Lean Presentation Design matrix, you are operating correctly both in the case of Lean presentations and in the case of reporting.
So, you can present orally with an essential presentation or you can enrich your presentation with content to make it understandable for reading.

However, you do not want to present text-rich slides, nor do you want to risk sending for reading an essential presentation developed to support your performance.

So, how do you satisfy the need to create a presentation that can be both presented and distributed?

In my opinion, it is enough to face the problem with intelligence.

Let's see three techniques to achieve this in the most effective and efficient way, if you never distribute the slides before the presentation.

3.1. FULL VS SLIM

When I design presentations to communicate my clients' projects, I often develop a *full* version and a *slim* version of the same presentation.

This way, the speaker always has the right presentation according to the occasion.

But if you must create it, you can't double the number of presentations to be developed!

The Lean methodologies applied to presentation design provide for the maximization of communicative effectiveness and efficiency in mental resources and time spent.

For this reason, this technique, although absolutely valid and effective, is not the most suitable in case you are developing your own presentation.

3.2. HANDOUT – THE RIGHT COMPROMISE

G. Reynolds suggests the most practical solution of all - and one of my favorites : the handouts.

What is a handout?

Have you ever used the PowerPoint note field under each slide?

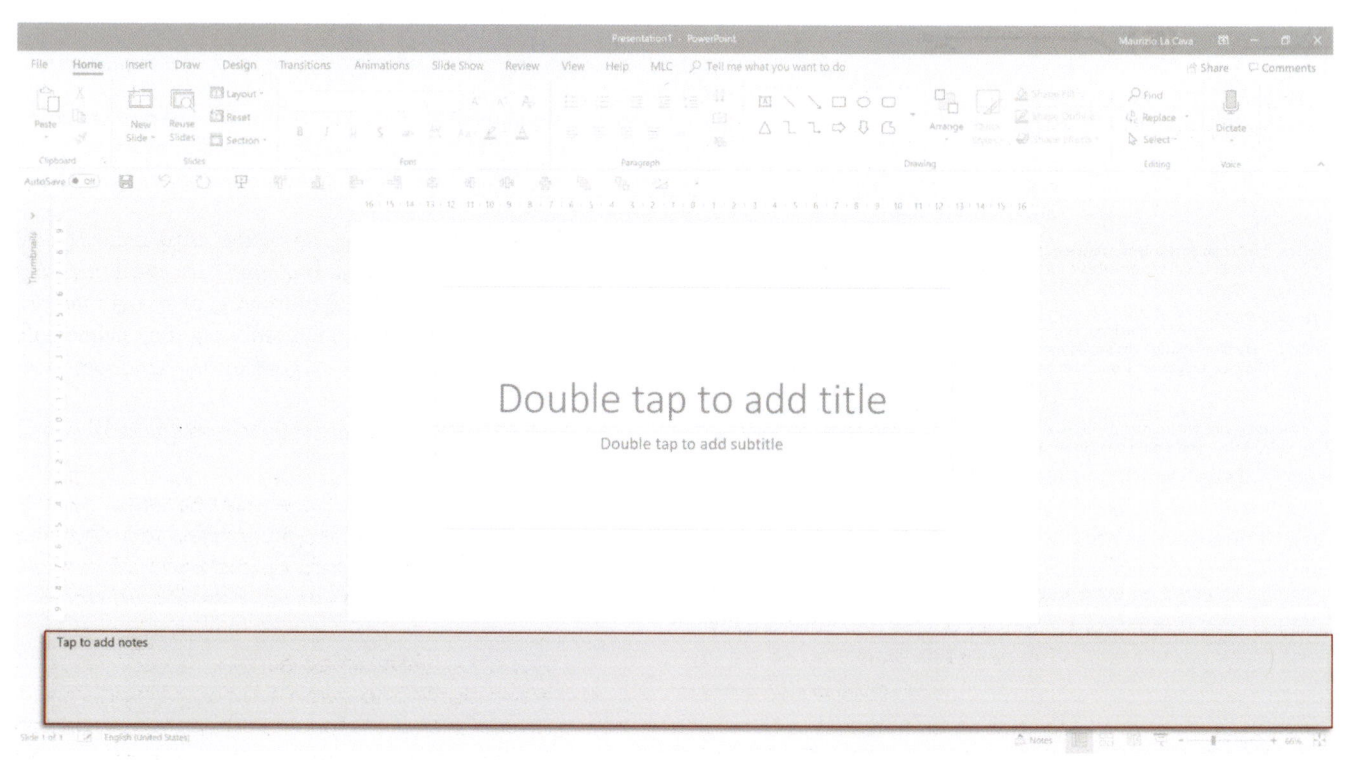

Image 7 - PowerPoint Notes

It is used for the most diverse purposes, but it has a phenomenal function.

In fact, you just have to write the speech you would have made as a speaker in correspondence with a specific slide and then switch to print mode with the notes on the page.

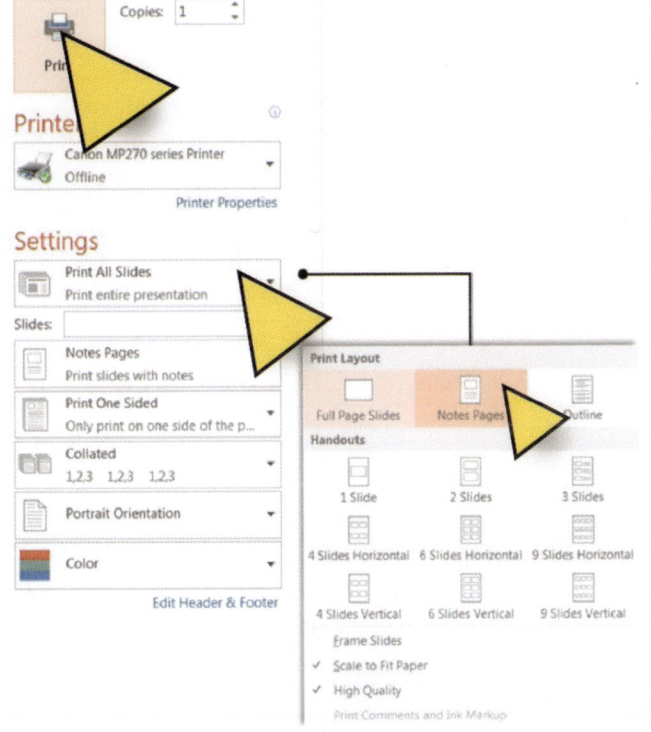

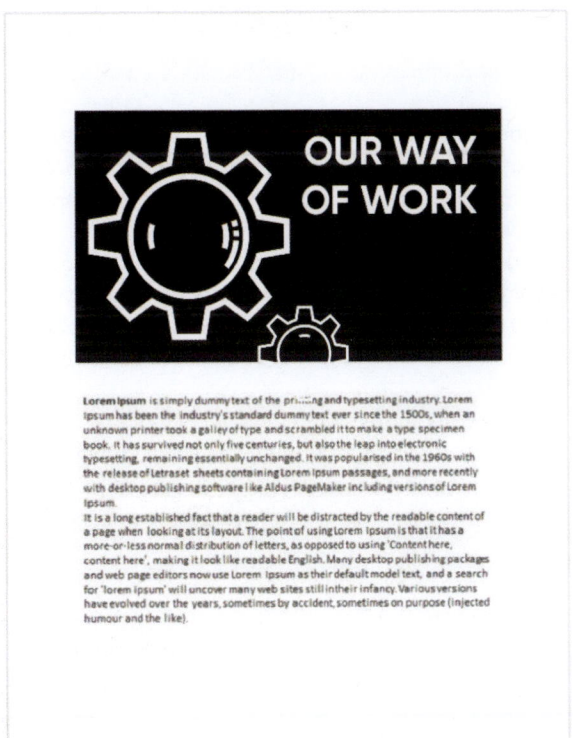

Image 8 - Print with notes on page in PowerPoint

If you print to PDF instead of sending the file to a printer, the result will be a PDF in A4 format with each page containing the slide and explanatory text.
I really like this technique because it generates a document that makes it easier for the reader to remember specific moments of your presentation.

In fact, the reader can easily link the text written in the notes to the slide to which it refers, memorizing the message for a longer time.

In addition, you no longer have to worry about having to create two presentations - one to present and the other to distribute.

You'll create a single presentation that will meet two different needs.

You will notice that writing in notes is very convenient, because you don't have to worry about positioning the text on a slide, formatting it, defining the color, size, position, etc.

This technique well balances the tradeoff between communication effectiveness and realization efficiency.

But be careful not to fall into the typical handout trap that I define "working for silos".

In fact, during a presentation in which you scroll the slides on the screen, your speech acts as a glue between a slide and the other, giving a logical sense to the speech.

Often, we write a comment to the specific slide forgetting that it really is a journey and that, in the absence of the speaker, the notes will connect a slide with the other.

I am proud to mention one of my students who, in creating a presentation with the handout technique, used bold to highlight the last sentence of the notes to point out the connection to the next slide.

See the last sentence in the notes in the following example?

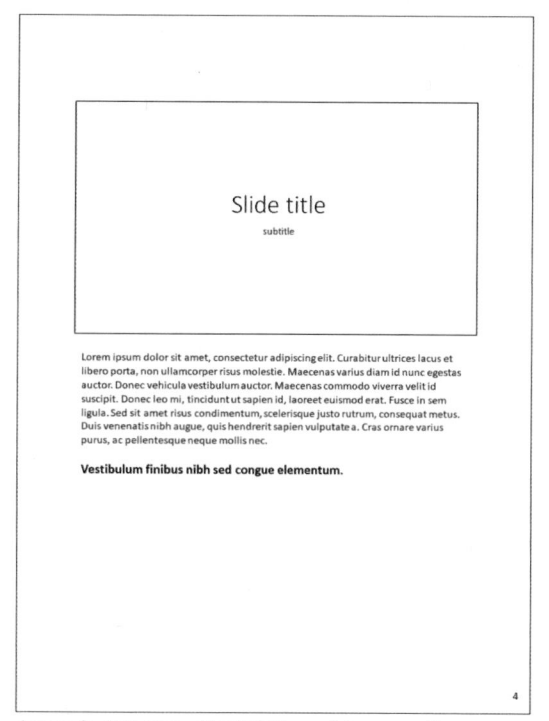

Image 9 - Handout - Highlighting a slide connection

The bold on the connecting sentence allows the reader to follow the conversation thread by jumping between one slide and the next, always having a clear general sense of the presentation.

In short, it is good to use self-standing presentations to share your ideas, as long as they are always designed to optimize the user experience for the final reader.

Later in the book I will share the techniques I use to optimize self-standing presentations that you will typically find in your day-to-day business.

Absolutely avoid presenting yourself with a deck developed to be read, otherwise I can guarantee that you will lose people's attention in record time.

Whether they are self-standing or not self-standing, the important thing is to always use the right presentation according to the context and the needs of the audience.

3.3. CASE STUDY:
PRESENTATIONS THAT DO NOT REQUIRE A PRESENTER

Have you ever read a presentation by Rand Fishking - Wizard of MOZ? If you haven't done so yet, I suggest you browse through one of the more than 50 presentations he shares on his SlideShare channel as soon as you've finished reading the case study (http://www.slideshare.net/randfish).

Moz is a Seattle, Washington, USA-based company that sells inbound marketing software subscriptions and marketing analytics. It was founded by Rand Fishkin and Gillian Muessig in 2004 as a consulting firm and dedicated itself to software development in 2008. The company hosts a website that includes an online community of over a million users worldwide in the world of digital marketing.

If I can recommend one, my favorite is "why content marketing fails" - even though I know it by heart, it excites me every time I read it again.

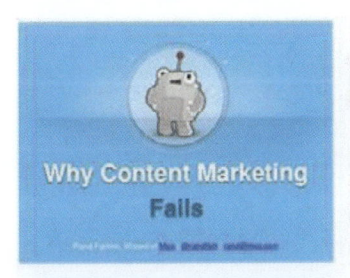

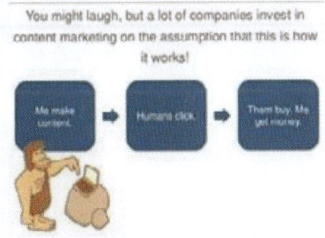

Image 10 - R.Fishkin Content Marketing Presentation

Beyond the more or less technical content, it is interesting to analyze the communicative structure of Rand's presentations.
In fact, they are neither handouts nor text-filled slides, yet they have an incredible social resonance, people love them!

So, I decided to contact Rand and ask him to reveal us his tricks:

Presentations can be used both as a speaker support and as an independent support for the player. I've created more than 50 presentations in the last 5 years, and they worked perfectly in both roles. When I noticed that during my presentations the audience shared (Twitter, Facebook, LinkedIn, direct e-mail, etc.) to another audience ten times larger, I realized that my presentations had to have the ability to play this double role and be educational even in the absence of a stage, a microphone and a presenter.

My main technique is to use descriptive text, often placed at the bottom of slides or in comics, to communicate the key message of the speech I would give on stage. Obviously, I can't include everything, but I do my best to distill the heart of the concept into one or two small sentences. When I present, I don't read the message (I hate it when someone does it while presenting) but I go into detail looking for the emotional connection with the audience.

There are two other techniques I use a lot:

1. I show the text on the slide only when I'm dealing with that point, to prevent the audience from reading and overtaking me as I speak

2. I create presentations with a large number of slides that run very quickly (at least 2 slides every two minutes) so as to keep the level of attention of the audience high and encourage them to get back on the presentation later so that they can review the visuals again (and maybe share them)

In short, Rand distributes the content in a way that keeps each slide focused on a key message.

In doing so, he produces a large number of slides that, however, flow quickly before the reader's eyes.

Moreover, by only showing the key message, the audience can only carefully follow it without ever having the opportunity to anticipate it.

In other words, Rand creates extremely engaging and emotional presentations that show a strong resonance on SlideShare.

Rand is obviously very skilled at giving the presentations two different roles, but I would like you to be careful.

In fact, these are very risky presentations because they distort the very concept of presentation as "support to the presenter".

I remind you that slides are born as a means for the speaker to trigger emotions in the audience using visual content.

If you don't have a deep knowledge of Presentation Design techniques and an innate ability to formalize content in an effective communication architecture, you risk wasting a lot of time and getting a poor result.

Rand has the ability to create a path, almost a split reading distributed through the presentation.

When you scroll through his presentations, it seems as if he is there to talk to you. This technique, if used correctly, allows to give the slides the double role of support to the presenter and support to the reader.

Have you ever seen Airbnb's pitch to investors?

The presentation introduced the problem/solution pair just after the opening slide with the following slides:

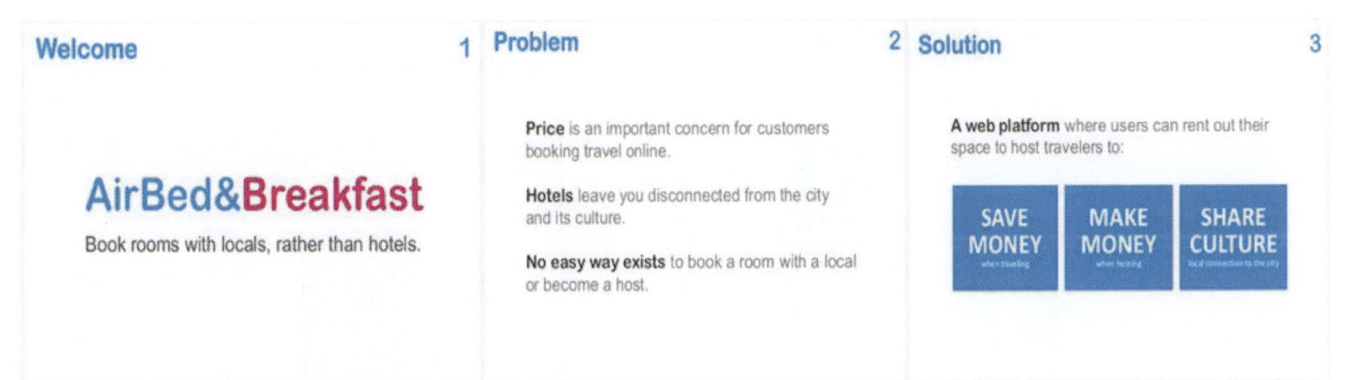

Image 11 - Official Airbnb Pitch Deck

Using Rand's techniques and a bit of Presentation Design, we could turn it into a direct dialogue with the reader that brings him, slide after slide, to discover the key message:

Image 12 - Airbnb pitch redesigned with R. Fishkin's technique

I tested these two alternatives on an audience of independent subjects and the result was surprising!

In the experiment I asked people to flip through the slides and stop when they were ready to explain the content to me.

In the first case (the original presentation) the average preparation time for the explanation was one minute and two seconds, and the readers went back in the slide stream to reread and make sure they didn't miss anything.

In the second case (redesigned presentation for the purpose of this experiment) the preparation time was reduced to 14 seconds, also considering the cases in which the readers went back and reviewed the previous slides.

However, readers in this case claimed to have gone back to review the photos and not to reread the content (as Rand predicted).

To quickly build this kind of communicative structures, you should distribute the messages on white slides, verify that the story goes on smoothly, and then add the visual content.

Later we will see how to correctly combine text and images in an effective presentation.

3.4. AUDIO PRESENTATIONS

What if, in addition to the slides, I could distribute your voice?

With PowerPoint it's not difficult to create a set of slides that represent your communication and record your voice.

You can record your presentation in slideshow mode and then send a document that will automatically scroll through your slides and play your voice.

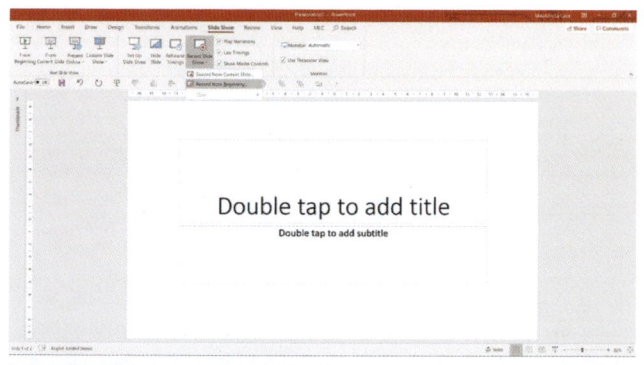

Image 13 - Slideshow on PowerPoint

Image 14 - Recording mode presentation on PowerPoint

As you can see from the screenshots, you can even interact with the presentation by highlighting areas of the slide.

That said, I personally believe that if you have to interact by highlighting areas of your slide as you speak, the slide is lacking in the way it was conceived.

As you speak, you should focus on your speech and the slides should follow.

In summary, I think recording the presentation is a great way to send a document that is self-standing, and therefore does not need the speaker.

Nevertheless, remember that listening to a recorded slideshow requires the recipient to watch the presentation from beginning to end without being able to quickly skip or read the parts that interest him least.

Maybe you want the recipient to enjoy your content in a linear way and therefore this method would be effective.

In short, like any technique, this one has its pros and cons.

I invite you, therefore, to reflect on the context, your audience and choose the most appropriate time to make the best of it.

3.5. IN SUMMARY

Not all presentations are made to be presented.

There are presentations that are born with the purpose of being read in the absence of the speaker.

From my point of view, this is a different experience from the traditional presentation, but since it happens on a daily basis, especially in structured organizational contexts, I firmly believe that it must be managed and optimized as best it can be.

If you have to create a presentation for an event and you also have to distribute it later, the best way is to use handouts.

Using the handout technique means writing in PowerPoint notes and printing in PDF format. Alternatively, you can always record your presentation and send a slideshow with your voice guiding its presentation.

4
CHAPTER

THE STRUCTURE OF A SUCCESSFUL PRESENTATION

« SUCCESS IS NOT MAGICAL NOR MYSTERIOUS. SUCCESS IS THE NATURAL CONSEQUENCE OF CONSISTENTLY APPLYING THE BASIC FUNDAMENTALS »

JIM ROHN

Which are, in your opinion, the fundamental components that make up the mix of a winning presentation?

A presentation is not just about slides.

Okay, slides are one of the components, but there's more. What are slides made of?

If you think about it, they are made up of content and the way in which it is displayed, that is, the design.

What else?

The way content is communicated.

In your opinion, does the order in which you present the information affect the communicative effectiveness of the presentation?

I can already see you saying yes.

In fact, the communication flow represents the order in which the contents are arranged and presented.

Remember when we used to say that "people make a difference" in presentations?

Well, you are the presenter.

The ability to speak in front of an audience is not obvious at all. Depending on the person, it can also be a real obstacle to overcome.

There are courses, techniques and countless public speaking coaches that can give you a lot from a technical point of view and therefore, if you think you must focus on this skill, don't hesitate to get to work.

The technique is certainly important, but it must be completed with the experience on the field.

You got it right.

I'm telling you that the best way to develop your ability to speak in public and manage stress is to present at every possible opportunity.

A few years ago, after deciding to abandon a business career in marketing to create my first real digital startup, I was invited to present my startup at a Mashable Social Media Day in Italy.

It was an important event in the digital world, with a large number of participants.

I still remember that, on the day of the presentation, I arrived at the event with my then Co-Founder, Davide, and together we entered the main hall.

We were in the main hall of a university where several hundred people were present.

As soon as we arrived at the event, we realized that we had been assigned the last slot of the last day of the week. In short, we were the last and umpteenth pitch for those poor people in the public who were, by then, tired and demotivated.

Certainly no one was pleased to hear the umpteenth startup asking for money and collaboration after a whole week of presentations.

Given the situation, I turned to Davide and told him that I had no intention of presenting and that I would have gladly given him the stage.

He looked at me as if to tell me that I had gone mad and that he had no intention of talking to hundreds of living dead.

So, we both chose an even or odd number, I won and introduced him!

Davide did something brilliant and totally unexpected that surprised the audience that day, as well as me. On that occasion I learned something very important that affected all my presentations from then on, and that's why I share it with pride.

I'll tell you what I learned that day.

As the last presenter of the day, Davide knew that he was in front of a tired audience with a low level of attention.

So, at the moment of presenting, Davide arrives on the stage smiling, brilliant and, just when everyone expects him to start pitching his startup, he says: "I know you're all too tired to put up with another presentation, so we will do the opposite, instead of presenting my startup to you, I'll leave the burden to you, you will present it yourselves!"

The first reaction of the people in the audience could be clearly read from their expressions: "this speaker must be crazy; what does it mean we should present?".

Davide pressed on and said: "You have understood well, don't be afraid, I'll leave you the floor and I'll give you a hand".

So, Davide jumps over a few slides on the deck and presents this one:

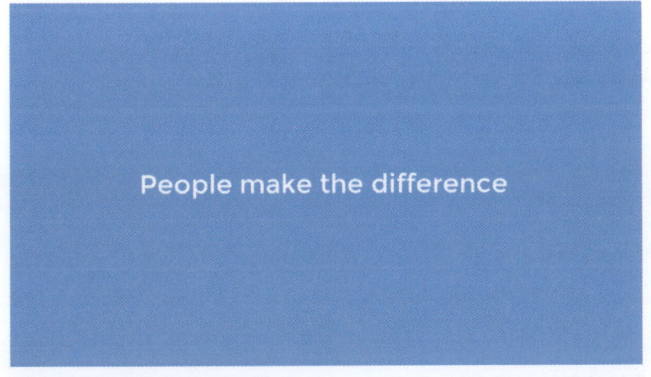

Image 1 – People make the difference

The audience becomes curious and, in some cases worried, begins to interact.

Image 2 - Davide talks at the Mashable Social Media Day

The first try to guess, and David begins to moderate the discussion.

The discussion continues guided by the speaker until the audience can guess what our startup was about.

What do you think Davide got out of this?
Exactly, people's attention.
By now, Davide had captured the attention of his audience. People were actually listening to him because they wanted to know how the story would end and if they had guessed what the startup was about (curiosity effect).

After finally turning hundreds of living dead into attentive people, David was ready to start the pitch presentation. So, he clicked on the wireless presenter to move on to the next slide, but something unexpected happened…

Image 3 - Slides quit the speaker

The next slide was blank, like all the others to follow.

The slides had just abandoned him.

Davide suddenly found himself in front of a tired audience, which he had laboriously awakened, only to discover that his presentation had just abandoned him.

This was really bad luck after so much hard work... Or maybe not?

It seemed all lost and I guarantee you that many presenters would panic at this point, but David, once again, managed to surprise his audience.

Very calmly, he began by saying: "the slides do not work, but you have seen too many slides these days, so we will take the opportunity to avoid them."

"If you want to receive the presentation, post a tweet and tag the name of our startup, and my team will send it to you quickly."

Davide: "I'll tell you our story in my own words". In an instant, I realized that Davide had managed to keep the audience's attention high despite the setback and had even taken advantage of the opportunity to distribute the presentation to all interested parties.

That day, sitting in the audience, I immediately turned on my computer, went on twitter and I saw hundreds of requests for a presentation that had never been presented, incredible!

At the end of this story, I can only confirm what Davide wrote on his first and only slide presented that day: "people make the difference".

Did you like the story?

As you can see, slides are certainly important, but it was Davide's public speaking skills that allowed him to improvise and manage a crisis in a cool and rational way.

Public speaking is a skill like any other and as such, in my opinion, you can learn it.

In summary, before any well-organized slide set there is an exchange between people: between you, the speaker, and the people who listen to you and, if they feel involved, they will interact with you.

You, as a speaker, have the task of interacting with your slides, but they must always be a background element that helps the audience to visualize and memorize your messages.

Remember - the leadership of the presentation is yours, not your slides'.

4.1. THE THREE MAIN PILLARS OF A PRESENTATION

Each presentation is like a real show and, as you know, there is no respectable show that does not have a carefully designed structure to entertain and engage people.

We do business, not cabaret, but this does not justify us from designing an effective communication flow, sewn on the goal we want to achieve.

Slides bring the concepts of the presenter to life, allow him to create a real emotional involvement by stimulating emotions in people and allow you to imprint lasting messages in the audience's memory.

The presenter runs through the flow and runs the slides animating the show.

In short, there is a speaker, supported by slides, who animates a performance in accordance with a carefully designed communication strategy.

We can therefore say that a successful presentation is made up of at least three fundamental pillars:

1. Public speaking
2. Visual content
3. Communication flow

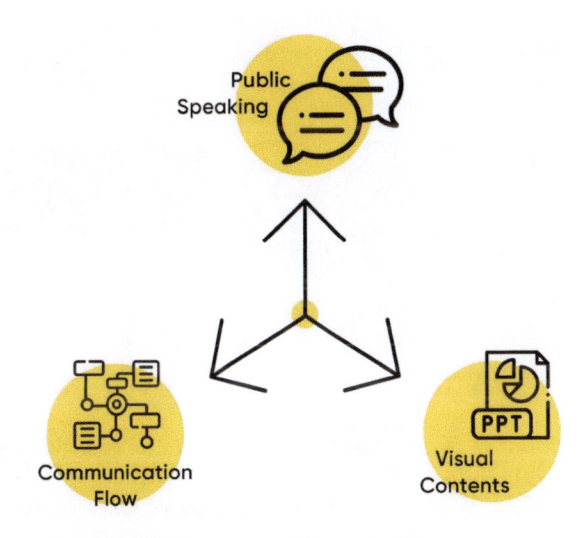

Image 4 - The pillars of a successful presentation

Slides only cover a third of the ingredients of an effective presentation: they are indisputably important, but it is the speaker who makes the difference.

When the speaker succeeds in combining the three components and making the most of them, we have an exceptional presentation.

The level of attention will be very high, the audience will be involved and attentive to receiving the messages of the presenter in all their aspects, communication will be effective and will remain imprinted in people's memories.

As long as these three dimensions coexist, the presentation will be well balanced and effective; while if these dimensions are missing, the presentation will be lacking and ineffective.

What happens in situations where only one of these dimensions is missing?
Let's see it together.

4.1.1. FEAR OF PUBLIC SPEAKING

Imagine the case where the presenter is very skilled at writing an engaging communication flow and creating effective slides, but is afraid to present in public, fails to be empathetic and does not do justice to his content when he gets on a stage in front of an audience.

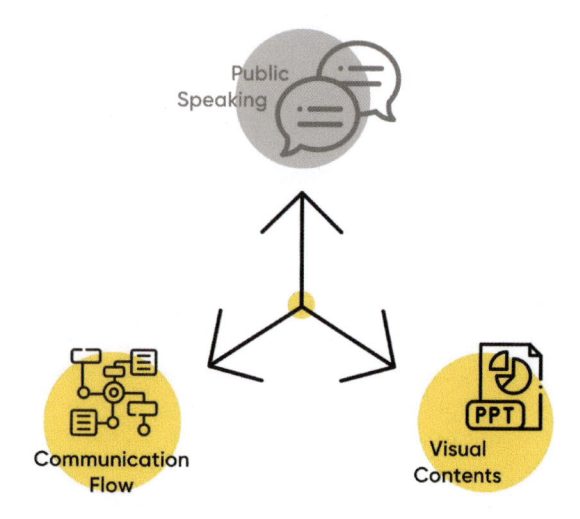

Image 5 – Presenter not up to the situation

Behind the scenes, the preparation phase will be handled very well, but the day of the presentation could destroy all the efforts made.

In these cases, it may help to completely eliminate the human component from the performance and create a self-standing presentation.

This would enhance the presenter's skills and avoid giving a bad impression.

After extensively analyzing self-standing presentations, you know that I'm talking about a presentation designed to be read individually by the recipient.

With a good design of an effective communication flow and an excellent design of the visual experience (slides) you can create an exceptional reading experience.
Easy?

Yeah, but be careful.

Public speaking is one of the most feared activities by most people. Therefore, I invite you to be careful and do not take this opportunity as an excuse to avoid presentations.

In fact, an excellent reading experience will never replace an effective oral presentation. Remember that a presentation is an exchange of ideas between people who interact, and the interaction between people is much more interesting and effective than the interaction between a reader and a slide.

4.1.2. INEFFECTIVE SLIDES

Let us now look at the case in which the speaker has an excellent stage presence and a good ability to speak in public in a structured manner.

However, he is not able to create a deck of slides that really enhances his content.

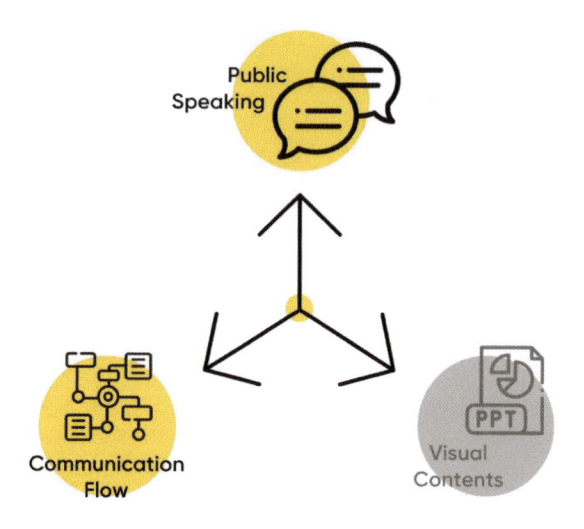

Image 6 – Ineffective slides

This is the typical case of a very senior speaker in his field, with many years of experience on his shoulders.

As the years progressed and his professional experience consolidated, this speaker has developed an extensive knowledge of his subject and knows how to talk about it in such a way as to interest the audience.

However, he has lost the train of technological evolution and is no longer, or has never been, agile in the rapid realization of effective slides.

Like many, he lacks a structured approach to presentation design and realizes he wastes too much time from the moment he launches PowerPoint.

In fact, this is the case for those who typically delegate the production of slides to their team or to the marketing/communication department.

In my opinion, it is correct to delegate the production of the presentation, but it is not certain that the brand manager of the team is the most appropriate person just because he is young and deals with marketing.

To create an effective slide deck, it is necessary to have a certain skill set:

1. Business understanding & critical thinking
2. Graphic, motion e infographic design
3. Strategic Communication

This mixture of skills is achieved by crossing very different training paths: there are those who study graphics, those who deal with communication and those who specialize in business aspects.

After all, you need someone who can understand what you want to communicate (business), who knows how to communicate (communication) and who has the ability to bring ideas to life and design effective slides (designer).

For this reason, when the director delegates his slides to the team, the result is rarely effective and often not efficient, considering the man hours wasted in using resources on a job that does not belong to him. It's not the team's fault.

It is often thought that if you are in marketing or if you are a former consultant, then you are good at creating presentations.

Neither marketers nor consultants possess all these skills from such different backgrounds.

Designing a presentation is a complex job that requires multiple roles.

The only alternative I find acceptable is to master a structured methodology, which as a professional (business) can help you to make up for shortcomings in communication and design.

Lean Presentation Design was born from this intuition.

After all, many famous approaches to the creation of effective presentations are, unfortunately, difficult to apply in everyday business because they do not take into account that slides are not necessarily created by designers but by all of us and that, often, time is a critical factor for success.

So, what should our speaker do in a situation where he is not able to create his own slides?

In my opinion, there are two solutions:

1. Delegate to those who are truly capable of making an effective presentation
2. Present without slides

Does it surprise you that I'm suggesting you give a presentation without slides?

Honestly, I think it's much better to have an effective presentation without slides than an ineffective presentation because of slides poorly created.

4.1.3. DISCONNECTED INFORMATION FLOW

Finally, we have the case in which the speaker has a good experience in public speaking and an excellent stage presence, he had exceptional slides made for him - perhaps by a designer - but neglected the communication strategy of the presentation.

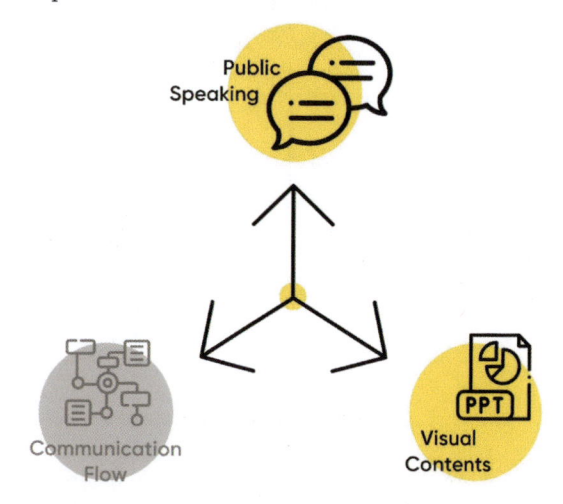

Image 7 - Disorganized presentation

In your opinion, does the order in which the information is presented make a difference in terms of effectiveness?

I can see you're saying yes.

I think it's quite intuitive that the flow in which information is presented has a significant impact on the effectiveness of communication.

After all, this is why I think it is useless to produce beautiful slides without studying the communication strategy.

Can you see how important the combination of multidisciplinary skills is in creating a presentation?

Achieving an effective flow is not an easy task, but of course there are techniques that can guide you.

I use some very powerful and easy to apply techniques in any area, from business to staff.

I'll tell you about them in the next chapters, when we'll see together what we are really talking about when we use the term "storytelling" in presentations.

4.2. A CANVAS TO VERIFY THAT YOUR PRESENTATION WORKS

When I prepare a presentation I always keep these three dimensions in mind, but it's not always easy to capture all the points of improvement needed because the three dimensions are developed at different times, and at the end of the process I may have missed some pieces.

The strategic communication part and the choice of the communication flow should be the starting point in the design of a good presentation. In the next chapter we will see in detail how to set up an effective flow according to the specific audience.

This is followed by the creation and design of slides, often with tools like PowerPoint.

Finally, we'll get to the part where you rehearse and maybe register yourself with a camera to evaluate your performance. When, in the final stage, I do the recording tests, to make sure that I have not forgotten anything and to evaluate the presentation according to all three key dimensions, I use the ***Presentation Assessment Canvas.*** [1]

The PAC presents, from left to right, the three main pillars of a good presentation in chronological order.

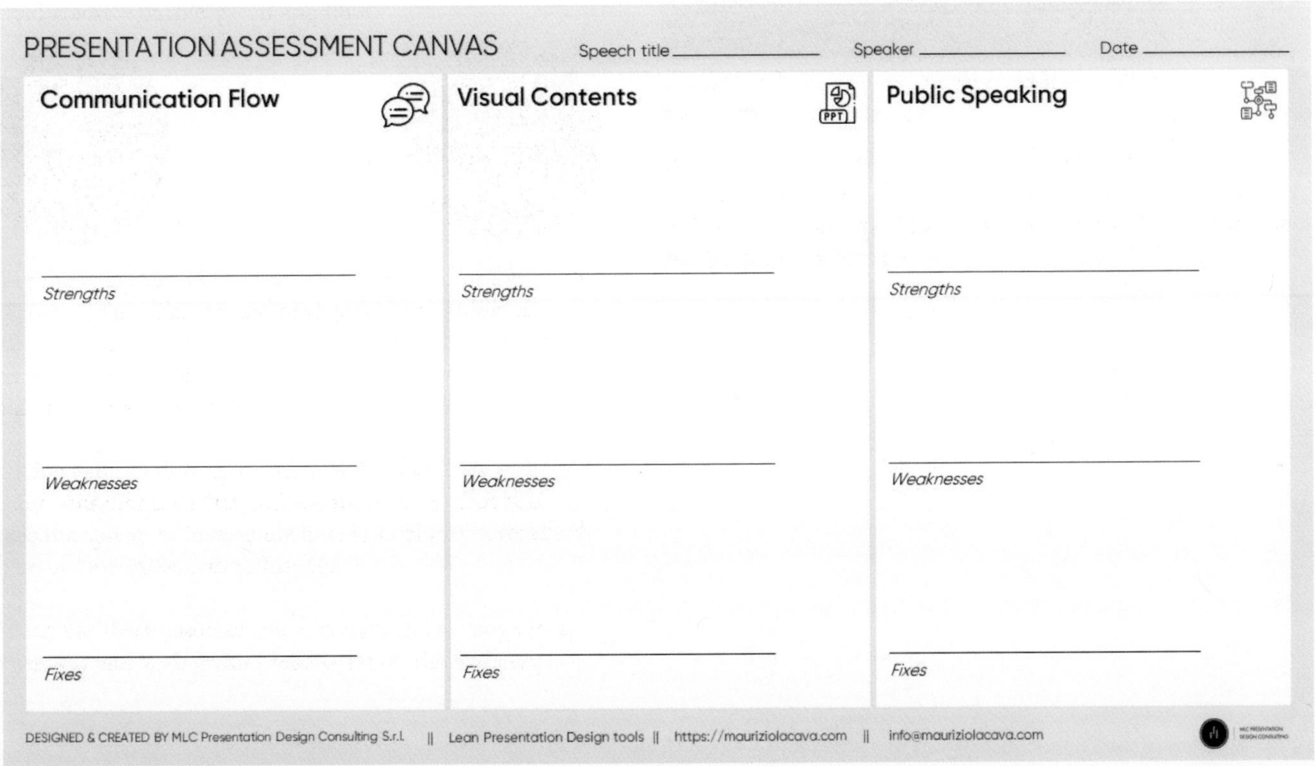

Image 8 - Presentation Assessment Canvas

[1] Presentation Assessment Canvas (PAC) – Available in PDF version on https://mauriziolacava.com

This tool allows you to assess, for each dimension, the strengths that need to be enhanced and the weaknesses that need to be resolved through appropriate corrections (fixes).

Be careful not to confuse weaknesses with corrections. The former clearly identify the problem, while the latter identify the solution to the problem.

Weaknesses and corrections are usually linked by corresponding numbers in order to make the associations evident.

When reviewing your presentation, this canvas is a handy tool to have printed, at your fingertips, to take notes in an organized fashion and to intervene in a targeted manner to enhance the effectiveness of your presentation.

4.3. IN SUMMARY

A successful presentation is based on 3 main pillars:

1. Public speaking
2. Visual content
3 Communication flow

The coexistence of these three dimensions ensures that the presentation is effective.

If one of these pillars is missing, there are dangerous intermediate cases that need to be managed intelligently.

The Presentation Assessment Canvas is useful to assess the progress of your next presentation, identify weaknesses and plan intervention actions.

CHAPTER 5

A LEAN APPROACH TO PRESENTATIONS

« EXCELLENCE IS A CONTINUOUS PROCESS AND NOT AN ACCIDENT »

A. P. J. ABDUL KALAM

5.1. THE TRADEOFF OF PRESENTATIONS: EFFECTIVENESS VS. EFFICIENCY

A bad presentation has two negative effects:

1. It requires an enormous cognitive effort from the audience and therefore lengthens the information processing time (=ineffective).
2. It generates a huge waste of time on the part of the author, who too often tries to find questionable graphic choices to make the presentation "more beautiful" (= inefficient)

There are therefore two main variables involved in the realization of presentations: effectiveness, that is the ability to transfer the message in such a way as to grab the attention and be remembered, and efficiency, that is the time required for the realization of the presentation.

Reasonably, these two variables define each other in trade off.

What does this mean?
That if you improve one of them, you will make the other worse.

Think about it: to create a good presentation you must spend more time (+ effectiveness, - efficiency).

I think it's all about method.

What method do you use to approach presentations? Usually, presentations are done out of habit, because when you started working your bosses asked you to do them and so it all started.

But no one has ever taught you a structured approach to dealing with them from start to finish in an efficient way so as to achieve an effective result.
Have you ever thought about it?

Follow me, there's more.
From time to time, during my classes, I enjoy questioning the participants about the starting point that everyone would choose to prepare a presentation.

From the answers, you can immediately see the difference in approach between people.

Everyone would start from a different point: some from the slides, some from the objective, some from collecting information, etc.

Different approaches emerge.
In your opinion, which one is the most efficient?

Above all, which of these leads to the most effective result? Hard to say.

It could also be that one of these approaches also leads to a relatively effective result, but can't be certain and, perhaps, it will cost an excessive expenditure of resources.

What if there is one approach, which everyone agrees on, simply because it is the most effective and the most efficient? In this chapter, I want to share with you the result of merging two seemingly opposing disciplines:

1. Presentation design & Communication
2. Lean Methodologies

The first studies how to transfer ideas in an effective way to people, the second studies how to reduce waste by maximizing the result.
When I talk about presentation design and communication, I refer to all the techniques that help you to organize and visualize your ideas in a memorable communication that affects people.

On the contrary, the "Lean" approach was born and successfully developed in the world of industry, health care, public administration and the service sector in general (factories, product design and administrative functions).

Working in a "Lean" way means achieving maximum results with minimum waste. It is a matter of using the few resources available in the most productive way possible with the aim of drastically increasing productivity.

In the immediate post-war period, Toyota was in serious conditions of lack of resources, as was most of Japan's industry, which had been defeated and exhausted by a devastating war.

At the end of the 1940s, it was a small Japanese car company, whose machinery was old and its market shares derisory.

The Taylorist-Fordist production criteria could not be applied in those conditions. Toyota's director, Taiichi Ōno, decided to adopt a new path, different from the rigid Western system, increasing the flexibility of the machinery to produce lots in short periods, trying to respond immediately to market changes, so that production would be continuously planned.

The Lean approach that made the success of the then small machine factory now known to all as Toyota is based on two fundamental principles:

1. Elimination of waste and low value-added activities through continuous improvement (*kaizen*).

From *kaizen* derive the activities of rapid prototyping and anticipation of the constraints of which you have probably heard of.

To create a value-added product, the activity must change the shape or function of the product making it as close as possible to the final product for which the customer would be willing to pay. It's frustrating when your customer/boss doesn't approve of the presentation you've spent so much time on. So, working with a focus on continuous improvement allows you to manage customer/boss expectations and reduce the re-working cycles of your work.

By working in a Lean perspective, you are not only reducing waste and therefore optimizing time and costs, you are above all improving the quality of the service / final product for the customer.

2. Respect for humanity

"Respect for the Lean approach is much more difficult to define than it seems," says Mark Graban, Lean Methodology Expert, who adds, "being respectful is not being nice and smiling all the time. Respect means encouraging others to do more and better by believing in them. It also means working together as a team, learning from mistakes and continuously improving (this is the practice of "kaizen")". The Lean leader doesn't send his own forward, but paves and shows the way.

The final customer of each presentation is the audience. You want to communicate a message that has the power to influence the behavior of the audience to change and improve themselves.

You will need to work closely with your audience to show them the way to change and encourage them to improve. Being able to present means being a Lean leader, and Lean leadership means bringing out the best in people and encouraging them to give their all.

"Lean leadership means helping people to evolve professionally and personally by becoming aware of a job well done and being proud of it. The Lean leader does not set goals and then returns to punish those who have not achieved them.

The Lean leader invests his time teaching others. A true Lean Leader spends very little time in his office, he is usually amid people getting his hands dirty, listening to others, understanding what's going on and acting to improve instead of being isolated reading reports. ("Graban")

Forget fear of public speaking, get down from your desk and walk among people.

Remember that the audience is the hero, your role is just to show them the way. Don't think about the judgment of others and don't let it affect your presentation.

You are there for them, to share a new point of view, the result of your discovery, an interesting opportunity. Communicating in an engaging way to people, putting them at the center of attention and motivating them to act is your role, the role of the **Lean Presenter.**

How can I not be afraid to speak in front of people when I am in public?

I understand that the theme may not be easy to deal with. I think it's natural that we've all suffered in the past, or still suffer the moment when we find ourselves giving a presentation in front of people.

Personally, I think that here, too, we can learn from the Lean methodologies.
The **Lean Presenter** is not foolproof and makes mistakes, like everyone else. What is different is the way he lives and deals with failures.

First, we need to develop the awareness that failure, sooner or later, happens.
Failure is inevitable, but there are different ways to fail.
I am not an expert in public speaking, but I will give you my point of view.
When I'm on stage in front of people, or even just in the classroom in front of my students, I'm always a little excited but never more than what's right.

The truth is that the **Lean Presenter** is a presenter who presents with the ambition to share an idea, a personal point of view, and is always ready to question himself.
If the discussion shows that there is a better point of view than that of the **Lean Presenter**, he will not hesitate to learn and proceed.

Unlike those who would panic because a pupil has surpassed them as a teacher, the **Lean Presenter,** in an open and humble way, is the one who appreciates sharing a better point of view than his own.

Every opportunity is good to learn and as an audience guide, the **Lean Presenter** has the task of sharing the best ideas with his audience.

If an idea was suggested by someone from the audience, the **Lean Presenter** would take the opportunity to develop the suggestion, perhaps by showing examples from his experience.

This way, the **Lean Presenter** will be perceived as one of the audience, completely breaking down the gap created by the stage or situation.

In doing so, he will create empathy with the audience. People will feel part of the presentation and will interact freely, without fear of making mistakes.

You know when the speaker says that there are no stupid questions and that he likes interactive presentations but then nobody talks?

It is typically concluded that the audience was not very awake or that they were not very keen on interaction.
I don't think so.
I think the audience interacts smoothly with a speaker who makes them feel comfortable.
It is about not punishing and therefore not judging who is wrong.
The atmosphere of exchanging ideas during a presentation must always prevail over everything else, but it is up to the speaker to create it.

In a context where the aim is to get better together, the speaker must not be afraid of public opinion and the audience can be part of the presentation, interact with the speaker and enrich the experience for the benefit of all.

5.2. A LEAN PROCESS FOR PRESENTATIONS

Lean Presentation Design learns from the practical experience of years and hundreds of presentations made by combining communication strategies and neuroscience techniques applied to design in order to formalize a unique methodology that balances the tradeoff between effectiveness and efficiency in presentations.

Efficiency is achieved through standardization, which is the definition of a logical, standardized sequence of activities that guides you in the realization of a presentation.

Effectiveness, in the case of presentations, is achieved through a paradigm shift.

What do I mean?

Presentations are commonly approached creatively, but not all of us are designers and not all of us are creative.

In fact, when the result of so many efforts is a presentation that doesn't work, we tend to defend ourselves by recognizing that we don't have the gift of creativity.

In my opinion, you don't need to be particularly creative to make a presentation effective, and that's why I think anyone can make presentations that influence people.

Over the years, after helping large multinational groups, entrepreneurs, doctors and professionals of all kinds create effective presentations that bring their ideas to life, I have developed an extremely efficient and result-oriented standard way of proceeding.

The idea is to approach presentations in a logical and no longer creative way. What is the most efficient starting point for an effective presentation?

As I told you before, when I ask the question in the classroom, I get many different answers. Everyone would start from a different point.

I suppose we agree that there is a better approach than the others, the difficulty lies in identifying and formalizing it in order to make it repeatable and transferable.

We are all aware that probably the best starting point is not to launch PowerPoint and start aggregating slides that already exist in an attempt to minimize the new layouts to be produced.

But isn't that exactly what happens every day in the company?

Some would start with the idea of a solution, others with numbers or, more often, their own experiences in an attempt to create credibility.

If you start off poorly, however, you will lose a huge amount of time, waste resources, concentration and, probably, the result will be an ineffective presentation.

Do you remember the endless days you spent on PowerPoint adjusting alignments, distributions and layouts?

I tell you that all this can end, and that creating effective presentations is just a matter of how you think.

How would your life as a presenter change if creating presentations became an easy to follow, repeatable and optimized process?

Let me show you the first Lean process applied to the realization of presentations:

The LEAN PROCESS for PRESENTATIONS

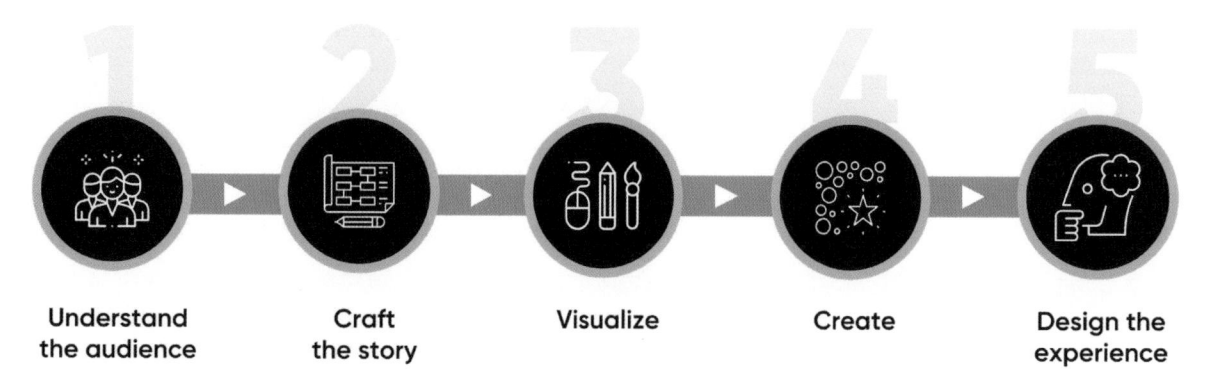

1. Understand the audience → **2. Craft the story** → **3. Visualize** → **4. Create** → **5. Design the experience**

Image 1 - Lean process for presentations

Have you noticed from where you start to create a presentation?

You don't start with PowerPoint, slides or a nice set of icons, you start with people!

Remember that the **Lean Presenter** speaks to people, about people and for people. Forget the spotlight on yourself and imagine turning it on your audience.
The audience is the hero who must make the change, not the speaker.

Remember that you are there for them, and that's why the right way to start a presentation is to carefully evaluate people.

However, talking to people and persuading them to act is not an easy task.
People have always exchanged ideas and told each other stories.

Think about it, you do it too, obviously.
When was the last time you told a friend something that happened to you?

Do you ever feel like your interlocutor can't feel and share the emotional importance that a story has for you?
It happens quite often.

Do you think it happens because your stories are not engaging, or because you have not told them in the best possible way?

In my opinion, the answer is the second one.
In the second step of the process you will learn how to create an effective flow to present your content through effective storytelling.

The third step is to visualize your ideas through the application of more or less advanced design techniques... You'll see!
Be aware, however, that only at the fourth step of the process ***Create the presentation*** you will really find yourself working with PowerPoint, not before then.

The last step is to study, design and implement the user experience on your slides. If you learn about the movements of the human eye when they observe a presentation, you'll also be able to guide them through the content through effective slide design.

5.3. IN SUMMARY

Regardless of our creative skills, we are all called to create presentations whenever we want to communicate our idea to the world with the ambition to influence people's behavior.

Working creatively without having the ability to do so means investing a considerable amount of time without any guarantee of achieving an effective result.

Lean Presentation Design is the first structured approach methodology that reinvents the paradigm of creating a presentation.

In fact, thanks to a series of techniques and a new perspective, you will learn to look at the presentations with new eyes, to see the fastest way towards the realization of an effective communication.

Understand to whom you want to communicate, prepare a story to transfer your messages in a clear and structured way, view the messages with all and only the necessary visual media, generate slides and finally design the user experience that maximizes the effectiveness of the presentation.

CHAPTER 6

UNDERSTAND THE AUDIENCE

« EVERY PRESENTATION HAS AN AUDIENCE AND EVERY AUDIENCE NEEDS ITS OWN PRESENTATION »

MAURIZIO LA CAVA

The LEAN PROCESS for PRESENTATIONS

1. Understand the audience ▶ **2. Craft the story** ▶ **3. Visualize** ▶ **4. Create** ▶ **5. Design the experience**

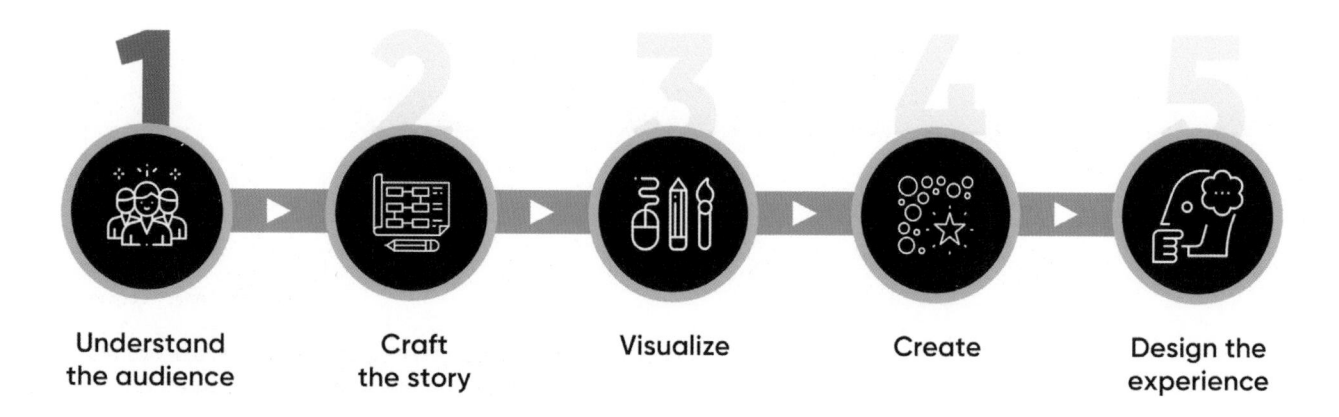

Image 1 - Lean Process for Presentations - Understand Your Audience

I don't think there's a single presentation that's right for everyone.

Even if you present the same theme, the point of view from which it can be declined can completely change depending on the people in front of you.

Think of the pitch to raise funds for a startup.

The project is always the same, but the communication can vary significantly if you are presenting to venture capitalists, business angels or even to the families of the friends who are supporting you in the first phase. [1]

The same could be said for a presentation within the company.

For example, if you're creating a presentation for the CTO, you'll probably highlight different aspects than the ones you'll focus on when presenting to the CMO or CEO.

So, the audience you present to can completely change the flow, content and display of your presentation.

All this means that a good understanding of the audience is essential for a successful presentation.

---

[1] Startup Pitch – Come presentare un'idea e convincere gli investitori a finanziarla, Flaccovio Editore

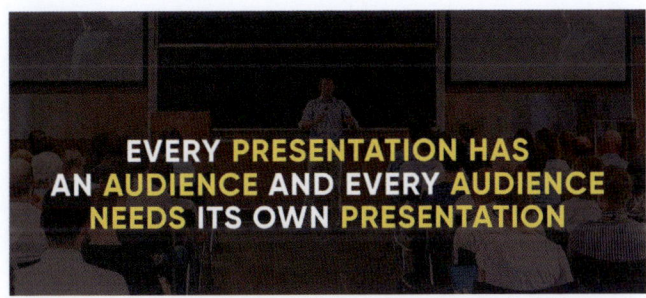

Image 2 - Each presentation has its own audience, and each audience must have its own presentation

After all, what would be the point of launching PowerPoint and drawing slides if you don't know who you're talking to?

You remember when your mom told you not to talk to strangers?

Image 3 - Mum

Well, she was absolutely right!
Have you ever wondered what people in the audience think, after they see you, in the moments before you start talking?

At that very moment, people will be thinking, "Give me at least one good reason why I should give you my attention rather than do anything else".

You want their attention, and they are waiting for a single good reason to come out of your mouth and convince them to listen to you.

People love to hear about themselves, nobody likes to hear about others [...] people are flattered when they find out that you did some work to find out who they are. [2]

According to P. Coughter, author of the famous book "The Art of The Pitch", people are only interested in hearing about themselves, they have no interest in hearing about others.

So, if you want to talk about them, you must really know them well before doing anything else.

We need to know all about our audience. Of course, we have to know the brand we work for, but this is obvious. I think we need to know our audience individually, as people, because our goal is to create an empathic connection with each one of them. The more we know about our audience, the better we will be able to create this connection. [3]

In short, you need to know your audience in order to talk to people about themselves.

However, most presentations start by introducing the speaker, enhancing his profile and trying to establish him as an authoritative figure in the relevant field.

Think of corporate sales presentations that begin with credentials, such as experience on similar projects, success stories, testimonials, an experienced, multi-ethnic team, etc.

Can I tell you how I feel about this kind of presentations?

I don't care!

Trust me, nobody cares why you think you are qualified to talk about a particular topic, at least not at the beginning.

People listen to you if you have something for them, if you are able to put them at the center of attention, not if the

---
2 Coughter P., The art of the pitch, Palgrave Macmillan, 2012
3 Coughter P., The art of the pitch, Palgrave Macmillan, 2012

first thing you do is introduce yourself and try to establish yourself as an expert or try to build your credibility in front of those who do not know you.

When you give a presentation, it's easy to fall into the "leading speaker's trap". The spotlight is on you, people are looking at you, and everyone is waiting for you to say the next words.

As a matter of fact, the protagonist of every presentation is not the speaker, but the audience.

The purpose of a presentation is to convince people to do something they would not have done without being infected by the ideas of the speaker.

It is the public who has to change, do something different, not you.

Who are you then?

You are nothing more than the facilitator of change!

The speaker is successful if his audience can overcome their resistance and accept the proposed change.

But let's go back to the moment when you still have to say the first word. The audience is looking at you and, individually, people are thinking: "give me at least one good reason why I should listen to you".

You need something from them, a very precious good and a scarce resource par excellence: attention.

They need a valid reason to give you attention.

Do you know the best way to get something from someone?

Be the first to give!
Didn't you expect it?

Well yes, if you want to get something from someone, the best way is to be the first to give something.

According to the principle of "reciprocity" of R. Cialdini, people feel obliged to return to others a behavior, a gift or a service they have received.

If a friend invites you to his party, you will feel obliged to invite him to yours. If a colleague does you a favor, you owe him a favor.

In the context of social obligation, people are more likely to say yes to those to whom they owe a favor.

One of the best demonstrations of the principle of reciprocity comes from a series of studies conducted in restaurants.

You may have been offered something after dinner: a digestive, a liqueur, a biscuit, a chocolate or something else.

It usually happens just before you get your bill.

It has been shown that offering something at the end of the dinner has a positive impact on the tip which, in the case of these experiments, increased by about 3%.

If two things are offered, the tip does not double but even quadruples, growing by about 14%.

It's probably even more interesting to note that if the waiter offers something, then walks away, turns around and says, "For you, special customer, here's another extra", the tip skyrockets with an increase of about 23%, influenced not by what was offered but by the way it was offered.

So, the key to using the principle of reciprocity is to make sure you're the first to give something, even better if it's something that's personalized and unexpected!

Do you want to make a personalized and unexpected gift to your audience to win their attention from the start?

Easy, start with the people!

Remember what Peter Coughter said a few lines ago? People are interested in hearing about themselves, and I might add, their problems and how you can help them in their personal or professional lives.

Almost any speaker introduces the speech by introducing himself and illustrating his experiences to justify his preparation on the topic.

No one starts from the audience.

If you want to stand out from the crowd and win the audience over from the very first words, speak about them, for them, and use their language.

The best way to present an idea is to have a sharing attitude. It's a lot of fun, you can see it right away. When someone wants to sell you something, wants something from you, wants you to register on their Facebook page, become a follower on Twitter, buy a product from them or invest in their company, the way they present their product is focused on themselves, they're constantly trying to sell themselves. I find it really unpleasant. When someone puts himself in a sharing attitude and shows the desire to give, to share an idea, a perspective, a new product, a new way of seeing things, people are much more receptive.[4]

You'll see that your audience will feel won over when they realize that you've worked to really understand their needs.

Did you notice that I wrote "in their language"?

How often does it happen that the speaker uses too technical a language just to show off his preparation?

It happens all too often, and it is absolutely ineffective.

Build your idea piece by piece with concepts that your audience already has. Use the power of language to unite concepts that already exist in the mind of the audience. Do not use your language, but their language. Your starting point is the level of knowledge of your audience. Speakers often forget that many of the terms they are used to are totally unrelated to their audience. Metaphors play a crucial role in showing how the different parts come together, because they reveal the desired form of the path on the basis of an idea that the listener already understands. For example, when Jennifer introduced the new biotechnology system called CRISPR she said: "For the first time we have developed a processor that allows you to modify DNA" and continues "CRISPR allows you to cut and paste genetic information very easily". Such a vivid explanation generates a moment of "aha" in the audience that sculpts the information in our minds. It is therefore important to test your presentation on as many people as possible, such as your friends, and see where you lose their attention.[5]

Your goal as a speaker is to make your ideas understandable to people. It doesn't matter if you are forced to simplify the language and use metaphors to make the concepts understandable to the audience, you won't be less appreciated for this, on the contrary!

People will be grateful to you and listen to you because they won't have to make any effort to follow you.

Knowing the people you are talking to is a fundamental prerequisite to be able to design an effective communication that pushes them towards your goal.

What goal?

The goal of the presentation!

The reason why you felt you had to block people in a room to listen to you for the duration of your presentation.

4 How To Begin Your Presentation with Simon Sinek | https://www.youtube.com/watch?v=e80BbX05D7Y
5 Chris Anderson: TED's secret to great public speaking | TED Talk

In short, the change you have in mind for your audience as a result of your intervention.

The starting point should be the identification of the goal: what you want people to do after your presentation.
Once you have identified the goal, you should ask yourself if there are any reasons why the specific target audience should resist.

Understanding resistance to change is crucial to the success of the presentation, and in fact is the basis for building a complete communication flow.

What do I mean?

I'm telling you that if you want your presentation to be persuasive, you can't ignore the fact that you must face and break down all your audience's resistance to the change you're proposing.

Let me give you a concrete example from my book Startup Pitch - How to present an idea and convince investors to finance it.[6]

If you, as an entrepreneur, are presenting a startup to investors for financing, you will not open the discussion with a request for financing.

Usually, there's a path you'll have to take your audience by the hand in order for them to accept your proposal.

In fact, investors may object that your idea does not have enough market or does not solve a significant problem or does not have a business model that generates value or maybe that the team is not up to the task.

These are what we call "resistance to change" in the audience.

Don't worry, it's normal for the audience to resist the change you're proposing.

What would be the point of presenting to a room full of people who already agree with you?

In fact, a good startup pitch has essential sections, including: Market Sizing, Traction, Team, Business Model, and others.

See?
I'm getting the information to introduce in my presentation from the questions that the audience will probably ask or, as mentioned so far, from the resistance.

So, start from a specific objective, study the target audience and analyze it to identify the main resistance to change.
Have you noticed?

In designing the communicative flow of the presentation I'm starting from the end and not from the beginning, and certainly not from the slides.

Do you understand?

For me, starting to work on a presentation doesn't mean opening PowerPoint and starting to recycle slides, but analyzing the audience and clarifying, first of all, who I'm going to talk to.

Following the Lean Presentation Design methodology, a good communication strategy starts from the definition of the objective that allows you to identify the resistances according to who you want to persuade.

These resistances will then be an integral part of the presentation in the form of reason to believe.

Don't worry, it's simpler than it seems - follow me and I'll explain you in the next chapter.

---

[6] La Cava M., Startup pitch. How to present an idea and convince investors to finance it, 2018

6.1. IN SUMMARY

There is no such thing as a presentation that suits all circumstances.

Even if you always present the same project, the content, flow and visualization of your ideas will change depending on the people in front of you.

When preparing a presentation, you need to understand the audience, in order to understand why they should resist in achieving your goal.

Usually, through a presentation, you're proposing to people to do something they wouldn't have done otherwise.

Understanding the audience and defining the goal allows you to anticipate the resistance they might raise against your proposal.

This way, you could structure the content of your presentation in such a way as to consider the resistance of the audience and thus break down the barriers to change one after the other.

CHAPTER 7

WRITE THE STORY

« PEOPLE HAVE FORGOTTEN HOW TO TELL A STORY »

STEVEN SPIELBERG

The **LEAN PROCESS** for **PRESENTATIONS**

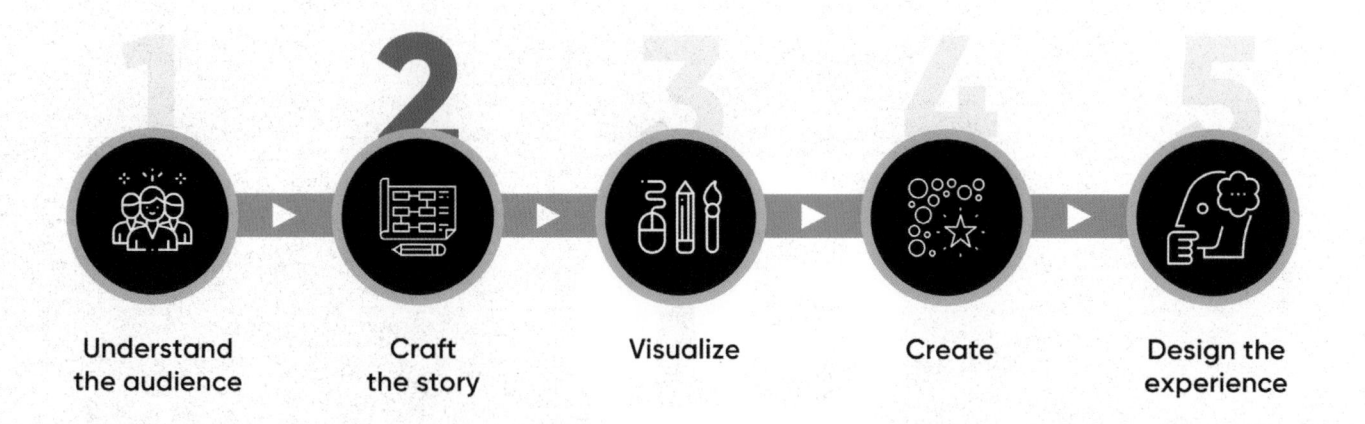

1. Understand the audience
2. Craft the story
3. Visualize
4. Create
5. Design the experience

Image 1 - Lean Process for Presentations - Write the Story

You defined your goal, studied the audience and identified all the resistances for which they might not accept your proposal.

By identifying the resistances, you have captured the key information that you will include in your presentation.

In short, at this point in the book, you are able to define the essential content of your presentation in relation to the audience to which you will present.

Being able to define the content that is really essential for a presentation is not easy at all.

How many times have you seen speakers who go into absolutely irrelevant details that lead to an attention drop?

Being able to define all the content that can't possibly be missing in the presentation is therefore a skill to be mastered and now you have it, bravo!

But be careful, it's still too early to celebrate.
In fact, while defining the essential content is necessary for a successful presentation, it is not enough.

What's missing?

The structure of the speech.
In your opinion, does the order in which the information is presented make a difference in terms of the effectiveness of communication?

The time has come to outline the route that will allow you to connect the buoy above wind to the boat below wind.
Are you ready?

Let's get started!

7. 1. STORYTELLING FOR PRESENTATIONS

How do you build a communicative path that takes the audience from a point A - where it knows nothing about what you are about to tell - to a point B - where it is ready to act according to your instructions?

I warn you; I'm going to use a very popular, powerful, dangerous and often misunderstood term.

What am I talking about?

I'm talking about Storytelling. After all, stories have always been the basis of communication between humans.
You always tell stories when you want to share an idea or excite someone. The problem is that all too often you think that to communicate effectively you just have to tell stories.

That's why we see these speakers presenting personal stories, jokes and anecdotes that nobody is interested in.

Attention drops, the speakers can't get the message through and they feel frustrated because they can't understand how, after telling a story, the audience got distracted and the storytelling didn't work.

Storytelling doesn't mean telling stories!

Image 2 - Storytelling doesn't mean telling stories

Surprised by my statement?

Well, that's right!

In my opinion, the problem arises from the wrong and often simplistic use of the word storytelling.

How many times have you heard things like "we do a storytelling to narrate the company event" or "we do a storytelling to describe our website" and so on.

Storytelling is not a way to tell a story.

In fact, I'll tell you that really effective storytelling would lead to no story being included in the storytelling.

In fact, the point is not to tell a story, but to exploit the narrative structure typical of stories to give order and structure to their contents.

Difficult?

Not at all, follow me.

Storytelling means structuring your communication, and therefore your contents, in the respect of the narrative structure typical of stories.

Let's get started.

Think about it for a moment, where does a story start?

Let me give you an example.
Have you ever seen the famous DreamWorks Animation movie with the green ogre?

Yes, I'm talking about Shrek.

Think about the story for a moment:

Shrek is a huge green ogre, living alone in a wooden house in a swamp, who carefully avoids any social contact, exploiting the prejudices against orcs, always considered bad. Although he looks cranky and lonely, Shrek is actually a good orc.

Farquaad is a ruthless dictator, who wants to make disappear from his feuds all the creatures of the fairy tales, which he considers useless.

During the hunt, the fairytale character Donkey manages to escape from the guards that chase him and enters the forest, where he runs into Shrek, intent on walking. The guards who were chasing him, however, frightened by Shrek's appearance, flee away.

Donkey is grateful to Shrek for saving his life and decides to follow him to honor his debt.

That same night, while Donkey is sleeping in front of Shrek's house, most of the exiled creatures pour into the swamp to camp there.

Shrek's peace has been violated by the invasion of the swamp.

Enraged, Shrek asks the many creatures present why they are so upset, and the latter make him understand that Farquaad has had them removed from their lands, thus leaving them without a home.

Shrek then decides to go and find Lord Farquaad to talk straight to him, and heads to his castle with Donkey, as he's the only one who knows where it is.

The two of them head to Duloc, the city-fortress of the ruthless dictator, to face him and solve the problem that prompted Shrek to do something he would never have done if there hadn't been a conflict situation.

Have you noticed how compelling it is?

It immediately attracts attention, and effortlessly takes you from getting to know the character to being immersed in his adventure and increases your desire to know how it is going to end.

Let's analyze together the narrative structure of the story.

The protagonist and the context in which he lives are introduced.

In this initial portrait, the protagonist is described through his habits and character.

At a certain point, it is introduced an antagonist who generates a problem.

The problem affects the life of the protagonist who, driven by this conflict, will do something he would never have done otherwise.

It is a problem so important for the protagonist to push him to a change.

So, Shrek, who would continue to live in serenity in his stinking swamp, leaves for the realm to meet Lord Farquaad and persuade him to give home to the creatures of fairy tales now lost.

Think about it, though.
Shrek and Donkey, do they immediately arrive at the realm and solve the problem, or do they get involved in a series of mishaps?

Exactly, I see that we have understood each other.

The two do not arrive immediately; on the contrary, they will encounter multiple misadventures that will hinder them from reaching their goal.

Whenever your heroes are involved in an unexpected event, you feel involved in the story and almost want to get on the screen to help them out.

Once you've overcome the difficulty, you always take a breath of relief.
Now let's try to extrapolate this narrative structure.

PART OF THE STORY	STORYTELLING	DESCRIPTION
CONTEXT	Shrek is a huge green ogre, living alone in a wooden house in a swamp, who carefully avoids any social contact, exploiting the prejudices against orcs, always considered bad. Although he looks cranky and lonely, Shrek is actually a good orc. Farquaad is a ruthless dictator, who wants to make disappear from his feuds all the creatures of the fairy tales, which he considers useless. During the hunt, the fairytale character Donkey manages to escape from the guards that chase him and enters the forest, where he runs into Shrek, intent on walking. The guards who were chasing him, however, frightened by Shrek's appearance, flee away.	Introduction of the initial context, of the protagonist and of all the habits that will soon be changed
PROBLEM	That same night, while Donkey is sleeping in front of Shrek's house, most of the exiled creatures pour into the swamp to camp there. Shrek's peace has been violated by the invasion of the swamp. Enraged, Shrek asks the many creatures present why they are so upset, and the latter make him understand that Farquaad has had them removed from their lands, thus leaving them without a home.	The protagonist's conflict. This part introduces a problem so serious that the protagonist is forced to change his way of acting and do something that he would never have done otherwise
SOLUTION	Shrek then decides to go and find Lord Farquaad to talk straight to him, and heads to his castle with Donkey, as he's the only one who knows where it is. The two of them head to Duloc, the city-fortress of the ruthless dictator, to face him and solve the problem that prompted Shrek to do something he would never have done if there hadn't been a conflict situation.	The resolution of a problem. Usually the time for releasing the tension created by the problem and questioning the success of the protagonist

Have you noticed this structure?

Here, impress it well in your mind, because this narrative structure does wonders in communication.

The story begins with the introduction of a context, a scenario and the introduction of a protagonist with his habits.

The audience begins to impersonate the protagonist and feel part of the story.

At a certain point, the moment of conflict arrives - what we have defined as the problem.

The problem is so important for the protagonist that it pushes him to change his habits to solve it.

Usually, this is the part where the protagonist is in danger and his routine is threatened.

There can also be very serious moments when, for example, the protagonist's life is at risk, which lead you to wonder if he will make it.

Do you know what I'm talking about?
Think of a movie you like.

These are the famous moments that leave you breathless.
There are movies that have such an engaging narrative

structure that they leave me breathless even if I know how they will end.

The classic example is historical films: you already know what the course of events is but, until the last scene, you remain with the doubt or the hope that things could have gone differently.

There's nothing we can do; humans always get caught up in this narrative structure.
Why is this narrative structure so engaging for us?
Why, for example, doesn't the story start with the solution?

Can you imagine a scene in which the main character is solving a problem that has never been introduced?

It seems to me that it wouldn't work, it's obvious.

7. 1. 1. DID YOU KNOW YOU HAD THREE BRAINS?

According to Paul MacLean, a well-known American neuroscientist, the human brain can be divided into three parts that have progressively evolved over the years:

1. Ancient or reptilian brain
2. Intermediate or mammalian brain
3. New brain or neocortex

The New Brain
Analytical

The Mammalian Brain
Emotional

The Reptilian Brain
Instinctive

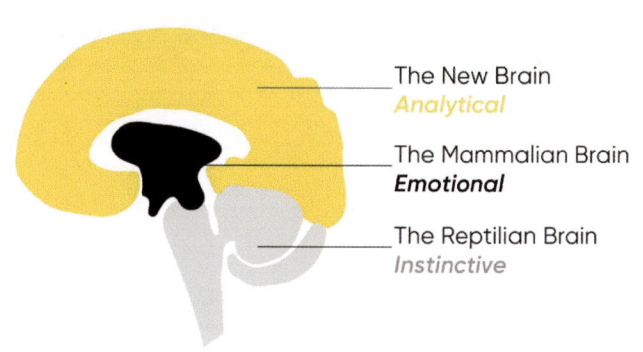

Image 3 - The three brains according to P. MacLean [1]

The reptilian brain lives on instincts, hunts prey and protects itself to protect our safety.

Do you find yourself there?

In practice, the reptilian brain has always been responsible for your survival.

The mammalian brain is home to all our emotions.

The new brain, on the other hand, is what distinguishes us as an evolved species because it allows us not to live the here and now of the present moment, but to see beyond and think in a prospective way.

In your opinion, which of the three brains consumes less energy?

We agree, the reptilian brain.

The other two brains play roles that require much more energy and it is precisely for this reason that the reptilian brain plays a filter function to protect the two.

What does "filter" mean?

It means that it will filter all the information that is not considered necessary for further processing.

So, if your communication does not attract the attention of the reptilian brain, it will simply be filtered out and you will not have captured the attention.

So how do you capture the attention of the reptilian brain? Let's think together about its nature.

This primordial brain basically wants to keep you alive and thus avoid painful situations (let's use this simplistic term, for the moment).

[1] The three brains according to P. MacLean - https://www.zeroseven.com.au/Blog/2018/March/Design-for-the-Brain

7. 1. 2. INTRODUCE THE PROBLEM TO CATCH YOUR AUDIENCE'S ATTENTION

For Shrek, "pain" is the moment of conflict in which his sacred swamp is invaded.

In storytelling, pain is generated by the introduction of the problem.

Do you start to see the dots coming together?

Follow me.

The context introduces a protagonist in which the audience sees itself, then it is introduced a problem that brings to light a "pain" that the audience perceives, and this pushes people into wanting to know the solution.

When the episode of your favorite TV series ends and the conflict or threat remains in the air, you absolutely want to know how it will end and you can't resist watching the next episode.

The problem generates tension, and the tension generates an urgent curiosity to know how it will end.

Do you realize what I just wrote?

Yes, I've just revealed to you how to capture people's attention.

So, if the problem generates tension and the tension generates attention, the reason why you start with the problem is precisely to catch the attention.

Think about it for a moment - it's the problem that generates interest and involvement, not the solution.

Let me give you an example.

Image 4 - Photo of a free and happy dog

This is a picture of a beautiful free and happy dog.

Nice, isn't it?

But it has nothing to do with the emotional impact of the photo I'm about to show you.

Image 5 - Dog in a cage - the disruptive force of the problem

Did you feel it?

This second photo is very powerful, the eyes of this poor animal pierce you deeply.

Why does the second photo have a disruptive force, compared to the first one?

The first photo could be assimilated to the solution, while the second to the problem.
The problem engages you and almost makes you want to intervene.

After all, think about it for a moment.

Isn't that exactly what you want to achieve with a presentation?

You want to persuade an audience to do something they wouldn't have done, and the way you do it is by creating this sense of urgency to act.

That's what a problem/solution attack is for.
Before you start talking, people are thinking, "Give me at least one good reason why I should follow you".

The reptilian brain is always ready to dodge information it deems superfluous.
At that moment you introduce a context, you introduce a problem and you make the audience live it to the point of making them think: "ok, I understood the problem and I absolutely want to know how to solve it".

Be careful, though!

It's not enough to introduce a generic problem and leave it there.
The keystone is to introduce your speech focusing on a specific problem of the audience.

As a presenter, you must understand the audience and find out which are the most significant problems that would lead them to act.

In short, returning to Shrek, you need to find out where your audience's swamp is and invade it as loudly as possible.

Slides are useful for making even more noise!

What do I mean?
I'm telling you that slides help you bring the problem to life and make the people in front of you experience it using multimedia content (images, videos, etc..).

Are you following me?

Let me give you an example.
Some time ago, I was pitch coaching a startup competition on the issue of energy.

As you can imagine, all the startups were working on a common problem: the reduction of air pollution.
However, one of the startups was able to decline the problem in such a particular way that it made itself indelible in my memory.

I'll tell you about it.
The founder tells me: "Since you live in Milan, do you know how many people died last year because of pollution in the city?".

By now, after having seen an average of 200 startups pitch per year, I've seen hundreds of attacks, so I'm not impressed anymore.

The founder tells me a number, he hits me, but he doesn't have my full attention yet.

At that point he says to me: "let's see if you are at risk too, there are two very dangerous moments in our daily lives: when you go jogging in the park and when you ride a scooter - is that something you do often?".
At that point I was shocked!

In fact, I always ride my scooter and I certainly jog in the park, thinking that if I run in the middle of the city's nature I can breathe cleaner air, but that's not the case.
At that moment, the founder had certainly captured my

attention and had intrigued me to the point of wanting to know what the solution was.

See?

If he had started from the generic problem and explained to me that I live in a polluted city, he wouldn't have really caught my attention because he wouldn't have told me anything new and nothing particularly personal.

Since he was able to decline the problem in such a way as to touch me personally, he got my attention.

Remember when I told you in chapter 6 that people aren't interested in hearing about others but about themselves, and that the best way to get something from people is to be the first to give?

Well.

Declining your communication on a problem that really touches the audience closely, personally, allows you to talk about people and tell them that you have something really useful for them.

Why is it really useful?

Simply because you solve a problem that causes them discomfort or suffering.

When people understand that you are not yet another speaker who talks about himself but talks about their problems, they will raise their antennas and want to know more.

7. 1. 3. OVERCOME RESISTANCE AND BUILD YOUR CREDIBILITY

So, the introductory problem/solution dynamic allows you to capture the attention in the opening and, if you can keep it, it gives you a window of opportunity to pass on your message.

To do this, the step of understanding the audience that we have seen in the previous chapter is essential.

However, there was another important point that we have defined as the identification of resistances.

Do you remember?

We said that, once you understood the audience, you would use the information about them to find out why they shouldn't adopt the change you proposed.

So, we defined these reasons: resistances.

The problem/solution dynamic is the basis of a persuasive storytelling, but it doesn't consider the resistances.

Do you think we can neglect them?

Absolutely not.

Responding to resistance means explaining to people the reasons why you are competent to implement the solution proposed to the problem.

If, for example, you were selling a startup to an investor, the investor may not believe that your team has the expertise to implement the solution proposed.
Here's how you, by illustrating your team's capabilities to them, will face their resistance and have the opportunity to convince them to do so.

If you were selling a project to a client, you may have to build credibility around your ability to deal with the project, your track record of successful projects over the years or testimonials who expose themselves to say that you are good at your job.

Do we do this to make ourselves look good in front of the client?

Not really.

We must talk about ourselves when it is necessary to support our audience in believing in our value proposition.

In practice, you are building credibility and giving the audience a reason to believe.

This leads us to add a further section to the storytelling structure that we have previously shaped. [2]

Simple, isn't it?

Yet, that's not how people present.

In fact, it is important to build your own credibility, but it should never be the starting point.

What do I mean?

I'm telling you that there is no point in starting the presentation by talking about yourself and your credentials to build credibility, because people are only interested in hearing about themselves and not about you and how good you are.

Therefore, starting a presentation by talking about yourself, in a vain attempt to gain attention with your background, is the quickest way to losing your audience's interest.

The credibility part is fundamental to overcome the audience's resistance but, remember, it always comes at the end and complements the overall structure.

STORYTELLING

CONTEXT	Introduction of the initial context, of the protagonist and of all the habits that will soon be changed
PROBLEM	The protagonist's conflict. This part introduces a problem so serious that the protagonist is forced to change his way of acting and do something that he would never have done otherwise
SOLUTION	The resolution of a problem. Usually the time for releasing the tension created by the problem and questioning the success of the protagonist
CREDIBILITY	Provides reasons to believe the implicit value proposition in the change presented by the speaker

---

2 SCoRe Model – The Presentation: A Story About Communicating Successfully With Very Few Slides by Abela Ph.D., Andrew V.

7.1.4. IF YOU WANT THEM TO DO IT, YOU MUST ASK THEM

Think of a web page dedicated to converting users to a product.

Have you ever purchased a book on Amazon?

The purchase page of a book is represented as in the following image.

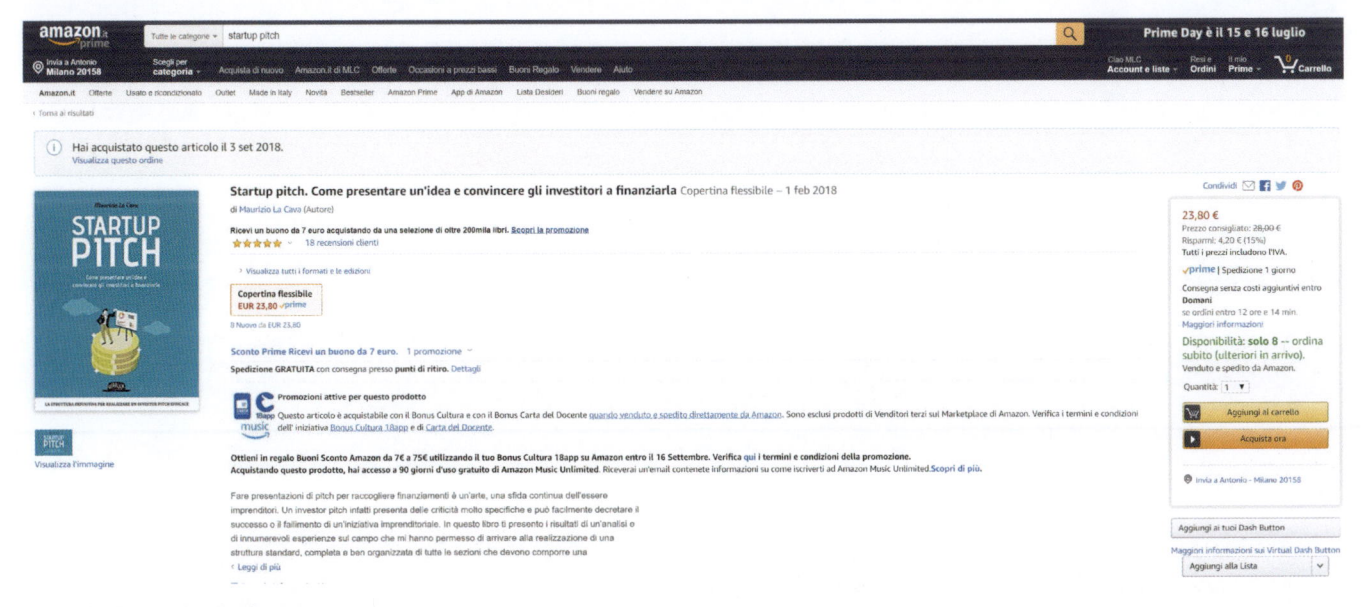

Image 6 - Amazon book sale page

What elements does it contain?

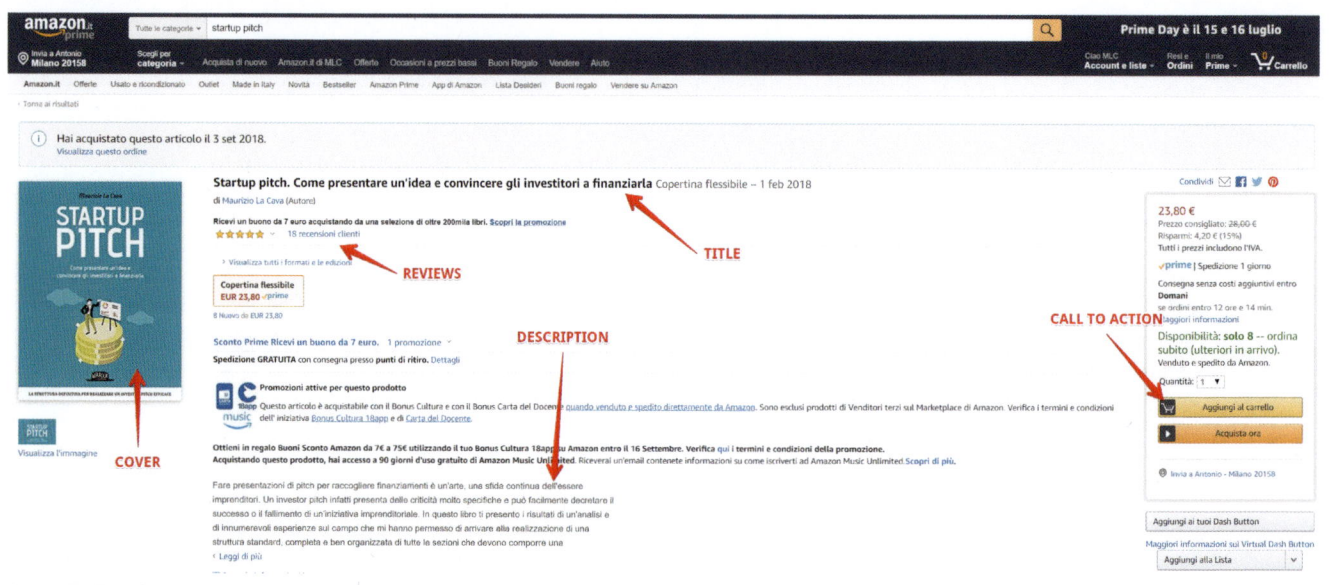

Image 7 - The elements that make up an Amazon page

First, there is the cover of the book that, with a possibly captivating graphic, tries to attract attention to the product;

There is an opening title of the page that represents the name of the product;

Below, a description adds more details to the product;

Reviews make it easier for people to choose because, having no time, we are led to trust the judgment of the masses and choose the solution that has received the best consensus from the public (= social confirmation).

There is still one element to describe.

The so-called *Call to Action*.
What am I talking about?

The product purchase button.
Think about it for a moment.

All the elements described above serve one purpose only, which is that you click on the purchase button and proceed with the order.

After all, what is the point of attracting the reader's attention with a good title, a nice cover and inviting him to read through a powerful description if, in the end, he doesn't click on the purchase button?

This is an excellent example of persuasive communication aimed at a specific goal: the on-page conversion of the user, that is, making the user buy the book.

The purchase is made through an action - the click on the purchase button.

The button is therefore called Call to Action.
What would this page be used for in the absence of the purchase button?

I'll tell you.

For a damn thing!
Why am I giving you this example?

Because I think that a presentation is a persuasive communication aimed at achieving a result.

You want your audience to do something they would never have done without your presentation.

So, you need to make them click on your purchase button.

But we are not on a website, and in a presentation there is no button to click on.

See, what I'm trying to tell you is that if you want people to do something they wouldn't have done otherwise your presentation plays a preparatory role, but you're the one who's going to push them to do it by asking them.

I'm going to ask them.

Imagine presenting your startup to obtain financing from an investor. At the end of the presentation, you will have to openly make your request.

If you are selling a product or simply giving recommendations for top management to adopt them, you must share the next steps and clearly indicate the way forward from the first.

In short, if you want people to do something, you must ask them openly.

For this reason, I believe that a good presentation cannot fail to conclude with a valid Call to Action.

Here is the narrative structure of a successful presentation.

STORYTELLING

CONTEXT — Introduction of the initial context, of the protagonist and of all the habits that will soon be changed

PROBLEM — The protagonist's conflict. This part introduces a problem so serious that the protagonist is forced to change his way of acting and do something that he would never have done otherwise

SOLUTION — The resolution of a problem. Usually the time for releasing the tension created by the problem and questioning the success of the protagonist

CREDIBILITY — Provides reasons to believe the implicit value proposition in the change presented by the speaker

CALL TO ACTION — The formal call to action to the audience

7.2. IN SUMMARY

The order in which information is presented significantly affects the effectiveness of your presentations.

The best way to organize the content of a persuasive presentation is to take advantage of storytelling, the peculiar narrative structure of stories.

This way you can win the attention of the reptilian brain and consequently that of the other two.

Get people's attention by putting your audience at the center of attention and make presentations that convince people to act.

8
CHAPTER

PRINCIPLES OF PERSUASION

« I THINK THE POWER OF PERSUASION WOULD BE THE GREATEST SUPERPOWER OF ALL TIME »

JENNY MOLLEN

A presentation is successful if the audience who listened to it will be persuaded to do something they wouldn't have done otherwise.

Did you manage to get them to achieve the goal you set for them?

As we said, it could be that an investor is interested in your startup or a customer wants to buy your product or service, but even if they simply adopted your recommendation and you were able to influence a business decision, it would be a success.

If I told you that persuasion is a science and that there are shortcuts that significantly increase the chances of success?

If so far, by defining the storytelling of a presentation, we have prepared dinner, now is the time to spice it up.

According to Dr. Robert Cialdini there are 6 principles of persuasion that, if intelligently exploited, can significantly increase the probability of receiving a "yes".

I also want to show you two others that come from my experience.

Are you ready?

Let's start.

8.1. RECIPROCITY

The best way to get something out of someone?

Simple, we've seen it before.

Just be the first to give.

If I invite you to my birthday party, when you'll throw your own, you'll feel compelled to invite me. If a friend offers you dinner, you'll probably feel compelled to pay the next time.

We are used to returning a good gesture to us.

In a presentation, this principle decrees the success or failure of the initial attack.

Do you remember what people in the audience think right before you start talking?

I'll remind you.

They'll be asking themselves: "Give me at least one good reason why I should pay attention to you and not do any of the other urgent things I have to do and to which I could devote my time".

If you want your presentation to work, you absolutely need people's attention. But nowadays attention is, as well as their time, a scarce resource.

So, by analyzing the situation, you're asking your audience for something before you even start.

Do you really want their attention?

Then answer their question.

What do you really have for them?

Start by giving, immediately create curiosity so as to lay the foundations for that relationship of empathy that will allow you to win their attention.

What do I mean?

I told you to start with the problem, remember?

True, but you must be careful, as starting from a problem that touches the people in front of you does not mean telling them something they already know, otherwise they will perceive that you have nothing interesting to say.

Are you lost?

You don't have to, it's much simpler than you can imagine, just use your head.

Follow me.

Use the sensitivities of your audience to one or more problems to decline your communication so that it is interesting for them.

For example, you could give them some information they don't know about the main issue. You could highlight the severity of the problem by means of interesting numbers.

Lately, I have become very sensitive to problems related to the impact of pollution on health.

Recently, a startup I'm following to improve their pitch opened the presentation by telling me that pollution is a serious problem, and we agree so far, nothing new, then they told me something interesting:

"a problem that cannot be measured is a problem that cannot be solved".

Interesting, I'm sure that in Milan pollution is detected and kept under control.

At that point, they explained to me that in the city where I live there are very few sensors for its detection, and that since the pollution should be measured in a capillary manner, unfortunately the data collected are often not significant.

At the same time, London has placed hundreds of sensors throughout the city and is heavily investing in the measurement infrastructure.

What can I say?

Interestingly, they told me something I did not know.

When they gave me the gift of letting me discover new information about a topic to which I am sensitive, they stimulated my curiosity and generated empathy because now I perceive them as more informed about the field than I am, and therefore they have my trust.

Remember, be the first to give if you want to be sure to receive.

8.2. AUTHORITY

You know when you enter the doctor's office, he shows up in a white coat, visits you, tells you what to do and you carefully take notes?

If necessary, you even ask a few questions to make sure that you can properly follow up all his recommendations.

You would never dream of questioning a decision made by your doctor.

He tells you what to do, you take note of it and you do it.

In that moment, you are under his authority.

The same thing happens when you enter a parking lot and the valet, wearing his uniform, guides you and tells you where to go - you won't argue with him, you will do as he says.

In these two examples there are people who gain authority based on the context and a wearable accessory, which in one case is a coat and in the second a uniform.

Have you ever seen the movie with Leonardo di Caprio and Tom Hanks: Catch Me If You Can?

That film is a hymn to this principle, in my opinion.

Frank Abagnale Jr is an internationally renowned con man who manages to pass himself off as a doctor, a lawyer, a professor and, as you can see in the film, often a flight attendant by simply putting himself in the right place and in the right context.

In one scene, his archenemy, FBI agent Karl plunges him into a hotel room with a gun pointed at him, and Frank just pretends to be a secret service agent, leveraging the fact that Karl had never seen his face.

Karl doesn't believe it immediately and orders him to put his hands up, but Frank continues to calmly explain to him that he, an American intelligence agent, has just captured the crook.

He gives him his wallet as a sign of trust and then distracts him by continuing to tell him how the story went.

Although it is a true story, the scenes are probably fictional, but it is very interesting to see how easy it is to convince people of your authority, changing your attitude and possibly equipping yourself with the right tools.

How does this happen in the world of presentations?

Simple, just be credible!

Do you remember the final part of the flow in which you build your credibility?

At that moment, you must give your audience a reason to convince them that you are competent in the matter you are dealing with and that they can trust the solution you are proposing.

Do you know when a consulting company tries to sell you a project and, to convince you, they show off their certifications and qualifications?

After all, isn't it like the doctor who displays his degree in his practice for patients to see?

Think about a physiotherapist who welcomes you to his clinic and has all the certificates he has obtained through specialization courses displayed in plain sight.

Obviously, authority must be built in contexts where you are not already recognized.

It would be pointless to show off your degree and your entire resume during a business meeting with your boss.

Instead, it would be advisable to show your entrepreneurial experience in front of a new investor you are asking to finance your last startup.

It makes sense on the website of a web marketing agency that sells consulting on Google Ads to show that you are a Google partner and so on.

Authority is easy to build and is very powerful towards your audience.

8.3. CONSISTENCY

The principle of consistency states the following: your future behavior is influenced by what you have already done or said.

It's also very easy to understand on a logical level: you always try to keep a consistency between what you say and what you do; nobody likes to be defined as an incoherent or a liar.

Imagine you decided to quit smoking.

As long as you decide this between you and yourself, even if you later decide to smoke a cigarette with your friends, nothing happens.

How does it change if you have publicly shared your choice on Facebook?

Imagine that you feel like smoking a cigarette and that your friends see you doing it, wouldn't you feel at fault?

Your friends will think that you are failing in your commitment, and this judgment will make you uncomfortable.

Micro commitments oblige you to be consistent in your future choices.

You know when they stop you on the street and ask you to sign up against world hunger?

Anyone would sign against world hunger but what happens when, immediately after signing, they ask you for a donation?

If you do not give, you will contradict your previous gesture, the signature, and this will create a discomfort that you will probably prefer to avoid with a donation.

To take advantage of this principle, you need to create micro-commitments in people.

These are simple commitments to which anyone would agree in the first place, but that will help you to bind future choices.

During a presentation, an easy way to get a micro commitment is to ask people to raise their hands.
To reinforce this effect you can ask, after having made them raise their hand, to look around to evaluate the answers of their colleagues.

This way they will judge each other, and the micro commitment will become public for each person in the audience.

Use these micro commitments later on, for example, to make your final call to action irresistible.

8.4. APPRECIATION

We're all more inclined to say yes to someone we like.

But what does it mean that we like someone?

I'm not talking about appearance.

We tend to appreciate someone who has something similar to us.

For example, imagine being on the subway in a very different country from your homeland. Suddenly, you hear a person speaking your own language, you approach her and ask her what part of the country she is from.

This is the beginning of a conversation that might never have started in your country.

In this case, however, you are both abroad in a situation where you have something in common, and for this reason you will like that person and you will tend to trust her accordingly.

This principle also applies in the professional or teaching world.

Imagine that you are working with your team.

The day comes for the review with your manager who, as soon as he arrives, starts to tell you what's good and what needs to be fixed.

You obey and do your duty, but there is no empathy.

Imagine if your superior had sat down with you and reasoned with you to achieve the best solution.

There is a big difference from looking at a machine from the outside and saying how the gears should turn and integrate with that machine as one of the gears that can facilitate its performance.

During a presentation, we start by sharing the problem because if people understand that we are aware of what problems are important to them, they will feel closer to us.

Tackling a common problem means working on common goals.

This is an excellent technique to build empathy from the very first seconds of the presentation and thus win people's attention.

8.5. SOCIAL CONFIRMATION

When people don't know what to choose, they rely on the choices of others.

Imagine that you are in a vacation spot and want to choose a restaurant where you can take your partner to dinner.

You google the restaurants in the area and then you check your profile on TripAdvisor and Google My Business.

First, you look at the photos of the food, you like the first one, you keep it in mind, and you proceed with your search. Of the other results, only one has good food photos and now you're undecided between the two.

What do you do?

You check which one has the best rating.

What does that mean?

That you simply select the restaurant that has the most positive reviews.

If the occasion is really important, maybe because you're inviting your partner to dinner for your anniversary, then you might even read the reviews to be sure.

Although we all know that reviews are not necessarily representative of the truth, they do influence our choices.

There are now reviews everywhere online, see Amazon for example (in the image, one of my books shows 18 reviews).

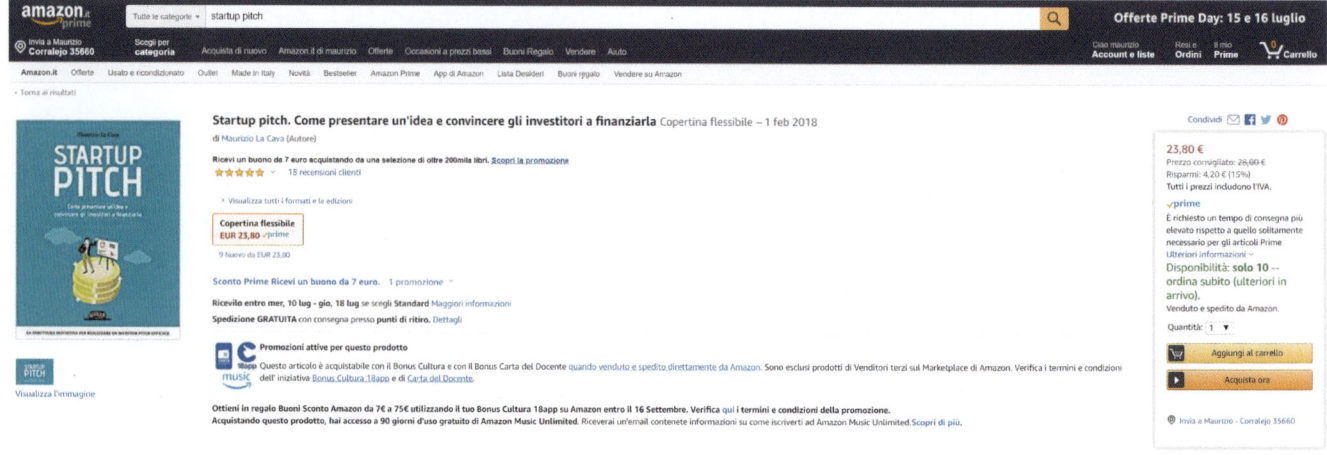

Image 1 - Startup Pitch reviews

TripAdvisor has built a business on this concept:

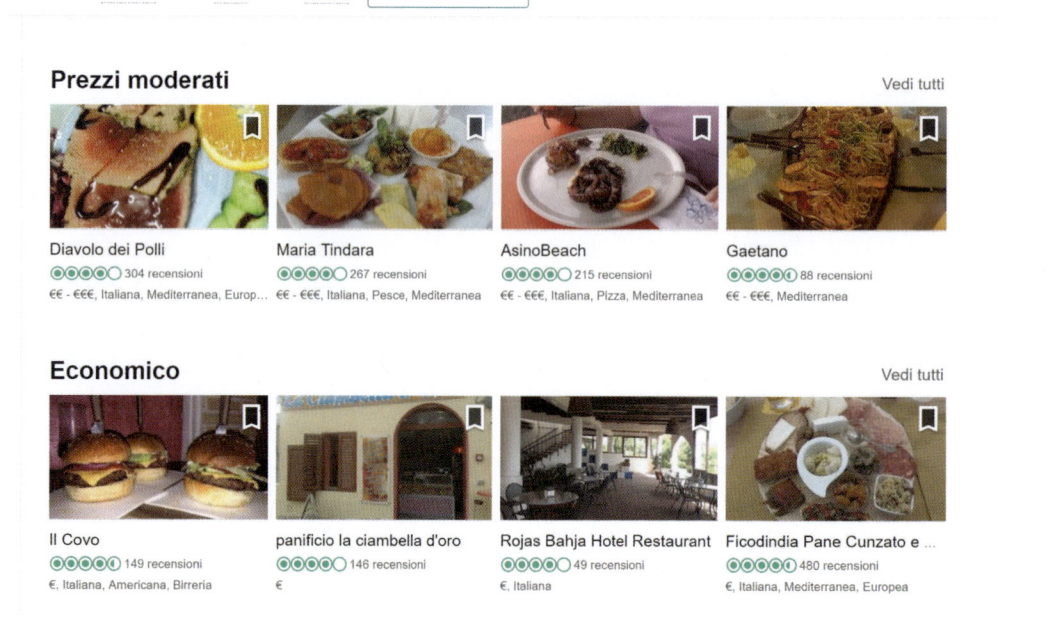

Image 2 - Restaurant reviews on TripAdvisor

Reviews seriously influence people's purchasing choices.

On the other hand, if you are writing a book or selling a product online, you probably know how important they are so that your product can find a market and be appreciated.

So, let's make a deal: I'm doing my best to share with you everything I think is useful to revolutionize the way you communicate through presentations and you, if you like it, can go on Amazon and leave me a sincere comment on the book you're reading.

Do we agree?

Okay, so I'll start by giving you the best through these lines.

How can you apply the principle of social confirmation in your presentations?

Easy, I'll explain.

Imagine giving a presentation in which you are selling a product or service. There will be a time when you will show your testimonials, other happy customers or, possibly, past success stories.

In short, you will show that other people are comfortable with your product or service and this will significantly improve the likelihood that your audience will accept the call to action.

8.6. SCARCITY

People want more those things they can have less.

Let me give you an example right away.

Have you ever heard of a brand called Off White?

It's an expensive streetwear brand that, recently, seems to have surpassed the likes of Gucci in popularity.

Off White has become famous for products developed in collaboration, for example, with Nike.

Let's visit their eCommerce to evaluate a purchase.

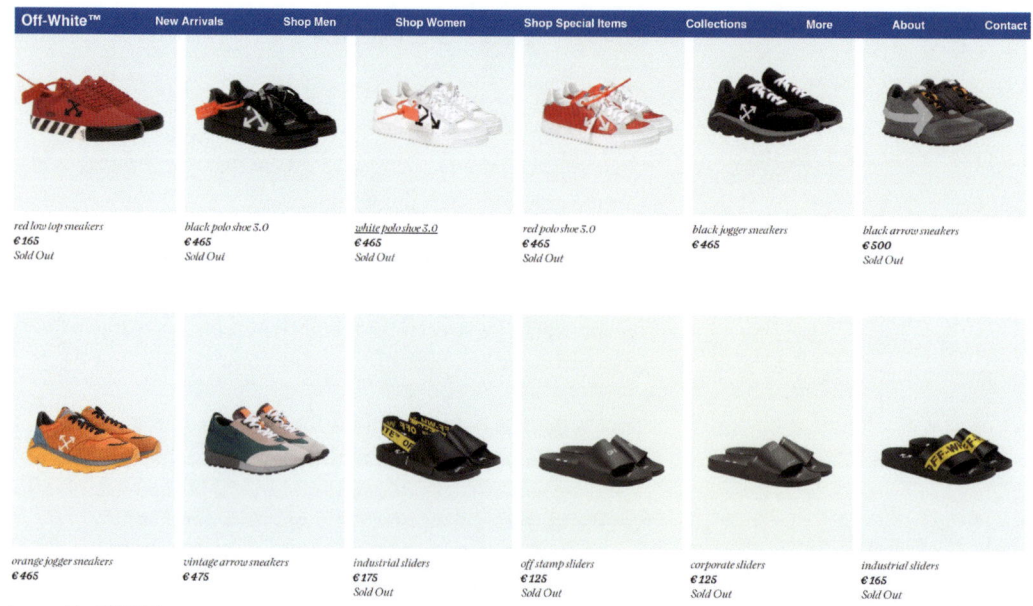

Image 3 - Off White

Practically most of their products are sold out.

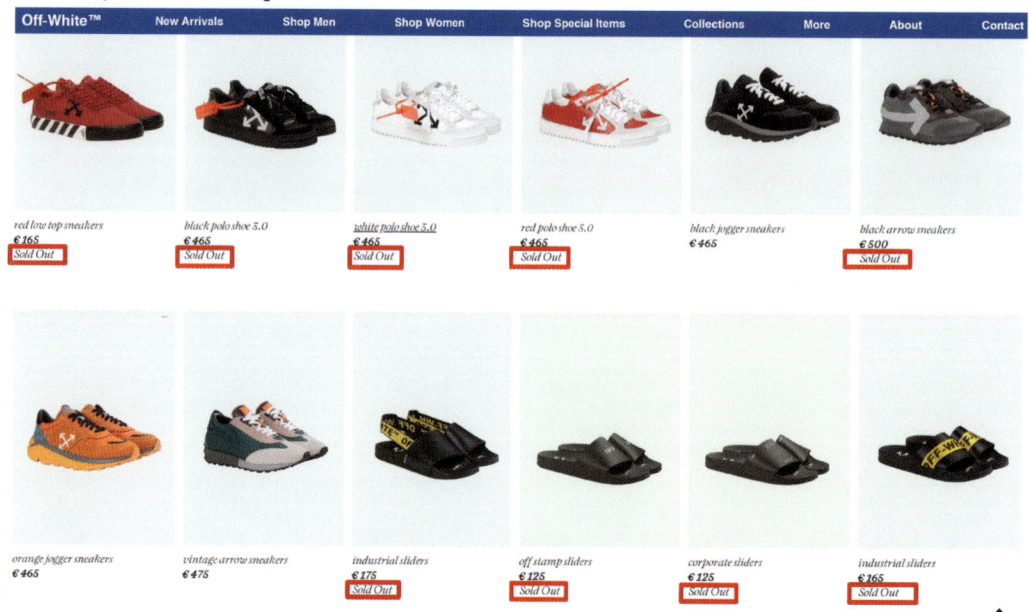

Image 4 - Scarcity on almost all products in the catalogue

Don't they want to sell?

On the contrary!

Have you ever seen how their launch works?

When they launch new shoes, they distribute a very limited number of units, for example, 80 pairs of shoes maximum.

As soon as sales open, on the day of the launch, hell breaks loose on their eCommerce and everyone tries to buy them.

Whoever gets them is practically a hero.

Think that these products are so rare that they are often found on other portals that resell them even ten times more than their initial price.

In short, if you can get a limited-edition Off-White model, you're a phenomenon because it's in fashion and because you somehow managed to win the day of the launch.

Are you following me?

I'm not a real Off-White fan, but I find this particular way of managing their launches extremely interesting from a marketing point of view.

Exploiting scarcity means leveraging a limited number of available products to boost their demand.

8.7. URGENCY

You know all those timed promos that urge the customer to buy so they don't miss the opportunity?

That is the principle of urgency at work.

This technique is, for example, widespread in online sales when you are offered a bundle (the product you are looking for plus something else that raises the perceived value of the cart) and you are told that the offer is valid until, perhaps, the evening of the day the offer came out.

The principle of urgency is often combined with that of scarcity, and that's how limited time offers come into being.

The combination works very well, and it is proven that it significantly increases call to action conversion rates.

It's no coincidence that Booking makes an extensive use of it.

Let's say you are going to Bali in the next few months, let's see what happens.

In the search you are already informed that there is only one room available (scarcity).

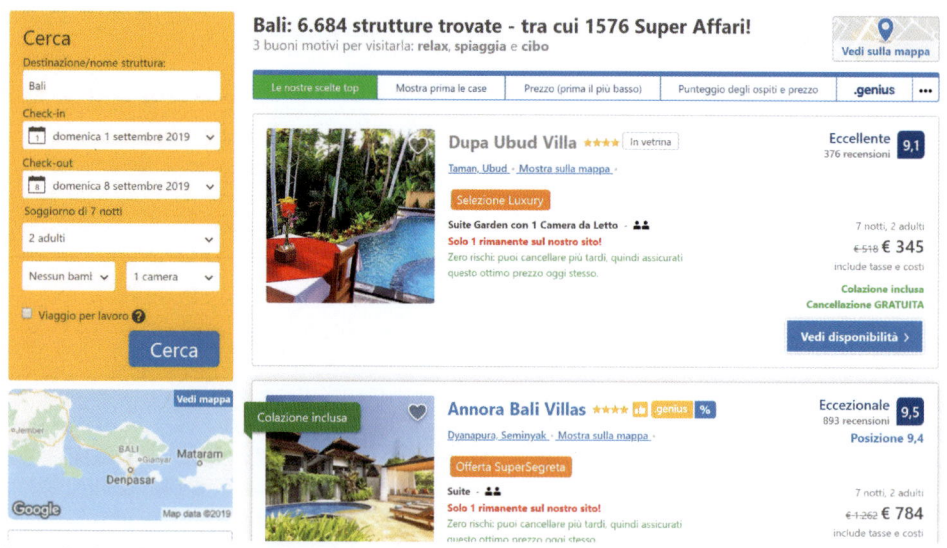

Image 5 – Scarcity on booking.com

You hurry up, open the tab of the villa and find a nice timer that shows you the offer of the day that will expire in 5 hours (urgency).

Image 6 - Urgency and Scarcity at work on booking.com

I mean, if you want this room, you really must hurry!

Also, I will not come out unscathed from this demonstration, because now I will be bombed by emails that will try to get me back to the page of the villa to make a reservation.

In presentations, you too will have a call to action on which you want people to act.

My advice is to limit as much as possible their space of action by telling them that the opportunity is not for everyone and is limited in time.

Are you wondering in which cases this principle applies?

For example, in sales presentations and, even better, in fundraising presentations.

How?

It's easy and powerful, follow me.

When you show the slide with the request for funding that illustrates how much you are collecting, the typical error is to present it as a request and not as an opportunity.

What do I mean by that?

If you make a request you put yourself in the position of having to win the consent of your audience, if instead you offer them the opportunity to jump on board the project, for a limited time (urgency) and for the maximum amount collected (scarcity), then it is your audience that must win the approval to become one of the few selected.

You are actually communicating the same information, but the way you communicate it can radically change the outcome.

Another example is the presentation of offers to sell new services.

The presentation closes with the opportunity to work together if, and only if, the offer is confirmed by a certain date, otherwise it will have to be remade.

This avoids sending out offers that will be waiting for months without getting a response and pushes people to make a decision.

In short, scarcity and urgency are two fundamental principles which are very powerful on people - do not hesitate to combine them when there's an opportunity to do so, because they really work well together.

8.8. TRUST

You have to buy a new laptop, and you want to be sure to spend the right amount on a good quality product.

You don't know where to start because there are too many parameters to evaluate, too many brands to consider and too many places to buy at different price points.

We all have the geek friend we call when our computer fails, or we have to make a new purchase.

At this point you may have done all the research you want, and you may have gathered endless information, but in the end your trusted friend's opinion will be the one that will really guide your purchase.

Trust is a matter of leadership.

Are you a person who inspires trust?

Don't take it bad, follow me.

When a new customer contacts you to solve his problem, he often asks you specifically what he wants but, just as often, the solution he asks you for is wrong.

In fact, the customer should not always be supported in my opinion, but rather guided towards the best solution for him. It is not certain that the customer knows the best solution in your field of expertise, otherwise why would he call you?

It's as if your home sink is leaking and you tell the plumber what he should do. You know that there is a problem, but he will be the one to propose a solution.

If you put yourself in a position of guidance towards your audience, you will be able to establish a relationship of trust and then more easily push them to act on the call to action.

If your audience trusts you, then they will follow you and trust you to show them the way to change.

Trust, however, is won in the field with continuity and determination.

It can take a lifetime to win people's trust, and it only takes a few moments to lose it forever.

I think that trust is gained by your attitude during the presentation - so it's up to you to be able to play your part well in the way you approach your audience.

There is another example of the application of this principle, which is the famous free trial of your product.

If, for example, you are selling a product/service, and you need to win the confidence of the audience in order to make them buy, a good strategy could be to let them try a demo (or shortened version of the product) to convince them of the quality and make them trust you enough to buy it.

Allowing you audience to try the product before buying also shows transparency, and therefore creates trust in the people who follow you.

8.9. IN SUMMARY

The effectiveness of presentations can be maximized if the principles of persuasion are applied to the presentation flow.

Among them, we have seen 8 very powerful principles that can be applied to the different sections of the presentation.

Learn to use these principles in an intelligent and balanced way, and you will see that your call to action will become irresistible.

CHAPTER 9

A STRATEGIC CANVAS TO STRUCTURE THE CONTENT OF PRESENTATIONS

« EVERY BATTLE IS WON BEFORE IT IS FOUGHT »

SUNTSU

This concludes the first two phases of the Lean process of approaching presentations.

In the first, you have learned to understand the audience and determine the resistance to your goal, while in the second, you have learned to structure your communication in an engaging and effective way through storytelling.

Finally, you learned how to use persuasion principles to enhance the effectiveness of your presentations.

Think of the principles as a checklist of elements to be ticked every time you used them. Of course, checking all of them will mean that your presentation is making the most of the levers of persuasion.

Use the principles wisely, without exaggerating or forcing their use.

Creating a successful presentation means having an eye on all these elements and possibly being able to share them with the team while you work.

In order to work in an organized way and eventually to be able to perform a collaborative work, I decided to summarize all these fundamental concepts for the realization of an effective presentation in a Canvas that I called Lean Presentation Strategy Canvas

LEAN PRESENTATION STRATEGY CANVAS — Speech title _____ Date _____

Audience	Objective	Resistances
The target of your presentation, who are you going to present to?	The reason why you are doing the presentation. What do you want the audience to do after your presentation?	The beliefs of the audience that prevent the audience to accept your change.

Context	Problem	Solution	Evidence	Call to action
Introduce the protagonist of the story and give a general understanding of the context to the audience	Create the conflict in the story introducing one or more problems and their impacts. The problem has to be declined into the audience' words and has to be relevant to the audience. The complication creates the necessary boost of attention to introduce the resolution	Present one or more solutions to the main problem/s. This section releases tension in the audience. The solutions need to perfectly match the problems.	Introduce the reason to believe to support the resolution. This section helps you to lead the audience to overcome its resistances to the change you are proposing them	Trigger the action of the audience by launching your request. This request represents the objective of your presentation. If you want them to do something you need to directly ask.

☐ Reciprocity | ☐ Authority | ☐ Consistency | ☐ Liking | ☐ Social Proof | ☐ Scarcity | ☐ Urgency | ☐ Trust

DESIGNED & CREATED BY MLC Presentation Design Consulting S.r.l. || Lean Presentation Design tools || https://mauriziolacava.com || info@mauriziolacava.com

Image 1 - Audience Assessment Canvas - Understanding the audience

I usually print a copy and then use a post-it for each section, letting all the ideas that come to my mind roam free in the first phase of brainstorming.

So, at first, I use it as a container to support the generation of ideas. Secondly, I write directly in the boxes the peculiar characteristics of the audience relevant for my presentation (only the information that really interests me), I identify the target, and finally I list all the resistances.

After building the base I can use the information collected to give life to my storytelling and then to the presentation flow.

Following the structure, I work from left to right starting from the section: Situation, which allows me, as seen, to introduce the context.

When you have completed the canvas, you will have very clear ideas about your presentation.

You will have made a careful choice of information and you will have defined an effective communication flow according to the specific audience.

There is another case where the canvas comes in handy, and that's when I assess someone else's presentation.

Why?

Simple, I'll explain.

When someone asks me to review their presentation, by following the canvas I am always able to ask the right questions and immediately identify the weaknesses to work on.

So, even if you're not the one creating the presentations, but you're delegating them to your team, the Lean Presentation Strategy Canvas is a useful tool to give structured feedback and guidance to those preparing your presentation.

You can download the Lean Presentation Strategy Canvas for free from the website https://mauriziolacava.com in the tools section, or use the tools you can find at the end of the book.

9.1. HOW TO STRUCTURE A SALES PRESENTATION

Imagine selling a software developed for management consultants.

You are given the opportunity to make an on-site presentation by the potential client during which you can explain what the benefits of the tool are and why it would make sense for them to buy it.

Here comes the interesting part!

The responsibility is all yours, you must prepare a presentation with the precise aim of selling a product to a defined audience.

Take the canvas and start writing.

For example, I use, develop and market a PowerPoint Add-in, which I introduced to you in the book's preface and which is called MLC PowerPoint Add-in.

It is a software that extends the functionality of PowerPoint and makes you much more efficient and precise in realizing effective slides.

Let's say it's a bit like the magic wand of any self-respecting Lean Presenter.

Since management consultants produce tons of slides (I've been there myself, and I'm well aware of that), MLC PowerPoint Add-in is a very useful tool for them.

Let's try using the Lean Presentation Strategy Canvas to structure the sales presentation of the MLC PowerPoint Add-in, assuming we are introducing it to the world of management consultants.

Complex?

No, don't worry,

We'll do it together. Follow me.

Let's start with the people.

The audience is composed of management consultants and the goal is for them to install the free trial.

Why shouldn't they?

Let's see together some resistances that I imagined as an example.

They might think that the software doesn't work well, that's why we'll have to explain how it works in detail and convince them of the quality of the product in the solution part.

This resistance may not crumble with a simple explanation of the features, and that's why in the Evidence part we'll include case studies.

They might think it's too expensive, but you'll justify the price after discussing the benefits in a dedicated section that we'll call budget in the canvas.

They may think that the tool is too difficult to use, and that no one has time to study a new software, even if it could be a life-changer.

For this last reason, we will introduce a detailed explanation on the operation and ease of use of the software in the solution part.

LEAN PRESENTATION STRATEGY CANVAS

Speech title: **MLC POWERPOINT ADDIN**   Date: _____

Audience: MANAGEMENT CONSULTANTS

Objective: INSTALL THE FREE TRIAL

Resistances:
- THE SOFTWARE DOESN'T WORK
- IT COSTS TOO MUCH
- IT IS TOO HARD TO USE

Context: Introduce the protagonist of the story and give a general understanding of the context to the audience.

Problem: Create the conflict in the story introducing one or more problems and their impacts. The problem has to be declined into the audience' words and has to be relevant to the audience. The complication creates the necessary boost of attention to introduce the resolution.

Solution: Present one or more solutions to the main problem/s. This section releases tension in the audience. The solutions need to perfectly match the problems.

Evidence: Introduce the reason to believe to support the resolution. This section helps you to lead the audience to overcome its resistances to the change you are proposing them.

Call to action: Trigger the action of the audience by launching your request. This request represents the objective of your presentation. If you want them to do something you need to directly ask.

Reciprocity | Authority | Consistency | Liking | Social Proof | Scarcity | Urgency | Trust

DESIGNED & CREATED BY MLC Presentation Design Consulting S.r.l. || Lean Presentation Design tools || https://mauriziolacava.com || info@mauriziolacava.com

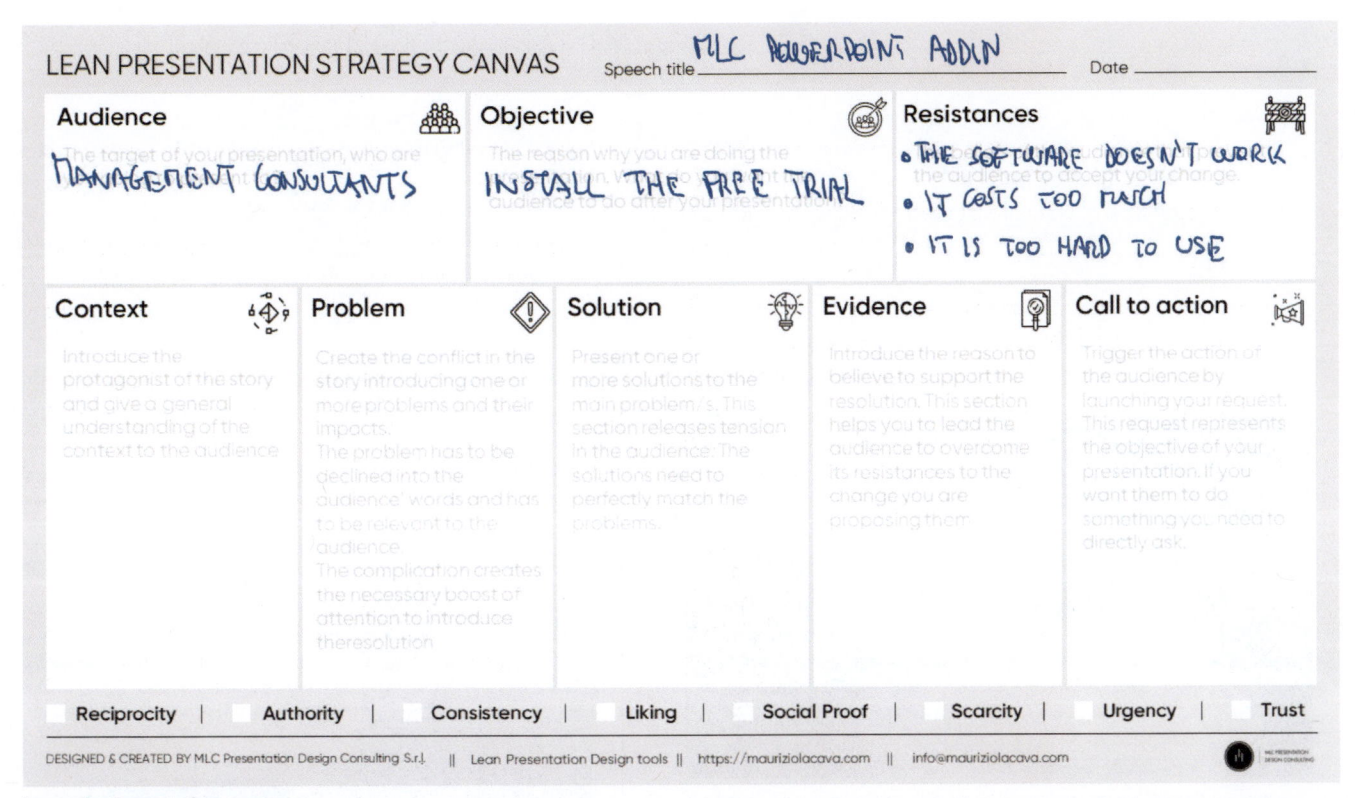

Image 2 – Presentation structure

Resistances should certainly be addressed during the presentation and define the essential minimum contents from which to start.

By asking yourself what resistances you need to overcome in order to convince your specific audience, you already have a list of points to be dealt with in your presentation flow.

Doesn't the audience think the software works? You will explain how it works and show how it solves problems.

Does the audience think it costs too much? You show them how much time they save and how much it is worth. People tend to underestimate the value of their time.

Do they think the software is difficult to use? You'll make a demo showing how anyone with minimal PowerPoint skills can easily benefit from it.

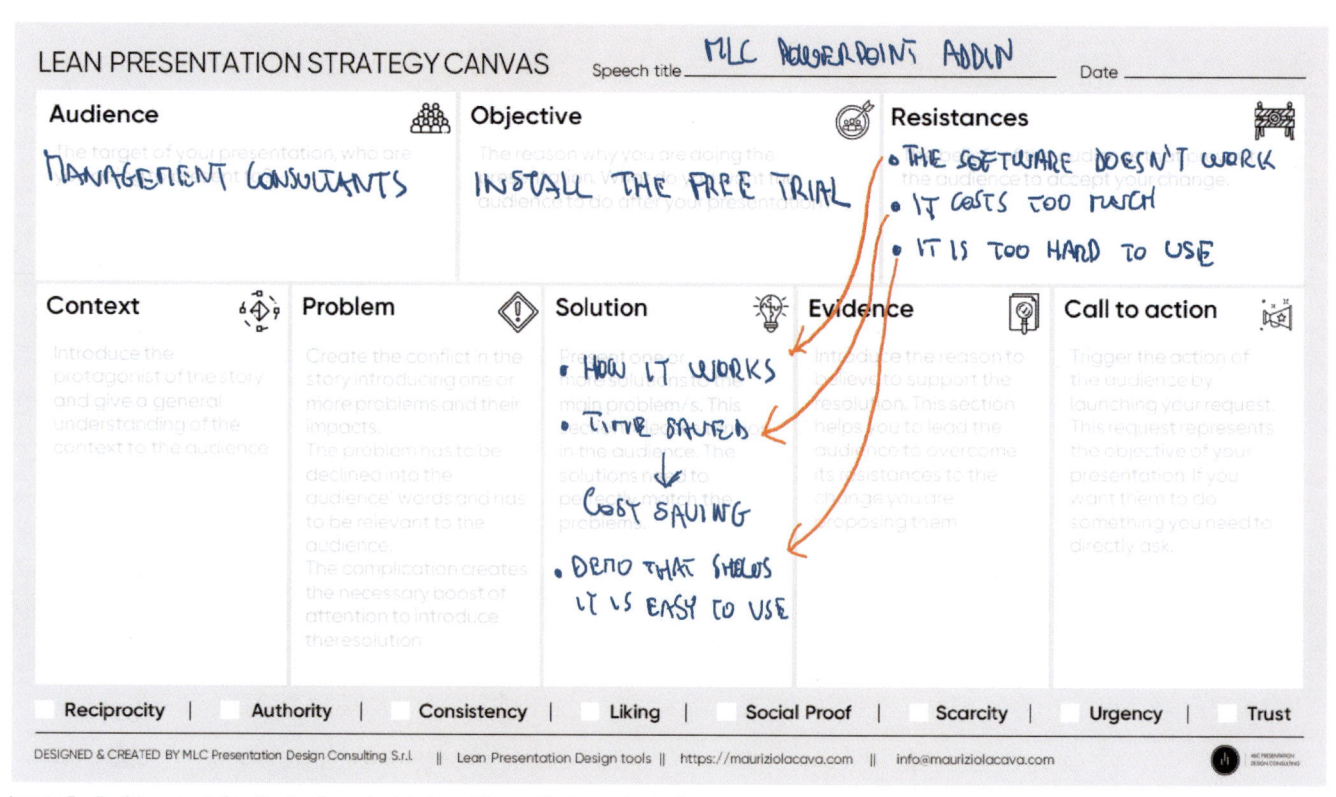

Image 3 - Resistances define the basic content to be addressed in the presentation

See how resistances allowed me to build the solution part of the presentation?
That's why a good understanding of the audience, and therefore of the resistance that they could oppose to the change that you propose, is fundamental.

After defining what information should be present in your presentation flow, you can build the beginning, introduce the context and prepare the ground for the solution through the Problem part.

In the problem you must create empathy with your audience by shedding light on the frustration that people feel when dealing with one or more of the problems in question. You will introduce the impacts, maybe even with some numbers to support it, to give importance to the problem and make the audience aware of something they don't know. This way, you will create curiosity and capture people's attention.

Why?
Simple.

Because you've given them some more information about a problem that's relevant to them.
In our example, the fact that they can save time and that this can result in cost savings is most likely related to the reason why people might want a PowerPoint Add-in.

The amount of time lost in making presentations, which, by the way, are also inaccurate, is definitely a good starting point to introduce the problem to your audience.

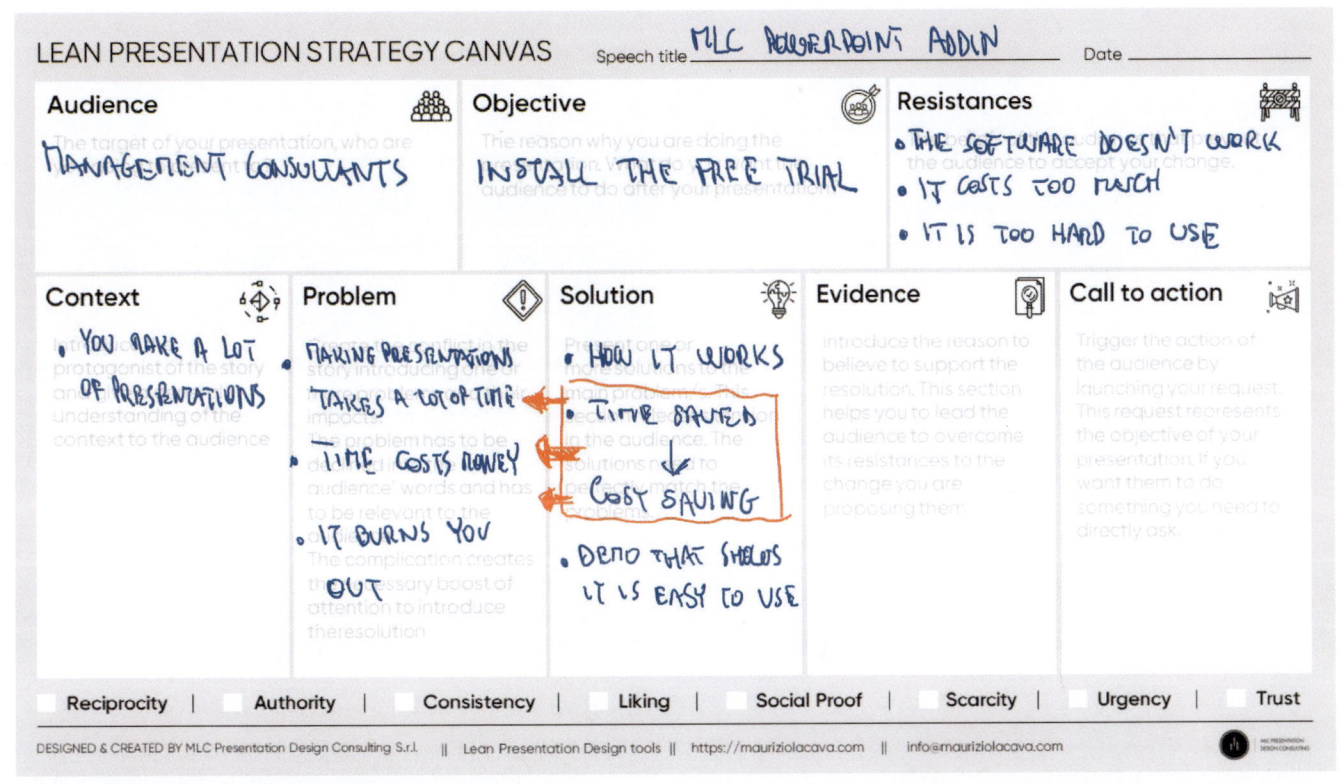

Image 4 – The problem is derived from the solution

The transition between problem and solution is crucial.

The solution can only start with a beautiful Unique Value Proposition.

UVP - the value proposition that a company makes to the market, expressed in terms of perceived benefits, tangible or not, that consumers can get from buying the solution proposed on the market. [1]

In essence, you have to explain what you are selling them in a sentence.

Want some examples?

Here you go:

The UVP (unique value proposition) of the MacBook Air plays on the lightness of the product.

---

[1] https://www.glossariomarketing.it/significato/value-proposition/

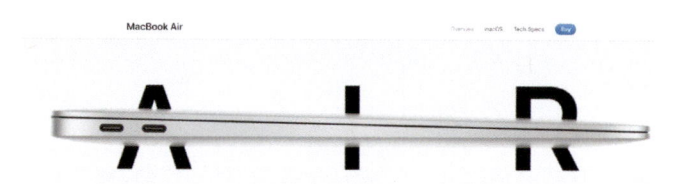

Image 5 - MacBook Air UVP.

Uber's speaks to drivers - get behind the wheel and make a living:

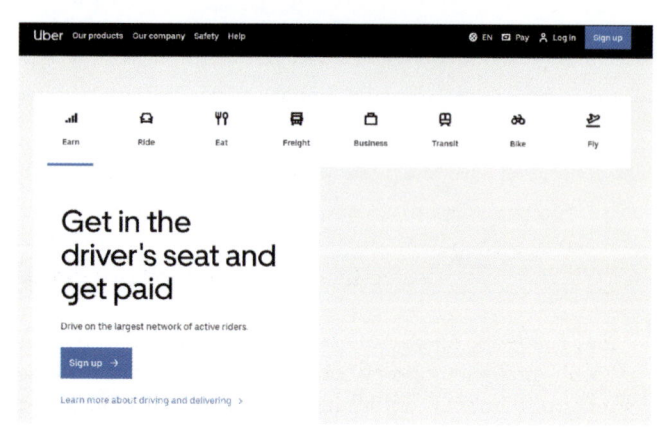

Image 6 – Uber's UVP

Evernote is also a good example - your notes effortlessly organized:

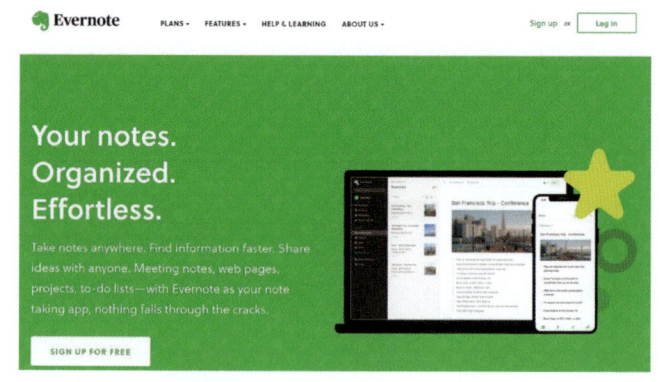

Image 7 – Evernote's UVP

What goes after the UVP?

You will certainly have to explain how your product works in a simple and intuitive way.

My advice is not to become too technical, let others follow you - if some technician has an extra curiosity there will be a way to give him an answer later - for now concentrate on not losing anyone until the end of your speech.

The budget part follows, and then the moment when you show the price of the product.

Before the call to action you can take advantage of it to try an upsell or just to create curiosity about the sale of accessories that increase the value of the customer's product.

An example of an upsell?

Recently I've been working on the new mini iPad and they proposed me to buy the Apple Pencil so that I could write and draw directly on the iPad.

The Apple Pencil is definitely an upsell, it extends the functionality of the product, adds value and allows you to raise the bill for the consumer.

Finally, you can launch your call to action to propose the free trial and the next steps to follow in order to proceed towards the final acquisition of the product by the customer.

You have finalized the entire content structure of the presentation - well done, but there's more.

In fact, the time has come to season your presentation with a little pepper, that is, the application of mental triggers.

Mental triggers form the basis of the Evidence section.

In the Evidence part, you play your credentials and do your best to build credibility.

This part can be more or less complex, depending on how well the customer knows you and trusts you.

The principle of reciprocity is inherent to the fact that the presentation is starting from the problem, and therefore from something relevant to people.

Give immediately something back in exchange for attention. The first one is gone; you can tick it on the canvas.

In the Evidence part I will strengthen my credibility by being presenting myself as an expert in the field thanks to my vertical experience ("why us" section). Through testimonials and case studies, I'll let others talk about me thus creating social confirmation.

All this leads you to strengthen your customer's trust.

Now you can check authority, social confirmation, and trust.

Finally, I will leave a maximum time beyond which the offer to install a free trial version of the software will expire, and in addition I will limit the number of licenses available to a small group of testers per customer.

I introduce the Call To Action - download the free trial version of the software as a limited offer.

By testing the software, I will demonstrate transparency and security towards it, and this will again gain me confidence.

Now you can check scarcity and urgency, as you already checked trust in the previous step.

The principle of liking will concern more my presence in front of people on the day of the presentation.

Considering that this is a presentation on which I have a great deal of experience, let us check the liking section, since I know that I will have go prepared.

Finally, I decided not to apply the principle of consistency because, being the first opportunity to sell the product to this audience, I have no previous commitments to leverage to appeal to their consistency.

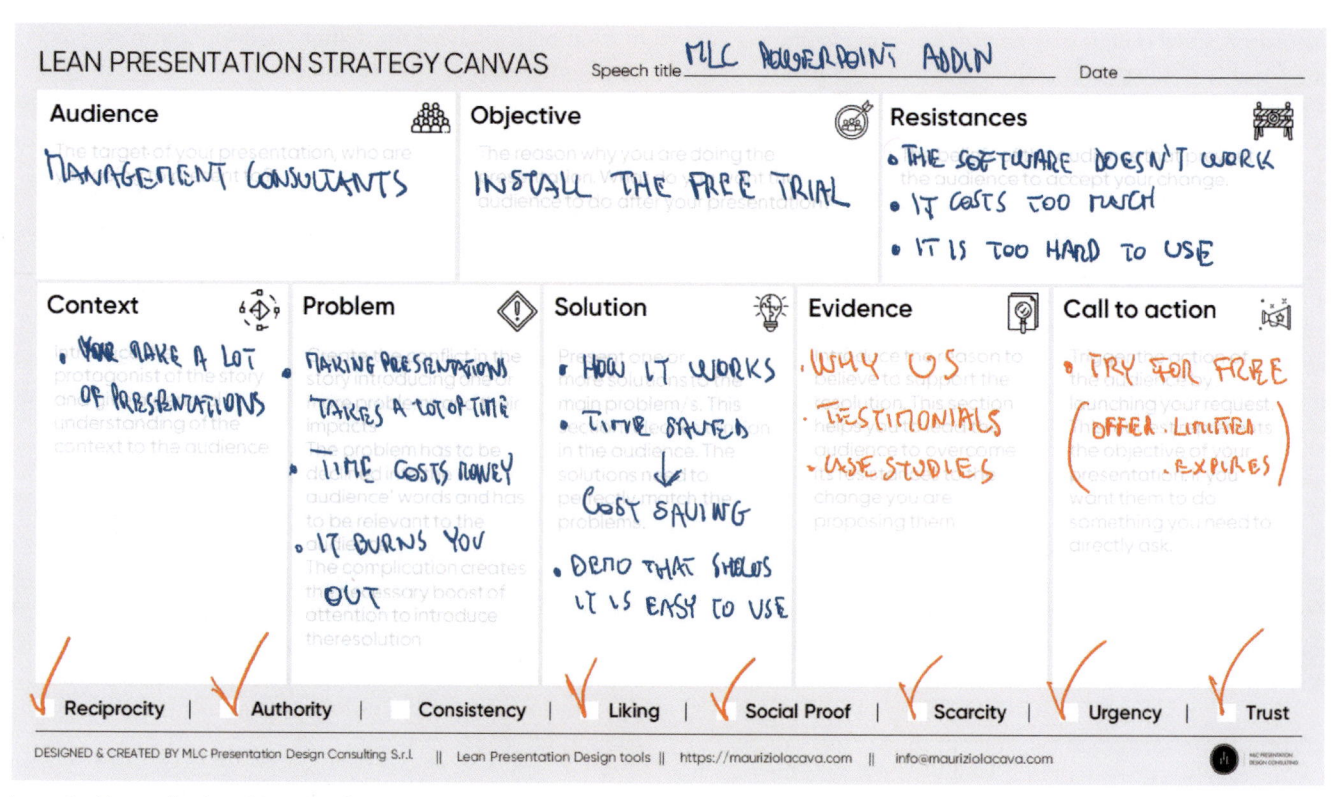

Image 8 – The application of the principles of persuasion in red

See?

The most amazing thing about all we just did is that we haven't even talked about PowerPoint.

However, we have laid the foundations for your communication flow by giving order to the information.

In short, thanks to a template that is on a single A4 sheet, from now on, you will be able to build the complete communication strategy of each of your presentations.

9.2. IN SUMMARY

The Lean Presentation Strategy Canvas is the main tool to build the strategy of each presentation and always have all the components under control.

Its use in brainstorming facilitates collaboration and stimulates teamwork.

The Canvas is also a formidable tool in case you are not the one who designs the presentation, but you still want to overlook the strategic structuring part of the communication.

Finally, it is also a very useful tool for assessing other people's presentations.

In fact, by having all the components under control, you are immediately able to understand what the weaknesses of a presentation are even if you're not the one who created it.

This allows you to give structured feedback and optimize the work of your colleagues or collaborators.

CHAPTER 10

HOOKING – THE INITIAL HOOKING STRATEGY

« THE FIRST BLOW
IS HALF THE BATTLE »

So far, we've been working to get people's attention, which is a key element of your presentation's success.

If you work properly on the structure of your presentation, you will be able to lay the foundations for winning the attention of your audience.

The foundations?

Yes, because you can go one step further.

You're almost there, but you need to take one more step forward.

According to Sequoia Capital, if you have a 60-minute meeting with a group of people, you don't have 60 minutes of their attention.

There is a significant drop in attention over the first 5 minutes.

What does that mean?

That if you don't start the game right, you've already lost it.

It is usually said that the audience is lost during the first 10% of the presentation.

You don't play the game of winning attention during the presentation, but at the beginning.

For this reason, we talk about initial hooking strategies.

Are you ready to discuss about them?

Let's start.

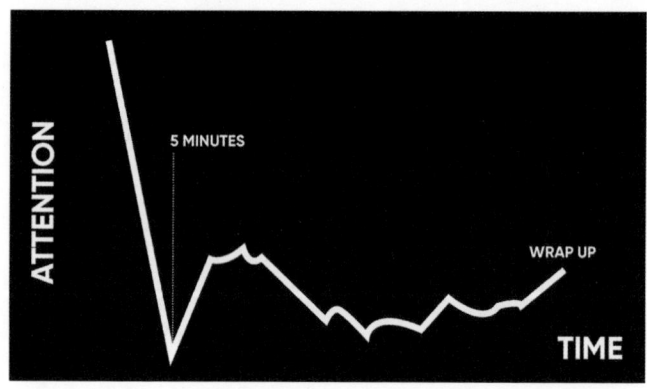

Image 1 - Decrease in attention during the first 5 minutes of the meeting [1]

[1] https://www.sequoiacap.com/article/how-to-present-to-investors/

10.1. INITIAL HOOKING STRATEGIES, WHERE DO WE START?

The first time I asked myself this question I did what anyone would do, I launched Google and did a quick search.

It's not hard to imagine what the result was.

A myriad of experts who suggested their initial attack strategy based on their experience.

I have analyzed a large number of them and have concluded that there are at least 13 effective initial hooking strategies used by the best speakers in the world.

Instead of just showing you my favorite initial hooking strategy, I want to give you a broader overview so that you can choose to use the one you feel most comfortable with.

Ready?

Let's see the hooking strategies in order.

10.1.1. TELL A STORY

When you give a presentation, the context naturally exposes you to the public in a position that can easily be perceived as one of superiority.

What do I mean by that?

You are usually standing in front of your audience; you could be in a meeting room or even on a stage.

In that position you risk creating distance with people in the audience and thus hindering the empathic connection between you and them.

There is a lot of talk about how to humanize the speaker in front of his audience.

I think one of the best ways is to share your experience just as you would do with a group of friends.

So, with the same simplicity and friendliness, tell something that happened to you.

Be careful, though.

The fact that I propose you to tell it in a cordial way does not mean that you do not have to adapt to the context, judge carefully the circumstances to avoid clashing.

Everything is simple so far, isn't it?

Quite the contrary!

How many times do you see speakers who tell personal stories and fail to attract attention?

All too often.

Why does that happen?

Simple, because they misunderstand the concept of storytelling.

But at this point in the book, you know that storytelling is not a simple storytelling but the ability to exploit a precise narrative structure that makes the stories really interesting.

So, when telling your own experience, I recommend that you use the problem/solution structure to create tension at the right times in the story.

Therefore, a context is introduced, and the protagonist is presented so that the audience can identify with it.

The protagonist, in this case you, will encounter a problem initially greater than him that will lead him to change something of his routine and the context previously introduced.

The problem and the doubt that the protagonist will be able to solve it will create tension, and tension will create attention in the story.

We've already covered this narrative structure in detail in previous chapters, so I won't go any further.

Instead, I take this opportunity to show you a new technique, famous, for example, in TV series.

Have you ever wondered how it is possible that finished an episode of a series that you like, you can hardly resist from watching the next?

Imagine that the beginning of each of your presentations is, for your audience, like the end of a TV series and that therefore they cannot resist from knowing how it ends after the introduction, and they want more and more.

The whole audience would hang on to your words and they would all be silent, listening to you.

Think that the simple technique I want to talk to you about is enough to succeed.

Are you ready?

Yes? Very well, then I'll tell you.

But I'll give you a quick introductory note.

No, I'm kidding, I won't give you any introduction, it was just to make you understand the technique!

If it worked, you were curious because I told you about the benefits you could have from using this powerful technique, but I never explained it to you.

This generates curiosity and interest.

Then, I took a break and proposed a premise.

If you are sufficiently intrigued, you absolutely want to learn about the technique, so you will read the premise, even if not desired at that moment, so that you can finally learn this new technique and have access to the benefits stated.

This technique is called: Anticipation.

Every year, millions of technical experts await the keynote presentation for the launch of Apple's new products.

Weeks earlier, Apple begins releasing powerful trailers to raise expectations.

The presentation of the new products then takes place in real events where the anticipation finds its climax and finally the products are revealed.

It's no coincidence that in front of the Apple stores there are people who sleep in tents to be the first to enter the morning after the opening.

How do you apply this to a presentation?

It's up to your creativity to find the right point of view.

For example, you could use the same logic that I proposed to you in introducing the concept of anticipation.

In practice, the technique consists in creating curiosity around something that is not said immediately but will be said at the end.

In fact, it's just like the episode of a TV series in which they start events that remain suspended and then find their realization in the following episode.

10.1.2. QUESTIONS AND INTERACTION WITH THE AUDIENCE

The fact that you, as a speaker, have the spotlight of attention on you should never make you think that you are the hero of the situation.

What do I mean by that?

During a presentation, who must change is not the speaker, but the audience.

Think about it for a moment.

For whom is the objective of change - for the speaker, or for the people who come to listen?

The presenter has a goal for his audience;

So, the hero of the situation is the audience, it is for them the adventure that leads to change, it is for them that you have prepared the whole presentation and it is up to them to act, if they are convinced, at the end of your intervention.

So, who are you?

G. Reynolds would say that if your audience were Luke Skywalker, you would be Master Yoda, a catalyst for change;

Do you want people to listen to you?

Be the first to listen!

What better way to start a presentation than to establish a dialogue with the people in front of you?

It often happens that the speaker in the room tries to force interaction by saying things like: "I like the lesson to be interactive, there are no stupid questions".

Personally, I think that if there is a need for such a statement, the speaker obviously has a problem in generating the involvement of his audience.

A little trick I often use is to start the presentation with a straightforward question, without even saying good morning to people in the classroom.

Too much?

Maybe, but it certainly has an impact.

Imagine you are sitting in the room waiting for the speaker to start talking and you get a direct question.

If you are still looking at your e-mails or are still distracted, you will feel that the presentation has begun without you and you will hurry to catch up and immediately pay attention.

What question to ask?

There are several possible alternatives that I'll let you explore in depth in the guide dedicated to the theme online on my blog (the blog is a valuable complement to the book, so I suggest you go and browse now that you're building the foundations of Lean Presentation Design).

I like to focus attention on people' problem, which is why they should be in the room listening.

In fact, when I teach courses on Lean Presentation Design, the first thing I ask as soon as I enter the classroom is:

"What is your relationship with presentations?".
Usually people, provoked on a hot topic, start to interact.

In doing so, the audience is at the center of attention.

This technique shifts the focus of the presentation to people and the problem they are looking to solve.

In addition, the dialogue lowers initial tensions, creates empathy and lays the foundations for good performance.

In short, the presentation is a dialogue, so let's treat it as such!

10.1.3. SHARE A SHOCKING FACT

Starting with a shocking piece of information for the audience is a classic.

To create this effect, use a surprising statistic.

It captures people's attention by evoking their fears. If you can exploit uncertainty, you can create anxiety about the unknown, and people will need your answers to overcome their fears.

In his TED, Jorge Soto begins by telling a short personal story that culminates in a chilling statistic: one in three people in that audience will find out they have cancer, and one in four will die from it.

It's chilling, isn't it?

You should see the video (I'll leave the link in the notes) [2]!

Slides, in this situation, play a fundamental role.

In fact, it is thanks to the slides that you can use a powerful combination of text and images to bring to life the shocking data and imprint it in people's memory.

What slides would you design for such a hook?

I would visualize it as in the next image.

---
[2] The future of early cancer detection - https://www.ted.com/talks/jorge_soto_the_future_of_early_cancer_detection

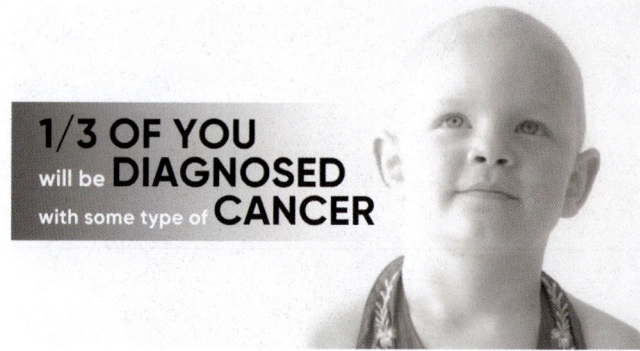

Image 2 - A possible hook slide on J. Soto's strategy

The combination of a powerful slide with a shocking message definitely makes people listen.

Don't forget, however, that it's not enough to give numbers at random but you must hit the curiosity of people with data that touch their interests.

There are two ways to surprise people with this technique:

The "Did you know that" formula
If you can stimulate the curiosity of the audience about a piece of data they were not aware of, you will have their attention.

Some examples could be:

• Did you know that food, if not mixed with saliva, would have no taste for us?

• Did you know that, on average, people fall asleep in 7 minutes?

• Did you know that, on average, every 40 seconds a person in the world commits suicide?

• Did you know that if you sum up the time you blinked your eyes in one day, it would be like having your eyes closed for 30 minutes?

The number first, the consequences afterwards

Exploiting people's fear of a fact that may affect them personally is a very common way of using this technique.

Suppose you're presenting a new car concept with an on-board computer that neutralizes smartphone use while driving.

It could be that the on-board computer connects to your phone via Bluetooth, allowing you to use the maps (as with Android Auto, for example) but making your smartphone unusable for safety purposes while you are driving.

You could introduce the theme starting from the problem you would solve.

How?

Nothing easier.

Launch Google and search for shocking statistics about smartphones on the road, you'll see that you'll really find everything.

Now, choose the most striking statistic and bring it to life with a powerful slide.

For example: 30% of accidents are caused by smartphones.

Can you imagine how this statistic could be represented by a slide?

I drew it like this:

Image 3 - Representation of the initial hooking message

You expected it to be worse, didn't you?

I could have been bloodier in the representation of this statistic; I could have depicted injured or even dead people.

Nevertheless, the slide works well.

Do you know why?

It works well because it's easy to identify with, as it's not so far from our everyday reality.

You decide how much you want to go far in the representation of a statistic and how much you want to be incisive, but remember, what really attracts people's attention is something that concerns them and in which they can identify.

Always remember that people are interested in hearing about themselves before anything else. So, it's not necessary to be bloody, just focus on people and learn to touch the right strings.

10.1.4. USE FAMOUS QUOTES

Quotes are a powerful opening tool for presentations. In fact, a famous quote carries with it a real belief system. What do I mean by that?

Using the famous phrase of a famous character or, possibly, the character of a film or cartoon brings with it the whole world of values and beliefs in which that quote is immersed.

Since you will be on stage, that system of beliefs and values will automatically be attributed to you.

That's why taking advantage of the quote makes you powerful in the eyes of your audience.

You can use different types of quotes: proverbs, famous people or even movies.

In this case, for example, we use a phrase from Einstein: once we accept our limits, we go beyond them and bring the concept to life.

Image 4 - Example slide for famous quote

Nice, isn't it?

This slide is really powerful.

I used some text and an image, but I know very well that creating slides like this is not an easy thing to do.

So, don't worry, I won't take it for granted.

I used a series of visual composition techniques that allowed me to give life to the quote by creating this WOW effect.

Are you curious to know how to do it?
Then read on, because it's going to be the subject of the next chapters.

For now, I want you to be able to appreciate the strength of a good, well-chosen and properly displayed quotation.

10.1.5. DEBUNK A COMMON BELIEF AND PROVOKE THE AUDIENCE

Surprise your audience by showing them that something they have always believed in is not true.

What do I mean?

Imagine a presentation on the theme of healthy eating.

I could structure a presentation as follows:

- Food production significantly affects our planet's health

- One of the main problems is the widespread use of pesticides in agriculture and the pollution they cause

So far, I have introduced the context and started to define the problem. Now I'm introducing the surprise hook.

If we want to increase our chances of survival, we must stop eating organic food

Image 5 – organic food

Image 6 – organic food, no thanks

Did you think I made a mistake?

Not at all!

I could continue by saying:

• Farmers who produce organic food use natural fertilizers which, it has been discovered, sometimes have worse polluting effects than industrial ones.

• In addition, after research conducted on 98,727 cases, it became clear that organic food does not have higher nutritional capacity than regular food

See how the presentation gets interesting?

Imagine that you are selling a new type of industrial fertilizer, this introduction would work perfectly for you.

Debunk a common belief and you will attract the attention of your audience.

10.1.6. GIVE LIFE TO YOUR MESSAGE

They say a picture is worth a thousand words - what about videos, then?

You could start the sales presentation of your new product by presenting features and benefits, but it would be very different if you used an introductory video that introduces the audience directly to the context and let them experience your product as if they were watching a movie.

Depending on the product or service you are presenting, the idea of a video fits more or less well.

In general, videos are a very powerful tool for bringing a message to life, but they need to be handled very carefully.

In fact, videos completely monopolize the audience's attention and create a strong detachment from the speaker.

When the video stops and it's up to you to talk, in fact, you could risk generating a brutal change of pace and quickly result boring to the audience.

Calculate your entry time at the end of the video and use a tone of voice consistent with the video you projected.

In addition, if you want to use a video in your presentation, I strongly recommend that you integrate it directly into your PowerPoint by downloading it, for example from YouTube, and not creating a link from PowerPoint to the online video, so that you are safe from connection problems.

I know, I know, downloading videos from YouTube is always an arduous task.

That's why I invented a software, integrated into PowerPoint, that allows you to do it by simply copying the link of the video you want to insert in the presentation - I'll leave the link in the notes . [3]

Always test the video before you start the presentation. The audio may not work, or the pc may crash due to insufficient memory, and it's never nice when you've bet on a video that doesn't start in your communication flow.

---

3 https://mauriziolacava.com/my-addin

As an alternative to the video, you could bring a prototype or objects that allow the audience to live the experience and make it indelible in their mind.
But keep in mind that every time you give them something to play with, you'll take a back seat and they'll get distracted.

So, work hard on organizing the presentation.

When you give them the experience don't keep on presenting, but support them yourself. Don't let your own techniques go against you.

In general, for us human beings, a lived experience is much easier to remember than an experience that has only been told to us.

Opening the presentation by creating an experience is equivalent to a nice change of gear in the opening, just be careful to keep up.

10.1.7. EXPLOIT HISTORICAL EVENTS

Imagine being CEO of a company that works with renewable energy and that you have to give a motivational presentation to the entire management team.

A good way to give meaning and value to your work is to refer to historical events and tie your business to them.

How?

You could open the presentation with a slide like this one, remembering the seriousness of the impacts of the Chernobyl disaster.

Image 7 – The Chernobyl disaster

You could then work on the impacts and consequences by bringing them into the spotlight in a rather strong way, but for the moment we'll leave this to your imagination.

Your speech could then go on to say that your company exists to make a difference, to put an end to disasters of this kind, preserve life and give a future to humanity.

See?

You have exploited a link with historical events to attribute a value system to your company's mission.

People will reflect themselves in these values and feel part of history.

Obviously, such a hook generates attention and curiosity in people.

10.1.8. TURN ON THE AUDIENCE'S IMAGINATION

Imagine a strong explosion as soon as you pass 3000 feet in flight, imagine an airplane full of smoke and the engine starting to squeak and about to go out.

Scary, isn't it?

Ric Elias, survivor of an air disaster, started his TED[4] by creating a strong involvement of his audience from the very first seconds.

People already feel part of the story, the engagement is strong and the imagination flies.

Now that everyone is on the burning plane, they are all attentive and eager to know how to save themselves.

As Ric tells the story, people will be wondering how he saved himself.

So, they're hooked to Ric's speech and waiting to get the answer.

How to create the slides?

Nothing easier.

In such a situation, you'd just need full-page photos, nothing more.

Slides must help you to bring the context to life, the story is already strong enough, with some photos you could even make someone dizzy!

Work on it, and don't be afraid to exaggerate.

The aim is to be a speaker unlike any other who has quietly presented his work.

There is also another, equally valid, way to stimulate people's imagination in the hook of the presentation, the "what if" technique.

How?

Let me give you a few examples, follow me:

---
4 3 things I Learned while my plane crashed – Ric Elias – Ted.com

- "What if suddenly cancer is no longer able to kill people?"
- "What if the tensions of war were resolved and peace reigned supreme in the world?"
- "What if there were no more thieves in the city?"
- "What if your car could drive itself?"
- "What if it were possible to live on Mars?"

The "what if" technique introduces a hypothetical situation and allows the imagination to run wild.

You could follow up the introduction by enriching the hypothetical context with all the benefits of the case in which it was reality.

But then you should return to reality, and this gap between dream and reality generates curiosity in people, and therefore, attention.

As you begin to use "what if's", the audience will be wondering if you're going to tell them that it's already possible or that you have a way to turn the dream into reality.

Let your audience's imagination fly and guide them through dreams that you will turn into reality.

10.1.9. GO STRAIGHT TO THE PROBLEM

As we said a few chapters ago, if you want people's attention you have to start from a problem that is relevant to them.

This is the case where the initial engagement strategy is based on the presentation of the problem and its consequences.

Let's say that this is the approach we could define as "straight to the point"!

Elon Musk, in the presentation of the Tesla Powerwall, gave a memorable speech using this initial hooking technique.

E.M.: "Tonight I'll tell you about a fundamental transformation of how the world works and how energy is distributed all over the world".

At this point, he showed a slide in which he clearly visualized the problem, representing the current reality.

Image 8 - Elon Musk presents Tesla PowerWall

E.M.: "It's really bad, isn't it?

I want to be clear with you, because often people get confused when they think about these things.

This is real.

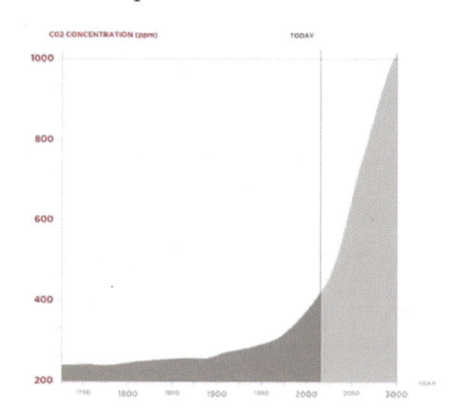

This is the way most of the world's energy is generated, with fossil fuel, and if we look at the trend, this is the famous curve, the Keeling curve.

I won't tell you what it says next, I'll let you go and take a look at the presentation online, also because it's a very interesting speech about our planet's future.

Image 9 - CO2 concentration in the atmosphere (ppm)

Where did Elon come from?

From the problem, without hesitation!
He started by going straight to the problem, without digressing.

He clarified how things stand in the world in which we all live, and then showed what the consequences of the current conditions will be if we do not act.

Elon is informing his audience of a serious situation that everyone knows about, but few really know what the cost of not acting is.

Therefore, the speaker defines a context in which acting is almost no longer a matter of choice, because not acting is already leading to devastating consequences.

Starting a presentation with the problem is a fairly traditional way of telling a story, as we have seen, it works well and engages people right from the start.

10.1.10. ALIGN EXPECTATIONS

Recently, I have had the opportunity to attend a presentation at a major event.

The speaker began by immediately showing a very long agenda with about 20 items that he would have liked to talk about in his presentation and started by commenting them one by one.

I can tell you that he spent half an hour describing each point on the agenda slide, without ever starting the presentation.

After the first quarter of an hour, turning around, I realized that he had lost more than half of the classroom.

Be careful to anticipate your entire speech, or you risk making it trivial.

If not anticipating the topics, how do you align the expectations of the public?

Let's say you could align expectations and then surprise them.

Remember the iPhone launch presentation by the legendary Steve Jobs?

S.J. "Today I want to introduce 3 revolutionary products:
- The first is a widescreen iPod with touch controls

Image 10 - Launch presentation of the first iPhone

- The second is a revolutionary phone

Image 11 - Launch presentation of the first iPhone

- The third is an innovative internet communicator

Image 12 - Launch presentation of the first iPhone

So, three things: a widescreen iPod with touch controls, a revolutionary phone, and an innovative internet communicator.

Image 13 - Launch presentation of the first iPhone

These are not three devices, but a unique device that we call iPhone.
Here the public began shivering and cheering.

Image 14 - Launch presentation of the first iPhone

Steve certainly anticipated the themes he was going to talk about, but then surprised the audience by triggering such a strong involvement that it sparked intense applause.

I understand very well that there was only one Steve Jobs, and not all of us are able to replicate such a performance.

But we can learn and take a cue.

Avoid depressing your audience by spoiling everything you talk about without creating any curiosity, and above all, avoid leading them through endless agendas of the day by telling them what you will talk about.

In my opinion, in presentations you must do what you'd said you would do and not keep telling them what you will do.

Remove things like: "this slide shows that, this graph says that, etc.." tell me directly what message you want to convey to me.

Please, do not forget to surprise people and create curiosity in every possible occasion.

10.1.11. USE A SURPRISING METAPHOR

Metaphors are a powerful way to create involvement and easily explain a theme to someone.

Let me tell you a story.

The CEO of a company in serious difficulty needs the involvement of the management team to be able to cut costs and try to save the company.

He begins the presentation by asking his audience what the cause of the Titanic's sinking was.

People, with confidence, replied that it was an iceberg that sank it.

At that point, the CEO says that the company is in the same condition as the Titanic, as there is a large iceberg straight ahead.

The only way to save the company is to cut costs and do it all together.

This way, that day the CEO of a multinational operating in the world of electronics generated a powerful public involvement and a deep desire to act.

10.2. COMBINE MULTIPLE STRATEGIES

If you're wondering what strategy to use for your presentations, stop now.

It clearly depends on the context, the content and the target audience.

What we can certainly say is that it is a good idea to start with an effective hooking strategy.

There is nothing to prevent you from even combining several strategies together and having one trigger the other.

Since this chapter is partially based on one of my most read articles online, I'll leave you in the notes the direct link to go and read about how to combine two strategies of initial hooking . [5]

---

5 https://mauriziolacava.com/lean-presentation-design-blog/presentations-delivery/13-successful-presentation-hook-ideas/

10.3. IN SUMMARY

When does people's attention drop during a presentation?

At the beginning, during the first 10% of the presentation.

So, if you want to fight this dramatic drop in attention and hope that at least some of the people in the audience remember your message, it is essential to start on the right foot.

How?

Using an initial hooking strategy.

We have analyzed 11 of them, and I'm sure that if you keep this book close to you while you create a presentation, there will be no lack of ideas.

CHAPTER 11

VIEW MESSAGES

« IF YOU ARE NOT READY TO BE WRONG YOU'LL NEVER COME UP WITH ANYTHING ORIGINAL »

KEN ROBINSON

The LEAN PROCESS for PRESENTATIONS

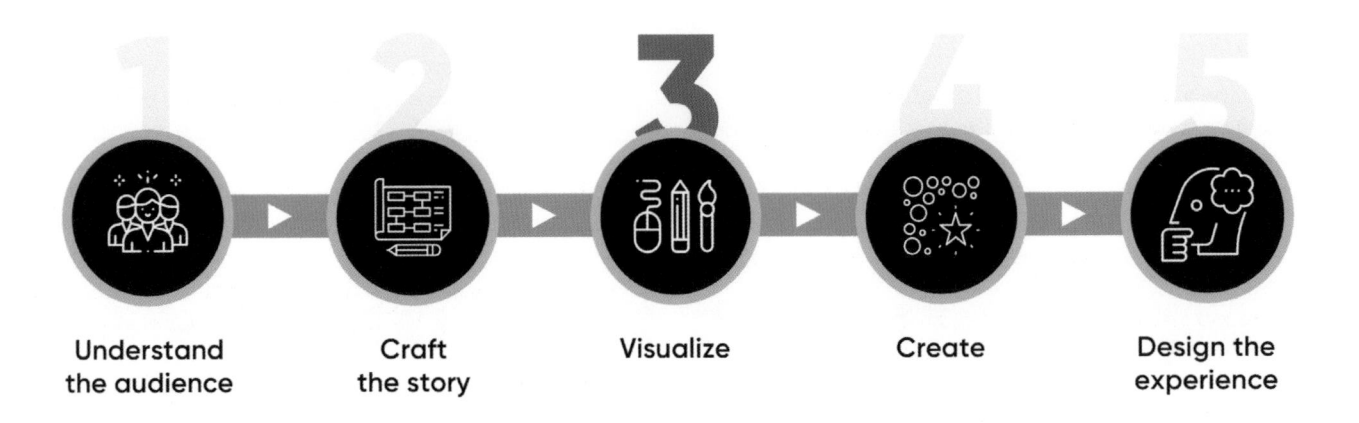

1 Understand the audience
2 Craft the story
3 Visualize
4 Create
5 Design the experience

Image 1 - Lean process for presentations - View messages

We have said that a presentation is not only made of slides but of a moment in which people exchange their ideas in an attitude of dialogue.

So what place do slides take in all of this?

Most presentations are made of slides that accompany the speaker and, in many cases, are even shared after the meeting.

Slides help the speaker to express the message and the audience to remember for longer.

In short, displaying messages is a good rule and slides are a great ally in this regard.

Where do we start?

11.1. FORGET POWERPOINT

In response to the question: "Where do we start to make a presentation?" usually, most people in the classroom talk about tools.

Many talk about PowerPoint, others refer to other tools such as Keynote or Google Slides but few give me the answer I would like.

There was a year when, at the Presentation Summit in the USA, there was talk about the quality of PowerPoint as a tool for making presentations.

I am clearly biased; for me, PowerPoint is the main tool.

Why own PowerPoint?

First of all because it is the most used and therefore working with PowerPoint means avoiding wasting time in compatibility problems.

Then, because, as you probably already know, I invented a software that integrates with PowerPoint and extends its functionality by customizing it with a whole series of additional buttons that I created based on my needs and that make me super fast in making a presentation.

If you want to browse I'll leave the link to MLC PowerPoint Add-in in the notes.[1]

But what exactly were they saying at the Presentation Summit?

It was said that PowerPoint is a practically perfect tool. Exaggerated?

Maybe, but the reason was that PowerPoint allows you to really refine your slides.

[1] https://mauriziolacava.com/my-addin

You can adjust the alignments to the pixel, manage the distributions and better organize your content for projection.

Are there any more precise tools?
Surely a designer would answer you that Adobe InDesign is a thousand times superior, and probably it is true.

However, in my opinion, it depends on what you have to do with it.

What's the point of using such a technical tool that only graphic designers can use it when working in a team of non designers?

If you're laying out a book I understand it but if you're making a presentation, PowerPoint has everything you need to make great presentations.

The only problem is that, once you open the tool, you will find yourself working on alignments, distributions, adjusting the size of the textand you will be distracted by the titles dancing between slides.

Why is that?
Because of course that's what the software wants you to do.

PowerPoint is a tool that drives you to aim for perfection but in doing so makes you lose sight of your communication strategy.

What do I mean?

I'm telling you that, with the work done so far, you have compiled the Lean Strategy Canvas, defined your storytelling and realized the hooking strategy and now it's time to associate a visualization with your messages in a logical sequence that approaches the structure of a presentation.

So, avoid getting lost in perfectionism on PowerPoint and keep your focus on the flow of communication.

11.2. THE LOGICAL FLOW OF MESSAGES

A presentation is a logical sequence of messages that you will need to distribute slide by slide.

Did you think you would do that in PowerPoint?

Let them prey on you.

Take pen and paper and write your messages one by one following the structure outlined in the Lean Strategy Canvas.

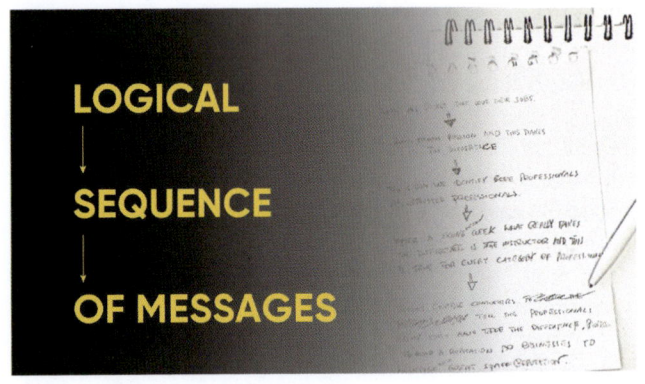

Image 2 - Logical structure of messages

In this way, you will see that you will not waste a second of time; you will remain focused on communication and on the weight to be given to each slide, quickly creating a logical sequence of messages, ready to be displayed.

These messages then go on display in a presentation.

It is not difficult to associate an image with a message but, once again, it is better to let PowerPoint go.

In fact, the moment you start working on PowerPoint is the moment you have to invest time to make perfect slides.

What happens if they are then rejected by your boss or if your client does not like them (inside or outside the organization in which you work)?

You need to secure approval before you invest your most valuable asset.

What resource am I talking about?

Your time.

To do this, you will work in a lean perspective; i.e. you will create a Minimum Viable Product of your presentation.

11.3. THE MINIMUM VIABLE PRODUCT

In Lean startup methodologies we talk about MVP or Minimum Viable Product.

You know what it is, you ever heard of it?

In any case, follow me while I show you an original example that I'm sure you have not yet seen.

In fact, I'm not going to explain what an MVP is: I'll illustrate it to you by example!

Have you ever seen the movie *The Founder*?

It's about the story of how McDonald's was born.

There is a part of the film, in my opinion ingenious, in which the McDonald brothers explain to Ray Kroc how the idea of the espresso system of the innovative cuisine of their restaurant was born.

Remember? Have you ever seen him?

At a time when drive-ins were in vogue in the United States, you'd go in with your car, order fish and after 40 minutes you'd need a hamburger, the McDonald brothers sensed that there was a clear need in the market and it was a need for simplification.

In fact, they said: "Why don't we give people what they ask for and serve it right away by cutting down on long queues?"

Image 3 - Drive In

To do so, however, they needed to standardize the products sold and, above all, rethink the layout of the kitchen.

They needed a very efficient kitchen in which every movement of the staff was thought out to the millimetre and allowed to be really efficient.

However, rethinking the layout of the kitchen means closing the restaurant, completely rethinking the kitchen, destroying the current one and creating the new one.

Imagine, for a moment, that once you've made your new kitchen, after closing your restaurant for six months, you've discovered that the layout you imagined on a piece of paper doesn't work.

What is the cost of failure?

Let's just say it could put the catering business at risk.

How can one validate such an important series at almost no cost?

No way?
Not at all!

This is precisely the teaching of lean methodologies, validating the assumptions as soon as possible at the lowest possible cost.

In the case of innovation processes failure is inevitable; it is part of the game.
How can you think of discovering something new, never done before, without making a mistake?

Innovating is an iterative process and necessarily requires failures.

> "I haven't failed; I've just found 10,000 ways that don't work"
> **THOMAS EDISON**

The point is not to avoid failure but to fail intelligently and, therefore, at the lowest possible cost so that we can gain experience and find the right path.

How do you put yourself in a situation of failure at no cost?

Here comes the concept of *Minimum Viable Product* to the rescue.

Do you remember how the McDonald brothers did it? With the tennis court!

Image 4 - Image from the movie "The Founder"

The brothers designed the layout of the kitchen on a tennis court, summoned the restaurant staff and tested the dynamics of operation.

It is said that they tested for an entire day, deleting and retrying the lines drawn with chalk to arrive at a layout that optimized the workflows of staff.

So, whenever they failed, they erased and redesigned the islands in the kitchen to solve the problems that emerged.

What do you think was the cost of every failure?
Exactly, zero.

Failing only cost them the time to erase the lines and redraw them, which is very different from investing in the creation of a wrong kitchen and discovering it when it was already assembled.

In this way, the McDonald brothers created the espresso system, the logic of building a super-efficient kitchen. Recently I found myself passing by McDrive, where you order food to be taken away directly with the car.

When I got in the queue, after placing the order, they gave me a stopwatch that counted three minutes and was already started.

Two minutes fifty, two minutes forty...

I asked what it was and the McDonald's staff told me that it is the bet they can serve me within three minutes of receiving the order.

If they fail, they give me a gift.
They won!

What does all this teach us?

The concept of *Minimum Viable Product* is therefore an intelligent way to make rapid prototyping, anticipate constraints and reduce waste.

11.4. SKETCHING

When you make a set of slides to support a presentation it often happens that your work is subject to approval.

It could even be that you're designing the slides for your superior, so you won't even be presenting them.

Or, it's a very important presentation for you and then you're looking for someone to share it with for advice.

Now let's speak clearly: what is the moment that requires more time to make a presentation?

It depends a lot on how good you are at the different stages - this is obvious - but I can assure you that the stage where you waste the most time is certainly the moment when you open PowerPoint or any other tool and you start working on the slides.

Why is that?

For the simple fact that a simple slide, the result of a good thought, can take twenty minutes to be made digitally, if not more.

But this is not the problem; it's just a design constraint to take into account.

In fact, the problem arises when, after having invested a lot of time in the creation of the slides, at the first comparison you are asked to make changes.

If the changes are extensive you can waste a lot of time making the slides again.

But redoing the slides means throwing away the time invested in the work done so far.

Time is the key resource to be optimized in the process of making a presentation and should not be wasted at all.

No one likes to be preparing slides for their boss late at night or at the weekend.

The idea is therefore to validate the views before investing all the time necessary to achieve them.

How do you do that?

Easy - with simple sketches.

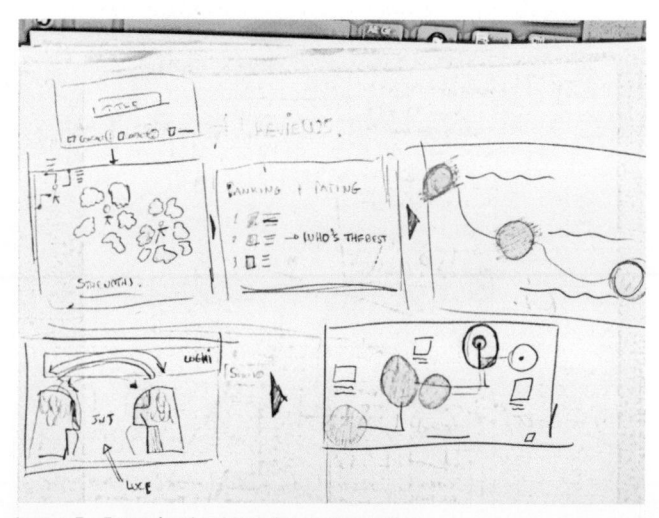

Image 5 - Example of a sketch for a presentation

It's the good old concept of the storyboard that is realized and shared before producing a video, if you think about it.

Every time I make a presentation, before anything else, I focus on the structure of the flow of communication.

I choose carefully what information I want to display and what I leave to the speaker's words, I define the best storytelling, I build the initial linking strategy and I do it without ever getting my hands on PowerPoint.

When it's time to view I don't launch PowerPoint but I use pen and paper or write directly on a tablet with a digital pen.

This way of working allows me to have an eye on the entire presentation, to divide the moment of concrete realization of the slide from the moment of conception and therefore to optimize my efforts and maximize the conceptualization while I work.

Above all, in this way I do not waste time making slides that my customer, or the person who has to approve them, does not like.

I can't hide from you the fact that I often make my own judgement on the sketches after I've made them and I realize, having an overall view, that some things need to be changed.

Tearing up a sketch and doing it again doesn't cost me anything and in this way I arrive quickly at the next stage where I have to do nothing but implement the graphics that I have already thought out.

11.5. IN SUMMARY

Working in a Lean way means anticipating constraints and reducing waste.

In the case of presentations, the primary resource not to be wasted is certainly your time.

The best way to make a presentation, then, is: develop the logical sequence of messages, sketch out how the presentation should be made, share the sketches with *stakeholders*, collect their feedback, refine the storyboard and, only finally, make slides in PowerPoint.

12
CHAPTER

CREATE THE PRESENTATION

«LESS IS MORE»

LUDWIG MIES VAN DER ROHE

The LEAN PROCESS for PRESENTATIONS

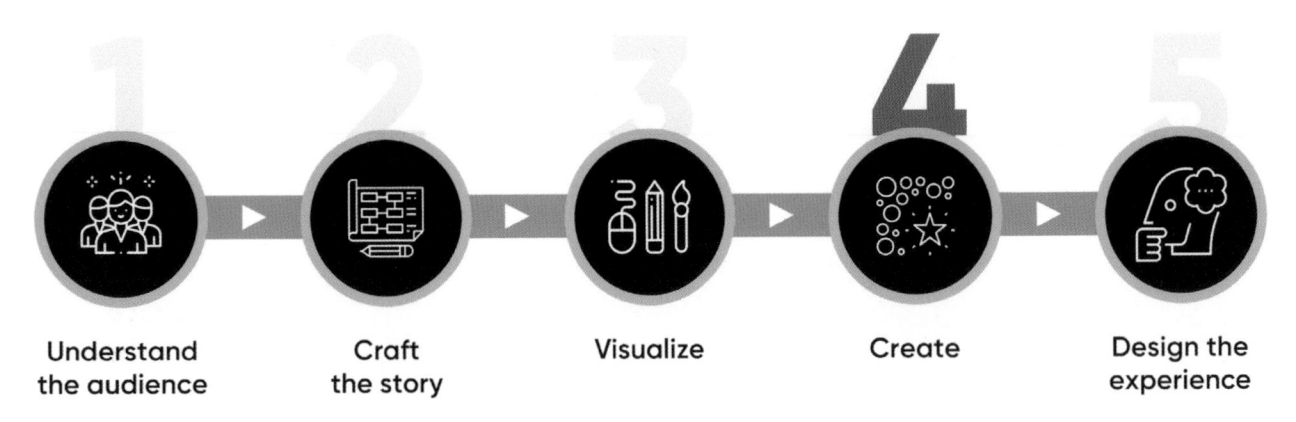

1. Understand the audience
2. Craft the story
3. Visualize
4. Create
5. Design the experience

Image 1 - Lean process for presentations - Create the presentation

The time has finally come to get your hands dirty.

I always say that this is the junction of the process because, at this point, you have defined the communication strategy, the initial connection, the essential information to be transferred and you have finally made some sketches of how you could view the messages.

Who said, however, that a presentation was necessary?

You could write an email, an article or go and talk without slides that support you.

I think there are far too many useless presentations in this world and, sincerely, I would like you to avoid adding yours to the long list that already exists.

Careful, I'm not telling you not to do the presentation; I'm just telling you to evaluate well whether the presentation is necessary or not.

If you need it then from this chapter onwards you will discover the best tools to make it.

Let's get into it!

12.1. NOISE IN PRESENTATIONS

Yeah, let's get our hands dirty, but let's keep the slides clean.

What do I mean by that?

Too often you see crowded or confusing slides where you do not understand exactly what the speaker wants the audience to look at.

The result?

Lost eyes of the public running up and down the slide in search of the message that the speaker is transmitting at that time.

But be careful: this spasmodic search for the message on the slides causes considerable fatigue to people.

Imagine it happening on a slide, on two slides or even on all slides of a presentation; how long do you think people keep trying before they throw in the towel?

When they give up, it means they stop following the slides, or they just stop following the presentation, they hold their dangerous smartphone and you, speaker, have come out of their attention range.

One-zero to the smartphone!

How to avoid all this?

I told you - keep your slides clean.

What does that mean?

Eliminate all kinds of noise.

There are two types of noise.

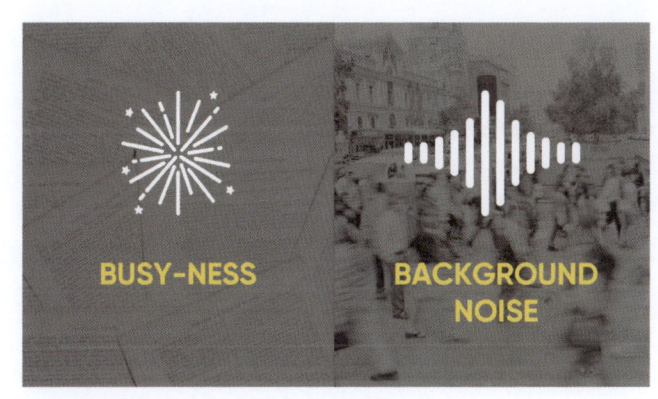

Image 2 - Two types of noise in presentations

We speak of busy-ness when we have an excessive amount of content on a slide, causing meaning to be lost.

Have you ever been to Japan?

The typical example is the number of advertising signs that stack on each other in centres with a high density of commercial activities.

Image 3 - Advertising signs in Japan

See? No one stands out more than the others, there is no order or hierarchy of reading and this creates chaos.

In short, I don't know which to choose and, probably, my eye can't even see them all because many get lost in the general confusion.

In your slides, at a glance people need to immediately understand which element to look at, which captures the message.

We talk about background noise when slides contain much more than they really need.

You know the famous quote:

"LESS IS MORE"
LUDWIG MIES VAN DER ROHE

That's exactly what I'm talking about!

From now on, every time you add an object, an icon, an image, a text or any other element to a slide, you have to ask yourself if that addition is really creating value for communicating messages to your audience.

How does an extra rectangle or an extra text, for example, make it easier for the audience to understand the message of that slide?

I'd like you to ask yourself why you put every detail in your slides.

If the answer is that the slide is nicer with the addition, then I'll give you some advice: delete it right away, before it's too late.
Eliminate everything you don't need inside your slides without delay.

On the slides there must be only and exclusively what is needed for effective communication; the rest is superfluous.

Do I seem too strict to you?
Let's take a real case as an example.

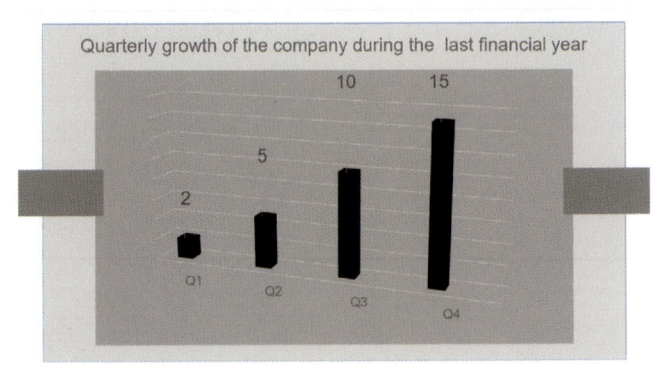

Image 4 - Example of slide with strong background noise

Now explain to me what is the point of framing a chart that you gave a background to, and then including a rectangle with a border and two bands that hook it to the slide?

Why draw the graph in 3D, with lines connecting bars and numbers, and what are the white horizontal lines behind the columns for?

I'll tell you, nothing!
Let me show you how I'd redesign this slide.

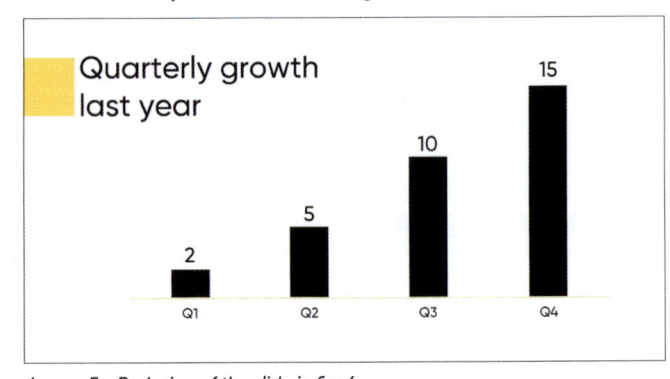

Image 5 - Redesign of the slide in fig. 4

See, isn't it much cleaner, lighter and easier to understand?

Try to keep the slides clean both for a matter of effectiveness, better communication, and for a matter of efficiency, do not waste time adding unnecessary objects.

12.2. THE IMPORTANCE OF EMPTY SPACES

The application of the *less is more* rule clearly leaves a good dose of gaps on the slides.

It should not be a problem at all, but unfortunately this concept is not so obvious and I don't want you to get it wrong.

Some time ago I came across a presentation created to convey the values of Italianism abroad.

I've extrapolated the most significant slide, which I'll show you in the next figure.

Image 6 - Italianism abroad

Do you like this slide?

As you can see, it's confusing, has a lot of content and works badly with images.

Why does it work so badly?

It almost seems as if the presenter is trying to hide, as much as possible, the gaps on the slide.

Blanks are filled at the cost of extremely small images.

What's with the crap?

The empty spaces are dear friends and not enemies to make disappear at all costs.

You see, spaces give breath to the content, enhance the contrasts and give elegance to your slides by reducing the busy-ness and background noise.

Image 7 - Redesign of the slide in fig. 6 - enhancement of empty spaces

Never accept feedback from someone who tells you that there are too many gaps in your slide; it would be a serious mistake to agree with that.

Make the most of the spaces, enhance the contents and don't be afraid to leave empty important parts of the slide because you are only highlighting the essential content you have decided to present.

12.3. IN SUMMARY

I promised you I'd provide you with the tools to handle every presentation.

I decided to start with some principles that limit the use of content in order to keep the slides clean and light.

The cleaner the slides are, the faster and more effective will be the eye of your audience to capture the message and return their attention to what you present.

Slides should not be crowded and should not have background noise; that is, it should always be very clear to the audience where to look to steal the message and to do so the slide should be simple.

Don't be afraid to take advantage of the empty spaces because they give elegance to your slides and help you create contrast.

13
CHAPTER

MASTER
THE USE OF FONTS

« TYPE IS WHAT
MEANING LOOKS LIKE »

MAX PHILIPS

When working with structured organizations, you will often have to use the institutional font approved by the communications department.

In these cases, you obviously can't choose the font, so you just have to adapt to the request, consider it a business constraint and adapt.

In all situations where the choice of font is at your discretion, you will have the opportunity to use the power of typography to enhance communication and highlight your messages.

However, there are hundreds of fonts available and no suggestions for directing your choice.

For typographical choices, there is an entire discipline that develops this field.

In this chapter we will take inspiration from some basic skills from the world of typography and use them to choose the most appropriate font for your type of communication.

13.1. CHARACTER ARCHITECTURE

The fonts available today all seem to resemble each other. However, the first thing on which they differ is the architecture on which they are built.

Each font has precise distances between the different height lines. Height adjustment allows us to change the appearance of the font to give it a more stretched or compressed shape:

- ascending line: imaginary line that delimits the maximum height of the body

- intermediate line: line that establishes the actual height of the body

- base line: line on which the base of each capital letter rests

- descending line: point on which the descending letters rest.

Image 1 – Height lines of a font

The font architecture includes not only the black parts that we all see, but also the white parts of the resulting spaces.

For example, one of the possible adjustments is to modify the kerning, that is, the white space between the letters.

Don't worry, in presentations you won't often find yourself changing the kerning or font structure.
This type of intervention is more specific to the world of editing, layout and printing on paper of magazines and books. PowerPoint allows you to edit kerning with both standard values (= pre-filled) and precise numerical values, but you can safely do without it for most common use cases.

What really affects the presentations is the type of font chosen.

You know when you open the font window and you're faced with hundreds of choices, which one do you choose?

The choice affects your communication and you just need a click to guide it, but you have no guidelines to make an effective choice, so you just have to proceed by trial and error.

Typically, you try one or more fonts until you find the one you like best.

But are you sure that the font you like the most is the most effective for your communication and your audience?

I wouldn't put my hand on it.

So, you spent time testing different fonts without even being sure of their effectiveness.

In fact, everything you need to know to direct the choice of fonts towards maximum effectiveness is a fundamental distinction in the world of typography.

There are two great font families: fonts with serifs and fonts without serifs.

Do you know what serifs are?

The serifs are those "tails" that soften the letter's appearance.

T CHARACTER WITH **SERIF** (serifs are in red)

T CHARACTER **SANS SERIF**

Serifs help the reader to follow the text by connecting word letter by letter. This way, the reader's eye will naturally flow through the text. In fact, serif characters are used in long texts that take a long time to read.

Presentations focus on understanding the content at a glance. Audiences need to be able to receive text and visuals at a very quick glance and then return their attention to the speaker.

Slides are not designed to be read.

Here that sans serif fonts become interesting: these are those fonts characterized by a clean letter cut. Sans serif fonts are very clean and tidy, and they enhance the white spaces facilitating reading.

However, sans serif fonts would not be suitable for long texts, such as for a book, because continuous reading would strain the eyes.

So, in slides it is recommended to use mainly sans serif fonts.

From now on you will see fonts differently, thanks to this knowledge. This way, you will be able to make the most efficient choice for your audience and not the one that you deem the prettiest, and you will be able to do it with just a glance.

Lorem Ipsum è un testo segnaposto utilizzato nel settore della tipografia e della stampa. Lorem Ipsum è considerato il testo segnaposto standard sin dal sedicesimo secolo, quando un anonimo tipografo prese una cassetta di caratteri e li assemblò per preparare un testo campione. È sopravvissuto non solo a più di cinque secoli, ma anche al passaggio alla videoimpaginazione, pervenendoci sostanzialmente inalterato. Fu reso popolare, negli anni '60, con la diffusione dei fogli di caratteri trasferibili "Letraset", che contenevano passaggi del Lorem Ipsum, e più recentemente da software di impaginazione come Aldus PageMaker, che includeva versioni del Lorem Ipsum.

ARIAL, 12pt
senza grazie

Lorem Ipsum è un testo segnaposto utilizzato nel settore della tipografia e della stampa. Lorem Ipsum è considerato il testo segnaposto standard sin dal sedicesimo secolo, quando un anonimo tipografo prese una cassetta di caratteri e li assemblò per preparare un testo campione. È sopravvissuto non solo a più di cinque secoli, ma anche al passaggio alla videoimpaginazione, pervenendoci sostanzialmente inalterato. Fu reso popolare, negli anni '60, con la diffusione dei fogli di caratteri trasferibili "Letraset", che contenevano passaggi del Lorem Ipsum, e più recentemente da software di impaginazione come Aldus PageMaker, che includeva versioni del Lorem Ipsum.

VERDANA, 12pt
senza grazie

Lorem Ipsum è un testo segnaposto utilizzato nel settore della tipografia e della stampa. Lorem Ipsum è considerato il testo segnaposto standard sin dal sedicesimo secolo, quando un anonimo tipografo prese una cassetta di caratteri e li assemblò per preparare un testo campione. È sopravvissuto non solo a più di cinque secoli, ma anche al passaggio alla videoimpaginazione, pervenendoci sostanzialmente inalterato. Fu reso popolare, negli anni '60, con la diffusione dei fogli di caratteri trasferibili "Letraset", che contenevano passaggi del Lorem Ipsum, e più recentemente da software di impaginazione come Aldus PageMaker, che includeva versioni del Lorem Ipsum.

GARAMOND, 12pt
con grazie

Lorem Ipsum è un testo segnaposto utilizzato nel settore della tipografia e della stampa. Lorem Ipsum è considerato il testo segnaposto standard sin dal sedicesimo secolo, quando un anonimo tipografo prese una cassetta di caratteri e li assemblò per preparare un testo campione. È sopravvissuto non solo a più di cinque secoli, ma anche al passaggio alla videoimpaginazione, pervenendoci sostanzialmente inalterato. Fu reso popolare, negli anni '60, con la diffusione dei fogli di caratteri trasferibili "Letraset", che contenevano passaggi del Lorem Ipsum, e più recentemente da software di impaginazione come Aldus PageMaker, che includeva versioni del Lorem Ipsum.

TIMES LT Std12
con grazie

Image 2 – Comparison of two serif fonts and two sans serif fonts in the drafting of a text

13.2. CHOOSING THE RIGHT CHARACTER

The choice of the character has a strong impact on the design of a correct user experience of the slides by your audience.

Creating presentations in a Lean perspective, we need a right compromise that ensures the usability of the content and optimizes the time to process the slides during a presentation.

In other words, your goal is to choose quickly, without risk of error, a font that facilitates the eye for the audience.

There are at least three big wastes of time caused by wrong font choices in presentations:

1. You use serif fonts to present, people read and don't listen, everyone's time is wasted.

2. You use fonts that are not compatible, and this causes time-consuming adjustments.

3. You waste time looking for a nice font but what really matters is its effectiveness, leave art aside, otherwise you'll waste time testing fonts choosing, probably, an ineffective one

Don't complicate your life, choose simple and well-known fonts.

I use very common sans serif fonts to create my presentations:

- Arial
- Verdana
- Calibri
- Tahoma
- Segoe
- Effra Corp

If you follow these simple guidelines, they will completely change the way you work in terms of efficiency and effectiveness.

What do I mean?

If you focus on choosing a simple and known font, you will be able to make an effective choice in a very short time.

If you plan a presentation of support to a speaker and you don't want the audience to read, then you will use sans serif fonts, otherwise, if you plan a report in which you want to facilitate reading, you can work with serif fonts.

Do you understand the point?

It's about making a careful design choice guided by the effectiveness and experience you want to achieve for your audience, not by your idea of what is nicer looking.

13.3. HOW MANY FONTS SHOULD YOU USE FOR A PRESENTATION?

One! Always and only one!

I think you can get excellent results by limiting yourself to a single font.

Remember that you are working from a Lean point of view, with the aim of minimizing the working time, the time of fruition of the contents by the public and maximizing effectiveness.

Working with more than one font would unnecessarily complicate your work.

So, choose a font and proceed with that throughout the presentation. Be sure to set the chosen font within the Slide Master so that you don't have to change it every time you draw a new shape or insert a new text box.

To set the font in the PowerPoint master, simply open the slidemaster from View > Slide Pattern and then go to Font from Slide Pattern > Font.

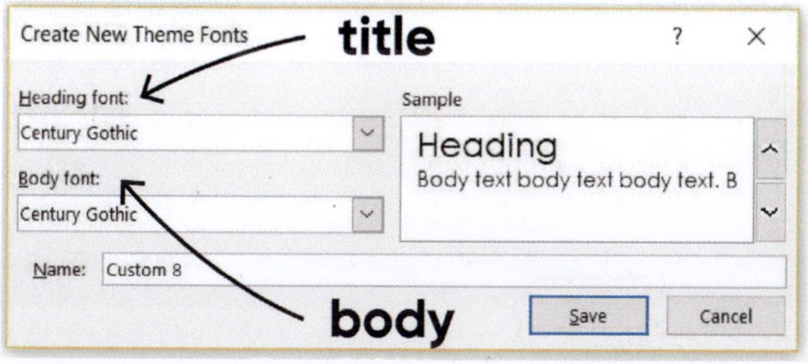

Be careful to choose the same font for both the title and the body of the text as discussed above.

Have you ever wondered why I guided you to set the font through the Slide Master?

Just to avoid an avalanche of adjustments typical of those who work with PowerPoint and do not use it.

Since this is a technical topic, I'll refer you to the guide about the Slide Master that I prepared in the online Learning Center on my website[1] that, as I told you in the preface, complements this book with all the technical knowledge necessary for a proper and efficient presentation process.

Image 3 – Configuration panel of a custom font

[1] https://mauriziolacava.com/lean-presentation-design-blog/presentation-design-technique/slide-master-powerpoint/

13.4. IN SUMMARY

Choosing a font significantly affects the experience you design for your audience.

Use sans serif fonts for speaker support presentations and use serif fonts when you want people to comfortably read long paragraphs of text.

Always work with one font per presentation and don't waste time with graphic artifices, choose compatible and known fonts.

14 CHAPTER

WORKING WITH IMAGES

« A PICTURE IS WORTH A THOUSAND WORDS »

Do you think it's right to use images in presentations?

Yes, I mean inserting images and photos into your slides and then presenting them to your audience to help you make your point.

Do you think it's a good way to present?

In general, no one would object to the contrary, more specifically it depends on what you are communicating.

However, we can say that the use of visual content in presentations helps the audience to understand.

Did you know that our brain processes images 60,000 times faster than text?

So, it's true that an image is worth a thousand words!

Yes, and in the presentations, for us, it becomes a mantra.

It's not just a question of understanding, it's also a question of memory.

In your opinion, what remains most impressed in human memory: images or text?

I think we all agree that human beings tend to remember images much better than any other textual content.

Human beings are naturally predisposed to process images.

According to the "Picture Superiority Effect" phenomenon[1], concepts presented visually are more likely to be remembered than concepts presented with words in text form.

Specifically, the PSE states that when information is presented orally it has a 10% probability of being remembered for the next 3 days, but if the communication is accompanied by visual content the probability rises to 65%.

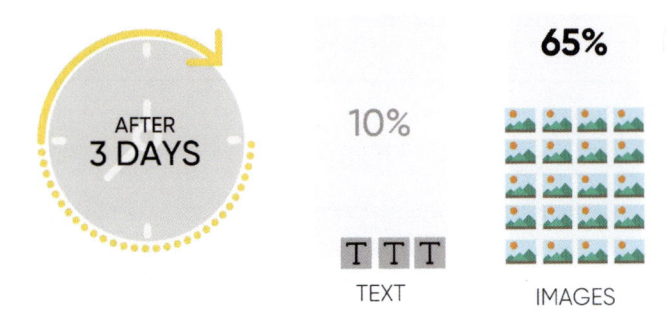

Image 1 - Picture Superiority Effect

The human brain naturally translates words into images so that they are remembered, so if you spare it a few steps, the result of the memorization process will be benefited.

Drawing with a pencil, for example, can be a very effective way of communicating.

"There is no more powerful way to prove that we know something well than to draw a simple picture of it. And there is no more powerful way to see hidden solutions than to pick up a pen and draw out the pieces of our problem". [2]

Think about how many times, during a meeting or brainstorming between colleagues, a simple blackboard makes the difference in facilitating understanding between people.

We are naturally inclined to communicate visually.

There's more - images have another, very powerful effect on human beings.

---

[1] The picture superiority effect in recognition memory: A developmental study using the response signal procedure, Margaret Anne Defeyter, Riccardo Russo, Pamela Louise Graham

[2] The Back of the Napkin (Expanded Edition): Solving Problems and Selling Ideas with Pictures

Images have the power to generate emotions in people, and emotions can make a message indelible in the mind of your audience.

It's not hard to imagine that an experience that excited you is, of course, easier to remember, right?

There are at least 6 types of images that have a clear emotional impact on people [3].

Follow me, I'll show you some examples:

PEOPLE'S EYES

Children are captured by a person's face more than by anything else. [4]

Probably for survival reasons.

After all, a child is much more likely to survive if he can recognize the face of the person who looks after and feeds him.

We are nothing more than children who have grown up a bit, from this point of view.

In fact, we are bewitched by the close-up portraits and often, the look of the subject penetrates us deeply.

I can't help mentioning the famous cover of National Geographic in 1985, where the famous photo of the Afghan girl by Steve McCurry was published.

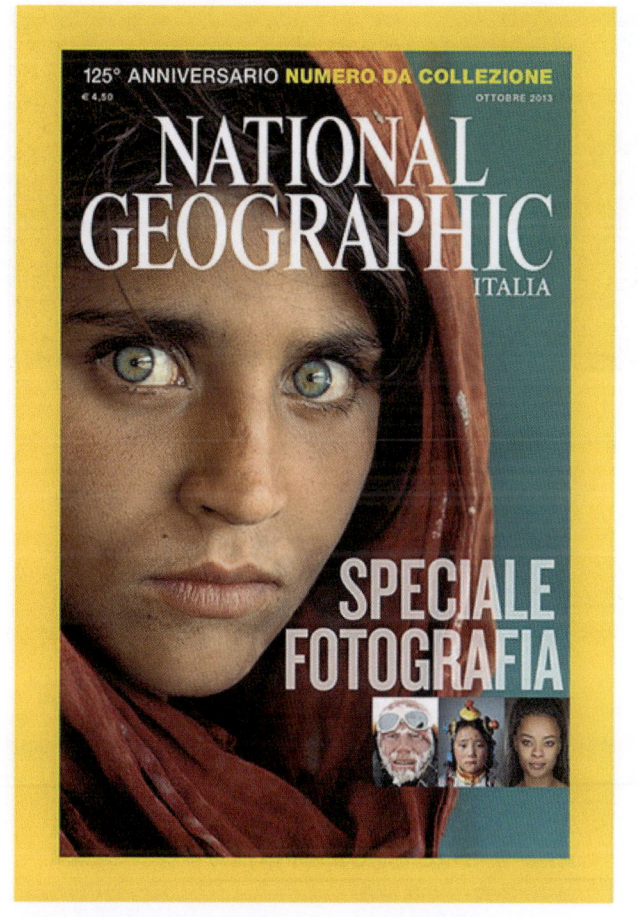

Image 2 - National Geographic Cover - The Afghan Girl

The intense, deep, frightened and suspicious look of this girl has literally gone around the world.

People's eyes communicate emotions to which the audience is exposed every time you decide to use this kind of images.

---

3 https://mauriziolacava.com/lean-presentation-design-blog/images-functions-in-powerpoint-presentations/
4 Robert Fantz, visual preference paradigm, 1961, Case Western Reserve University

Image 3 - People's eyes generate emotional involvement

Identify your message and ask yourself if a person's gaze is not enough to go straight to the point.

Remember, an image is worth a thousand words.

IMAGES OF ANIMALS AND CHILDREN

You know how kittens look on social networks?

The British alone share more than 3.8 million kitten photos every day, compared to 1.4 million selfies.

Doesn't that sound incredible to you?

Image 4 - Photos of cute kittens

There is a lot of talk about kittens, but the same goes for puppies - especially when they are portrayed in human poses.

Image 5 - Dogs acting like humans

As a rule, dogs and kittens hit us straight in the heart when they are very small and so damn soft.

Image 6 – Dog puppies

Not to mention when they look at you with those sweet eyes

Image 7 – Sweet eyes

Dogs, cats… That's it?

Absolutely not!

You know who else hits us in the heart?

Speaking of puppies, it's not hard to imagine.

In fact, we are talking about children.

Image 8 – Sweet baby

What do all the pictures you're looking at have in common?

The tenderness factor, which generates the emotional stimulus that engages us.

According to Konrad Lorenz, there is a pattern of elements that generate the tenderness effect: wide forehead, big eyes, rounded shapes, a rounded body bigger than the head, and soft shapes.

- Wide forehead
- Large eyes
- Round forms
- Body bigger than the head
- Rounded body
- Smoothness

Image 9 – The key elements of tenderness

INSPIRING IMAGES

There are images that generate inspiration and motivation in people.
Typical examples are images of extreme sports or, in general, of people achieving incredible results.

Each image can convey a different message, depending on the context in which it is used.

The image of a boy helping another could communicate the message of teamwork.

Image 10 - Teamwork

Or the achievement of a goal that costs sacrifice and determination.

Image 11 – Sacrifice and determination

The achievement of a goal and the satisfaction that follows:

Image 12 – Achievement of a goal

Associating a powerful motivational image with a key message within your presentation can generate emotional involvement and imprint the message in the memory of your audience.

IMAGES DEPICTING EXPRESSIONS

Obviously, we are talking about disruptive and engaging emotions.

Do you know how contagious a smile is?

If you are amid people you don't know and you start laughing, it's very likely that someone else will laugh and a viral chain of smiles will be triggered.

Emotions are contagious, and with them messages are conveyed.

Image 13 – Unexpected happiness

Image 14 – Image depicting a success

14.1. IMAGES IN PRESENTATIONS

Images are a powerful tool but are often not correctly used in presentations, and this causes ineffective communication. In my opinion, there are 3 main recurring problems in the use of images in presentations:

1. GRAINY IMAGES

Image 15 – Slide with grainy image

typical case in which the images are downloaded from the web in low resolution and then brutally pasted on the presentation without any care for their quality.

Sometimes you even notice the low quality but the time available is always short, searches on the internet do not give better results and then you settle for what you have.

2. WATERMARKED IMAGES

Image 16 – Watermarked image

How many times have you searched for images you can't find and finally surrendered to downloading the preview from paid sites?

The problem?

Simple, if they are purchasable images, they'll be protected by the watermark - the annoying transparent overlay plot that indicates the origin of the photo.

3. TOO SMALL IMAGES

5 things not to say during your next presentation

- I have a lot of information to cover so let me get started
- I will keep it short and not bore you
- I didn't have too much time to prepare but...
- Sorry I'm very nervous of being in front of you
- I'll be back to that later

Image 17 - Lots of small images

Typical slide in which text and images are clearly unbalanced in favor of a rich amount of text that forces you to reduce the images to small stamps.

Wanting to use so many images in a small space leads to an ineffective slide with so many small photos that do not generate any emotional involvement on the audience, also because, other than those who are close to the screen, others probably cannot even see them.

Do you find yourself in at least one of these three typical cases?

If so, don't worry, it's normal.

How do you get out of it?
Simple, follow me.

If you think about it for a moment, what you need is high definition images (that don't get grainy), free (without watermark), copyright free (that you can use without legal problems).

In practice, you just need to know where to find them and how to put them into your presentation.

Of course, if you have access to paid portals of the shutterstock.com or Envato Elements level, you're already starting from a good base - but what if you don't have a budget for your presentation images?

There are obviously many online portals to refer to, I'll tell you the three that I use most often.

The first of these is Pixabay.com, which offers over a million free, high quality and copyright-free images.

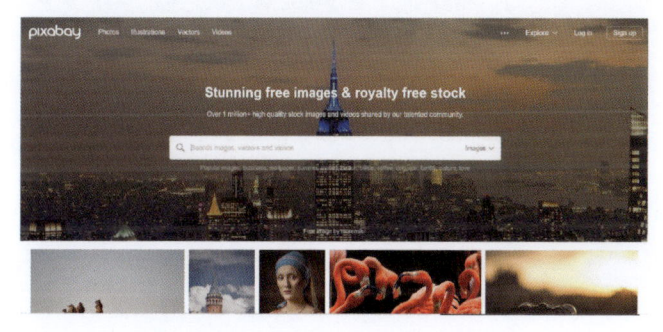

Image 18 - pixabay.com

Nowadays, on Pixabay you can also find illustrations, vector graphics and video parts for your editing.

If you're looking for more exotic images with more specific shots, you can definitely look into Unsplash.com

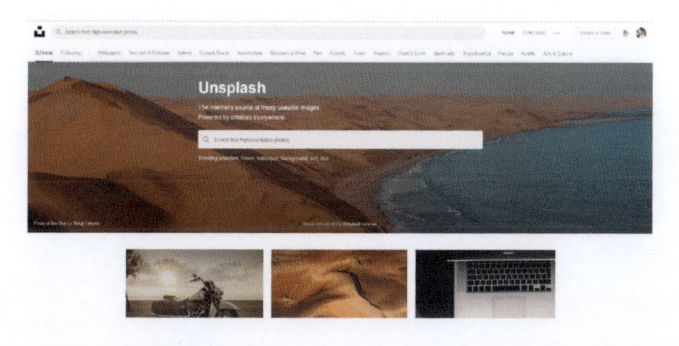

Image 19 - Unsplash.com

Unsplash is less equipped than Pixabay, but it has a completely different cut. See for yourself, have a look and let me know.

Finally, you can refer to Pexels.com, which offers a large amount of free high definition images, ready for your presentations.

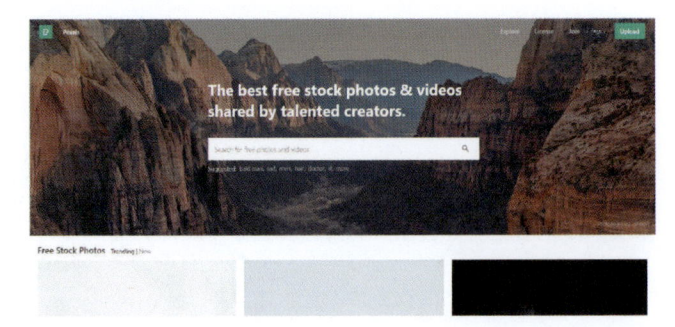

Image 20 - Pexels.com

Once you access one of these portals, you just have to download the selected image file and drag it to PowerPoint to quickly import it.

Keep in mind that once you have imported images to a tool like PowerPoint, they need to be processed.

Of course, in this case, having taken care of the source you're starting from a very good base - but how to enlarge the image to the whole slide without wasting time, how to correctly work with cropping frames or with the powerful filters made available to saturate or desaturate the images according to the specific context (like your company template, for example)?

I suggest you refer to the online guide about the use of images in presentations to learn all the techniques for creating high-impact visual slides. [5]

---

5 https://mauriziolacava.com/lean-presentation-design-blog/presentation-design-technique/free-images-for-powerpoint-presentations/

14.2. COMBINING IMAGES AND TEXT IN SLIDES

You have learned to display messages by inserting high resolution, high quality images, but this is not all.

In fact, slides allow you to go further and associate text to these images.

After all, think about it for a moment - slides are a constant combination of media content such as images, videos, icons or other graphic elements and text; this is the strength of slides, combining content of a different nature.

Easy?

Not at all!

Problems arise when you combine content of a very different nature, and you need to be able to combine them effectively.

Let's assume you want to create a slide that displays the claim - people make the difference.

We want to bring to life the idea that, in a specific situation, it is people who make the difference, more than anything else.

For example, in the case of a celebration, we want to explain that it is not the gifts or the party, but the people who make the moment special.

Here is a high-resolution image from pixabay.com of a girl who is about to wish you a happy birthday.

Image 21 – Image from Pixabay.com

We enlarge the image to cover the entire slide.

Image 22 - Example of a high-resolution photo in a centered, full-slide position

The image is of excellent quality, the photo is well centered and extends over the entire surface of the slide (to extend the image in a single click and perfectly cover the slide I used the Fit to slide feature of the MLC PowerPoint Add-in).

The problem?

This slide could mean a lot of things, not necessarily what you want to convey.

That's why it's so important to add text.

You just have to enter the phrase "people make the difference", that's all.

But where do you write this text on the slide?

The problem with combining text and images is that images are often not designed to superimpose text on them.

How many times, in fact, do you see images with superimposed texts that you can't read?

Also, searching for an image takes time and effort.

Once the image has been identified, inserted in the slide and processed (with resizing, application of filters, etc..) it would be a huge waste of time to have to find another for the simple fact that there is no space where you can write clearly.

First, do you know why text on images is not often readable? Because it lacks contrast.

Images have a complex background made of many different colors.
For this reason, the very first thing to do is to assess whether the image has spaces with a roughly uniform background.

In this case, you have a dark uniform space on both sides on which you could write, for example, in white.

Image 23 - Space with uniform background on the sides of the photo

Interesting, but the space is still not enough to write on.

For this reason, we use the cropping functions to move the image outside the slide frame, on one side only, and increase the space for writing.

Image 24 - Extending the image beyond the cropping frame

Be careful, the frame delimited by black handles, in PowerPoint, represents the cropping frame.

That is, everything inside the frame is shown, the rest is hidden.

To make it simple, it works like a mask.

In this case the mask corresponds exactly to the size of the slide, and therefore we have a full-slide image.

Image 25 - Example of free high-resolution image

Applying the cropping, the image will be moved to the right and, as they say, cut raw on the edge of the slide.

Have you noticed that on the left you have now obtained the space needed to write?

Now you can finally add the text, paying attention to use a color that clearly contrasts the background.

Image 26 - Text overlaying on an image

See the result?

Thanks to this simple image manipulation you have managed to create a well-balanced slide that perfectly combines a high definition photo with a clearly legible text.

Always remember to take a critical look at the photos you're working with, because sometimes a simple cropping is enough to get an excellent integration.

More examples?

Here they are.

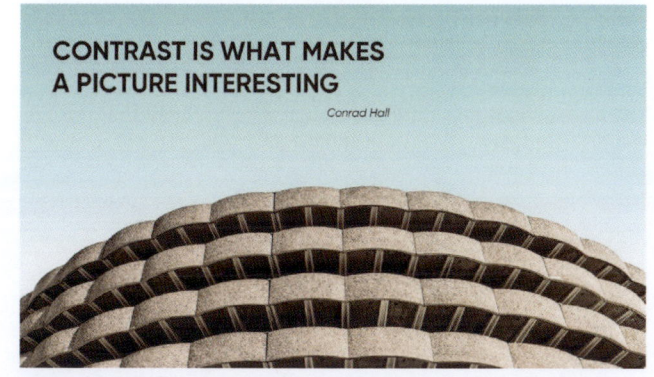

Image 27 - Write text in areas where it contrasts with the background

Image 28 - Full slide image with no free areas for writing text

In this case, since we don't have where to write legibly, we'll use a simple technique that gives you the flexibility to write on all kind of images.

The "transparent box" technique.

What is a transparent box?

Very simple, I'll explain it to you.

As you can see, on this image you lack a uniform background on which you can write the message so that it is uniformly readable.

Since it is missing, we'll create it!

Just insert a simple shape and give a transparency that, in PowerPoint, can vary between 20% and 30% in order to create a background on which to write.

We insert the box.

Image 29 - Box introduction

The box creates a uniform background but is rather invasive when superimposed on an image.

First, let's work on the color.

You should assign it a color that matches the image, unless you are bound by a particular branding, such as that of your organization.

In this case, using a simple dropper tool, you can sample a color. All the latest versions of PowerPoint provide the dropper tool.

I selected a dark blue from the jersey of the second person from the left and applied it as a full, uniform fill to the box.

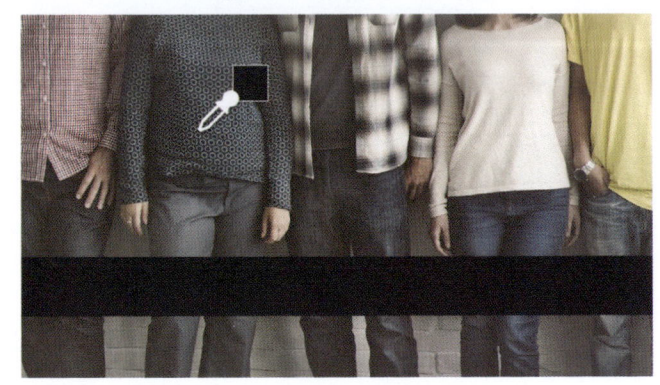

Image 30 - Box filling color consistent with the image

To maximize the box integration with the image I applied a slight transparency to the filling, which as we said, can vary from 20% to 30%.

Image 31 - Box with 20% transparency

Now you can finally bring the text back into the box, confident of its contrast and therefore of its legibility.

Image 32 - Contrasting text inside the transparent box

If you look carefully, I applied to the text the beige color of the second jersey from the right.

See how well you can read it?
There are no contrast problems, and I did not have to look for the image a second time, I used the one we had already found.

I could give you endless examples in this regard.

Image 33 - The transparent box technique makes the text readable

Now, thanks to the cropping technique, the new way of looking at and analyzing images, and the transparent box technique, you can combine text and images on slides in an effective and efficient way.

14.3. THE SEMANTIC RESONANCE OF IMAGES

Combining text and images is a very effective and basic technique for presentations.

Although it seems the easiest thing in this world, especially now that you've seen the techniques to use to graphically solve the problem, it's not trivial at all.

Why is that?

Let's play a game, I'll show you some slides and you'll think about the feelings that they'll bring to your mind. Focus them well before moving on to the next one.

Are you ready?

Let's go start with the first.

Image 34 - Slides supporting the concept of semantic resonance (Ex.1)

I guess you've felt your mouth watering, unless you're a vegetarian or even a vegan. On average, when I show this slide in the classroom, people get an appetite and think of an exclusive restaurant and elegant cuisine.

Ready for the next one?

Here it is.

Image 35 - Slides supporting the concept of semantic resonance (Ex.2)

Yes, I know, to many this would look appetizing too but, you will agree with me, that it is a different kind of appetite.

In this case, when you interrogate the room subjected to this visual stimulus, words such as: junk food, fat, fattening, etc. emerge.

The meaning begins to shift from the first example, but wait to see what I'm about to show you.

Image 36 - Slides supporting the concept of semantic resonance (Ex.3)

Don't tell me you're still hungry!

Usually, this is the moment when your appetite passes and you begin to feel for the poor, frightened cow.

Imagination runs wild, and one wonders how terrible what's about to happen can be.

Should we pass on to the last image?

Come on, I'll show you.

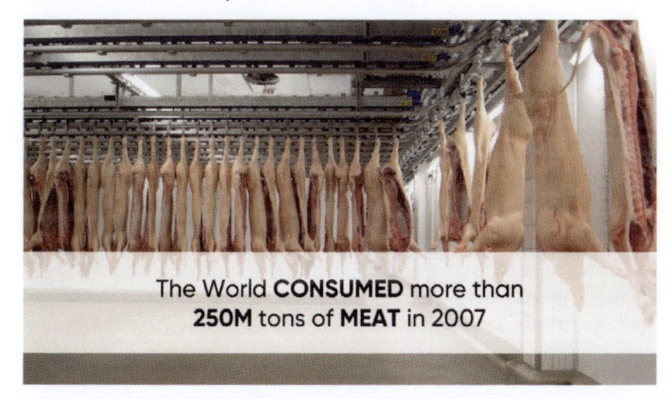

Image 37 - Slides supporting the concept of semantic resonance (Ex.4)

You knew it was going to end like this.

I know, the example is a bit raw, but I exaggerated on purpose, you'll see that this will help you remember.

Have you noticed what the 4 slides I showed you have in common?

The meaning has changed radically, to the point that between the first and last you may even have lost your appetite, but the text has not changed by a comma.

Image 38 - The 4 slides express different meanings, but the text does not change

Did you realize that the text never changed?

This is a useful example to summarize the concept of semantic resonance and the importance of images.

The concept of semantic resonance explains that words can take on different meanings depending on the context in which they are placed.

In this example, images represent context and give words a meaning, sometimes even opposite ones.

Be careful when combining images and text - if you use the combination cleverly you can leverage the concept of semantic resonance and leave your message imprinted in people's memories for a long time, but if you miss you risk leaving a different message imprinted than the one you were hoping to convey.

I invite you to pay even more attention if you operate in the context of a multinational company, where you can find yourself interacting with cultures that can be very different from yours and therefore, a context that for you has a meaning, for others it can assume a very different significance.

14.4. IN SUMMARY

Images are a powerful tool in presentations: they help to emotionally engage the audience, to imprint a message in their memory for a long time and speed up the transmission of a concept.

Therefore, it is good to use images in presentations, but it is essential to work with quality images - and for this reason it makes sense to use, for example, the online repositories that I reported in paragraph 14.1 where you can find images free, high definition images not subject to copyrights.

Presentations allow you to combine images with text, but it is essential that you preserve legibility and maximize contrasts by studying images or using the transparent box technique.

Remember that images define the context in which the text is inserted and can therefore completely change the message perceived.

15
CHAPTER

VECTOR GRAPHICS - ICONS

« SIGN AND SYMBOLS
RULE THE WORLD,
NOT WORDS, NOR LAWS »

CONFUCIUS

As far as we've learned so far, if you want the audience to remember your messages longer, it's better to communicate through visual rather than textual content.

The Picture Superiority Effect says just that.

That's why we used images, learning how to find them on the web on dedicated portals.

Slides with images work well because they make it easier to get the message across and engage the public.

But this can't always be the solution.

How many times have you seen slides on which is contained much more than a message?

I should tell you that every slide must always and only convey a single message, but let's be realistic and face reality... We know how things are.

When on a slide there are more messages and each message must be displayed, the solution is not certainly to insert many small images in stamp style (which unfortunately is often seen).

This is one of the cases in which, instead of images, you can use icons.

Icons are visual contents that allow you to give presentations an infographic style, different from what is provided using images.

What am I talking about?

Follow me, I'll explain it to you.

15.1. ICONS IN PRESENTATIONS

Icons are a powerful graphic medium that allows you to symbolize messages and significantly improve the fruition of your slides.

The typical example of icon application is the resolution of an evil that is all too common in the world of presentations: bullet points.

Bullet points are an excellent tool for synthesizing reading points in a text to be read... To be read!

If you have a slide made of bullet points, like the one I'm about to show you, you can be sure that people will read it and stop listening to you.

Imagine having to present 3 initial hooking strategies for presentations. After reading chapter 10 you have identified the 3 you prefer and created this slide:

Image 1 - Traditional slide presentation of a list of points

We agree you can do better than that, right?

When we see a slide like this, we are naturally led to say that we do not like it.

Actually, what we say is not entirely true.

In fact, the truth is that this slide does not work and, not knowing how to identify the causes of design ineffectiveness, we say what we feel and what we do not like.

If you were able to understand what the reasons behind the malfunction of a slide are, you would also be able to quickly redesign it effectively.

Technical analysis of slides is at the heart of a Lean approach to presentations, but we'll talk about it in a few chapters, when you've acquired all the tools you need to make a proper redesign.

For the moment, let's try to reduce the reading effect of the audience on this slide.

The slide contains a list of 3 points of equal importance.

So, you can't use a full slide image to solve this layout, you need something else.

Since each point is key to the presentation, I suggest you display all three of them, and do it with nice icons.

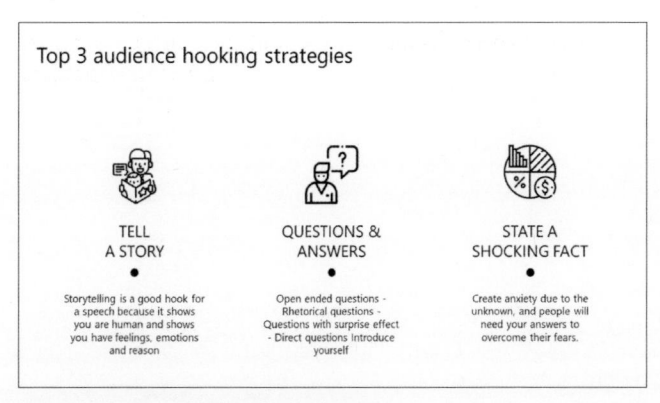

Image 2 - Image 1 redesigned using icons

See how the slide already has a different face?

I'm trying to limit the redesign only to the application of icons.

What do I mean?

That if I had to redesign this slide, the icons would be just one of the interventions to do, but for now we'll stop here.

The reason why I'm limiting the example is to show you the powerful impact of using icons in the resolution of a typical layout without anticipating techniques that I will explain in the next chapters.

The icons symbolize the three points, facilitate understanding and therefore help the audience to remember longer, but above all, they summarize the content and make it usable at a glance.

You see, you don't have to waste time processing the message, because thanks to the icons it is easy to identify and focus it.

Thus, icons simplify layouts and improve the comprehensibility of your slides.

15.2. WHERE TO FIND ICONS

The first place to look for icons is just a click away while working on PowerPoint.

If you have one of the latest versions, you will see that in the insert menu you have a small icon representing the icon menu.

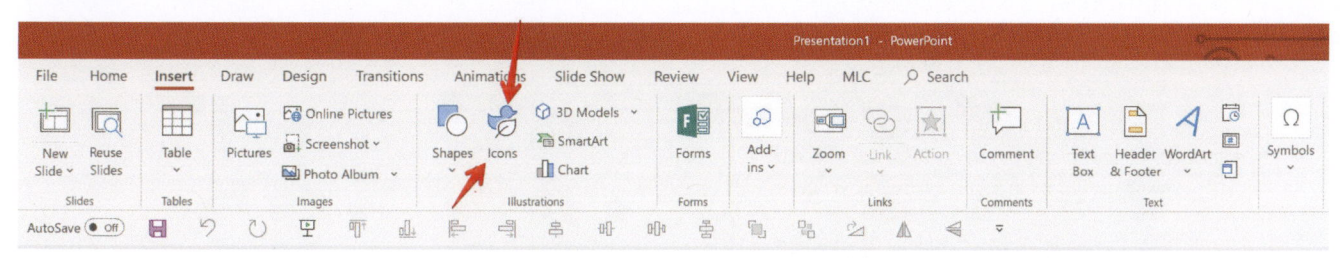

Image 3 - PowerPoint icon menu

From there, you can easily access a small library of icons organized by category.

Interesting?

Definitely, but it's not my favorite resource.

Why?

There is little choice and they are rarely updated.

There are dedicated portals online that make available, for free or for a fee, millions of icons and collections of icons with a far greater choice.

Want some examples?

Let's start with the ones I use most often.

The first one is called flaticon.com.

I'll show you a screenshot I took today, but consider that when you'll read this book, probably, there will be even more icons available because, like all the portals, it's constantly updated.

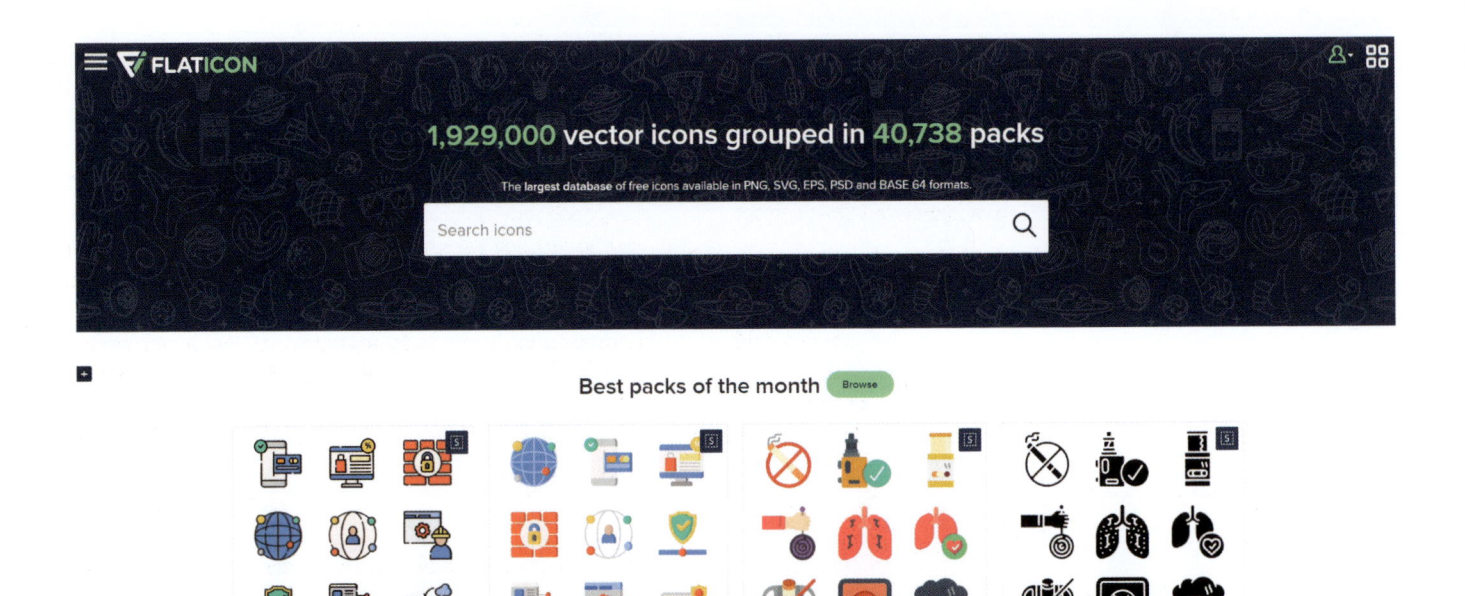

Image 4 - flaticon.com

Flaticon is interesting because it provides a large amount of icons, many of which are free of charge.

Paid icons are currently marked by a crown, while others are available to you.

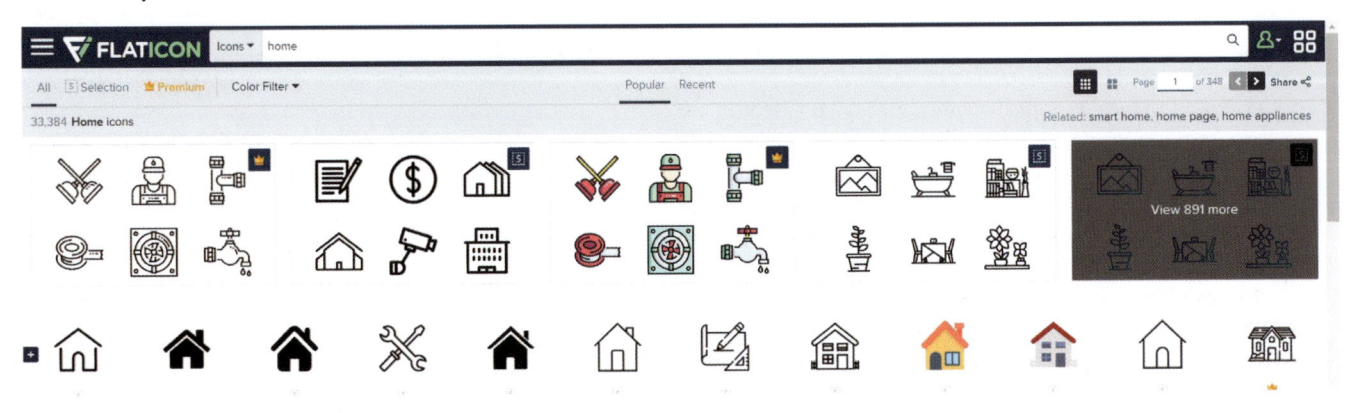

Image 5 - flaticon.com, search example

There are colored icons and monochrome icons.

What do you think I usually opt for?

Careful, a single color does not mean black and white, but only one color.

You can assign a color of your choice.

You could color the icons, for example, according to the color of the brand you are presenting.

Are you already guessing the solution?

I prefer to work with monochrome icons for a matter of graphic consistency.

What do I mean?

Icons are usually used in quantity in a presentation, imagine what happens if you insert a large amount of multicolored icons, you can say goodbye to any glimmer of graphic coherence.

If you're working for Coca Cola and you have a presentation that works with red as a brand color, then you might need all the red icons to create consistency with the official theme of the presentation.

Remember that, in many cases, you may find yourself working in compliance with a corporate template that you can enrich with beautiful icons, but always respecting its visual identity.

Consistency, working with icons, is not only created with color but also with style.

Each icon has its own style, and that's why you must be careful when combining them.

How to combine them without mistakes?
An intelligent way is through the collections that Flaticon offers you.

These are icon collections with the same style, so sometimes downloading the entire pack can help you maintain the graphic consistency of your slides.

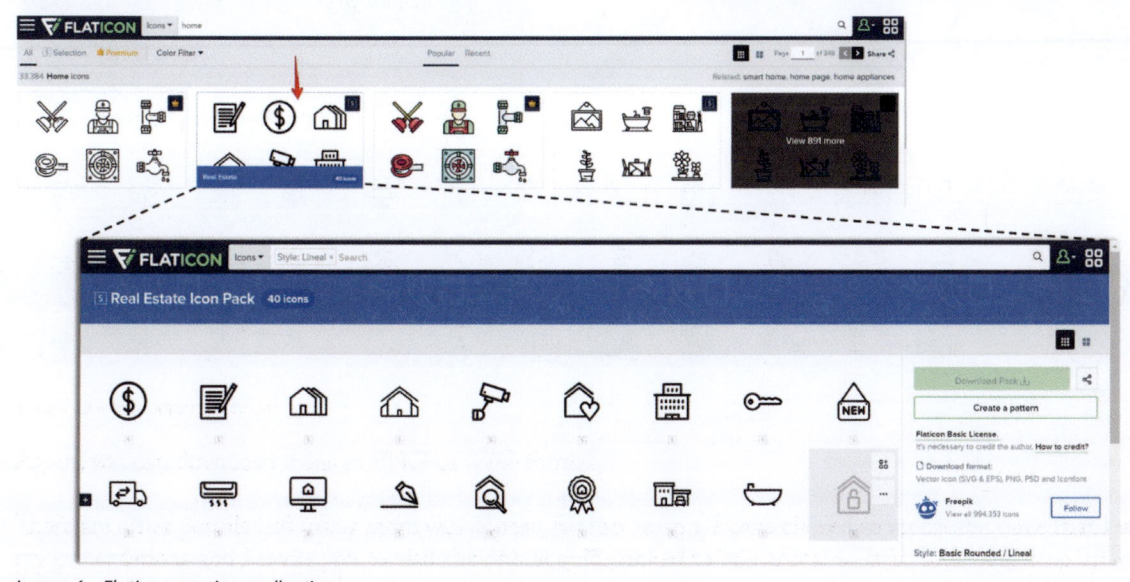

Image 6 - Flaticon.com icon collections

Flaticon is not the only portal where you can find and download icons for free, there are others.

Iconfinder is definitely a very good alternative.

Image 7 - Iconfinder.com

On the whole it is less equipped than Flaticon, but it stands out for its editor that allows you to customize the icons to your liking.

Image 8 - Iconfinder icon editor

Iconfinder, like Flaticon, allows you to download icons in the two formats that interest us: PNG and SVG.

What's the difference?

I'll explain it to you in the next paragraph.

Let's finish our portal overview.

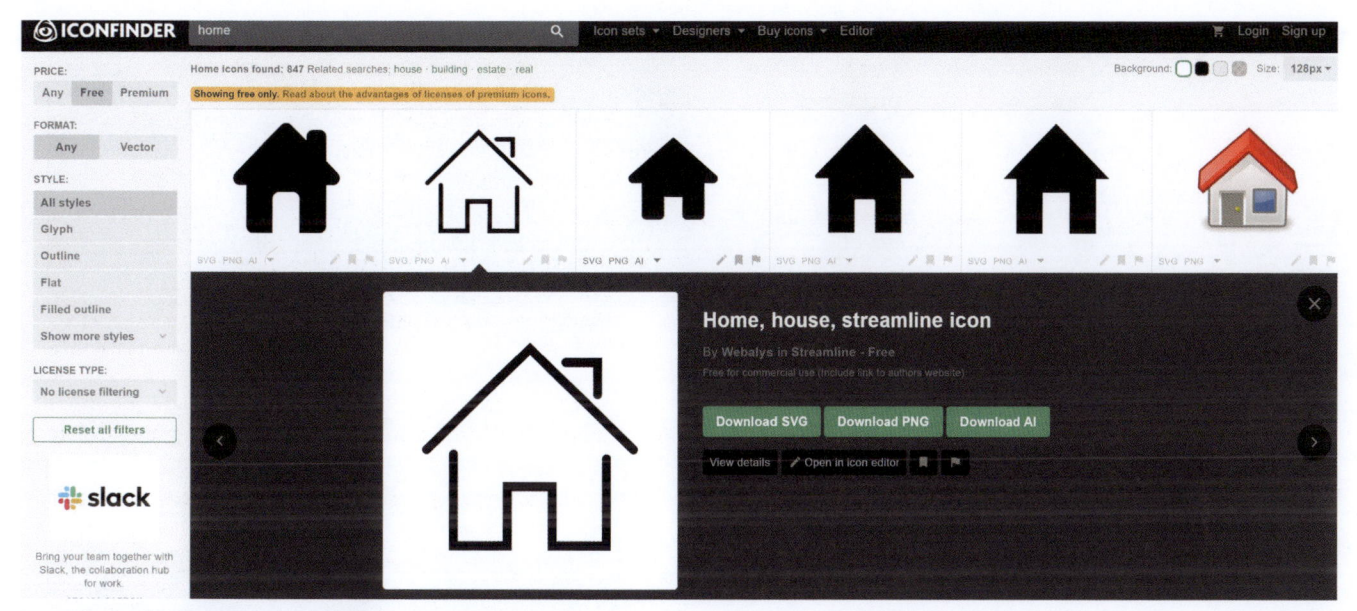

Image 9 – Available formats on Iconfinder

The last interesting portal is The Noun Project.

Image 10 - thenounproject.com

Again, you can download icons in PNG or SVG format.

There are other portals and many more will appear; for this reason, I have chosen to report the three that I use most often for my presentations and I invite you to visit the online guide linked to this article to learn more and keep up to date.

15.3. ICON FORMATS

When you'll try to download an icon, for example from Flaticon, you'll immediately notice the possibility to download it in different formats. The most common formats, and in fact those at your fingertips, are always PNG and SVG.

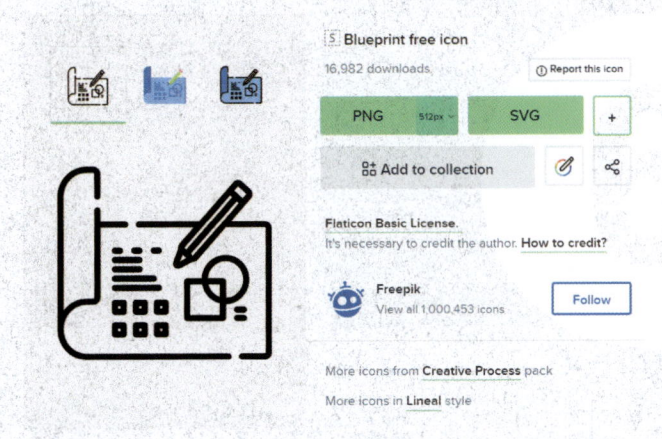

Image 11 - The most common icon formats used in presentations are PNG and SVG

PNG (or Portable Network Graphics) is a format for saving raster images, with lossless compression, primarily designed for the creation of graphics on the web. [1]

The PNG format supports the so-called alpha channel, which allows 256 levels of transparency.

This time I was pretty technical, wasn't I?

Don't worry, I'll explain.

PNG is the image format that allows you, through the alpha channel, to give transparency to the background of the images.

You know when you have those images with that annoying white background?

Allow me to modify the bullet point slide seen above so that I can immediately show you what I mean.

I'll add a black band with a transparent image.

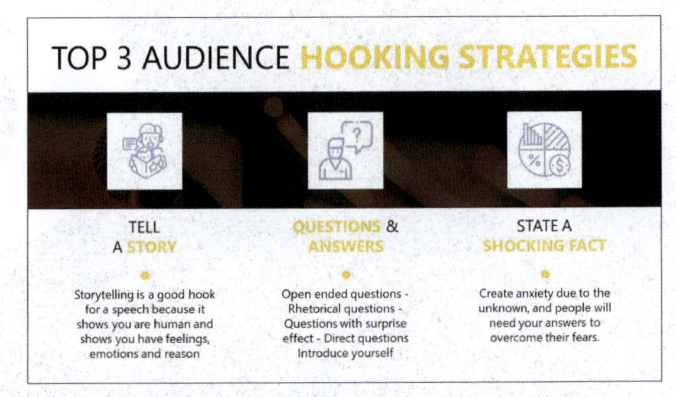

Image 12 - The problem of the background of non-contoured images

Did you notice what happened to the icons?

This is the typical case of JPG icons, an image format that does not manage the Alpha channel, making it impossible to change the background of the image.

In the case of PNGs, you can assign a color to that background and then, in this case, we could assign the transparent color, instead of white, so that it disappears.

So, replacing all the icons from JPG to PNG and setting the color fill to transparent you will get non-contoured icons.

---

[1] https://www.html.it/articoli/grafica-per-il-web-con-il-formato-png/

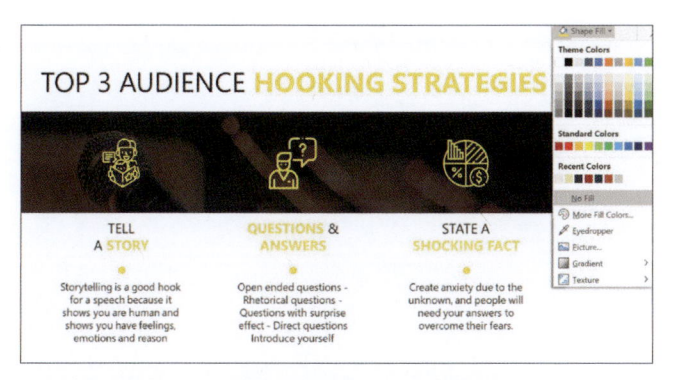

Image 13 – Icons without background thanks to PNG format

What if I now wanted to change the color of the icons and not the background color?

Applying a yellow to the icons you will find yourself with colored backgrounds.

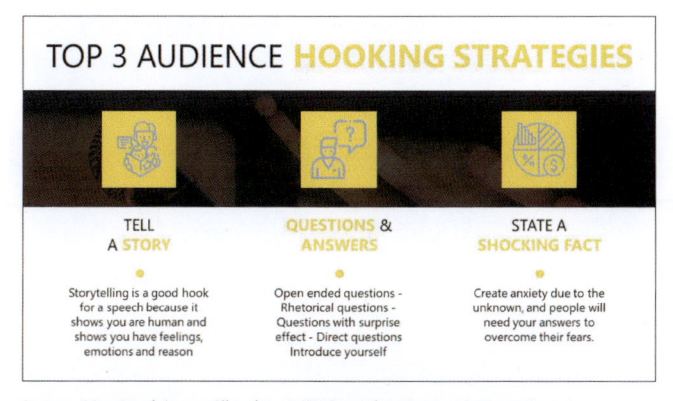

Image 14 - Applying a fill color to PNGs colors its background

This is because the icons are in PNG format, which is an image format. So, the PNG format helps you make the background disappear, but it's not enough in case you have to change the color of the icons.

Here comes to your aid the SVG format - Scalable Vector Graphics, a technology that can display objects of vector graphics and, therefore, can help you manage dimensionally scalable images.

Unlike images, vector graphics can never get grainy, which is why it makes no sense to talk about resolution in these cases.

Let me explain.

If you enlarge an image, sooner or later, depending on its quality, it will appear grainy on the screen. This is because the image is like a grid of many-colored dots that, if moved away, leave holes between them.

Vector graphics, on the other hand, work differently. Imagine it as a formula that takes dimensions in input and returns the part of the colored screen in output.

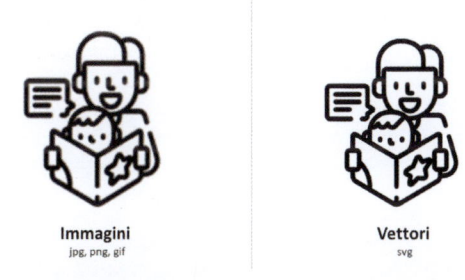

Image 15 - Vector graphics, unlike images, never get grainy

Thanks to the use of the SVG format, you are now able to change the color of the icons, directly in PowerPoint, by simply using the color fill function.

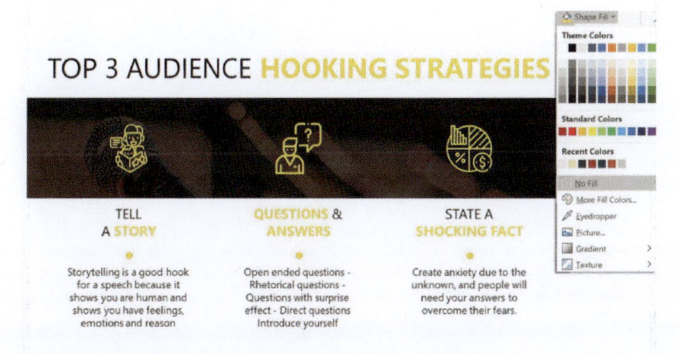

Image 16 - To change the color of SVGs just apply a filler

In conclusion, the PNG format is useful when you create a presentation and want to prevent others from changing the color of the icons.

If you need to be able to quickly change the color of the icons directly via the fill function in PowerPoint, then the PNG format is not the right solution.

Personally, except in special cases, I always work with SVGs because they give me more flexibility and I can always change the color of the icons, if necessary.

15.4. IN SUMMARY

Icons are a powerful graphical tool for solving complex layouts. They help you simplify slides and get the message across with a single glance.

Icons are available for free on different portals in different formats: image (PNG) or vector (SVG).

The SVG formats are the only ones that allow you to change the color of the icon via the color fill function on PowerPoint and, for this reason, are the most flexible.

16
CHAPTER

**GIVE COLOR TO
YOUR PRESENTATION**

« A COLOR DOES NOT ADD A PLEASANT QUALITY TO DESIGN, IT REINFORCES IT »

PIERRE BONNARD

We all have a general understanding of colors; you've learned to play with them at school and, when you were a child, you've had fun using them to draw or worse... Create a mess all over your house! Colors are one of the most natural and powerful tools to support communication, when used correctly.

I will now teach you how to use them in the most efficient way to enhance the communicative effect of your presentations.

16.1. THE COLOR WHEEL

The understanding of colors starts from a very simple concept: the color wheel.

The color wheel has 12 basic color shades. In color theory, a shade or dye is a "pure" color, that is, a color made without the addition of white or black pigments.

Blue, yellow and red are called primary colors, and they are the basic colors used to form all the other colors.

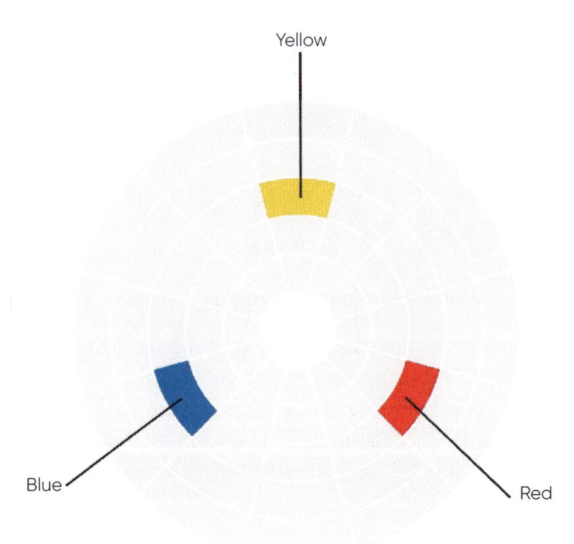

Image 2 – Primary colors

Secondary colors are halfway between the primary colors that generate them. Each secondary color contains the same amount as the two primary colors of which it is composed (e.g. Orange contains 50% yellow and 50% red).

Image 1 - The color wheel

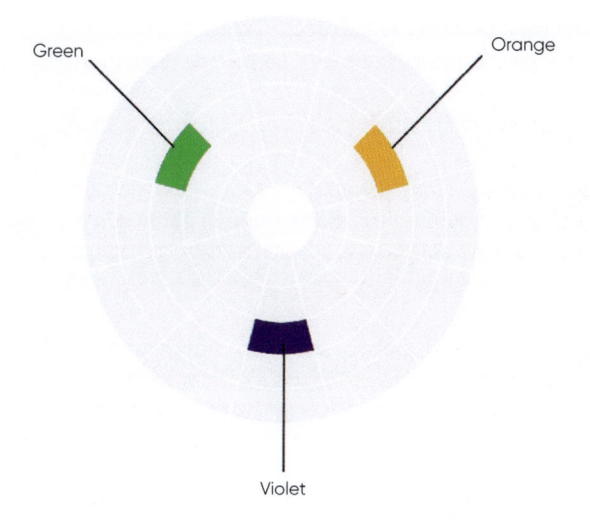

Image 3 – Secondary colors

Figure 4 - Tertiary colors

Tertiary colors are composed in equal parts of primary colors and secondary colors.

The real strength of the color wheel is that it teaches us how to manage the relationships between colors and choose them in order to obtain always effective combinations.

16.2. LIGHTS AND SHADOWS

Adding black and white to the color shades results in light tones and shadow tones, respectively.

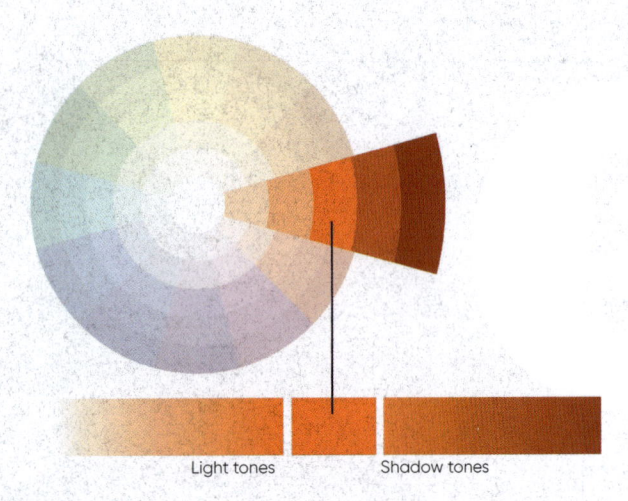

Image 5 - Light and shadow tones in the color wheel

In PowerPoint you can easily adjust the amount of black and white to add to a color via the color panel:

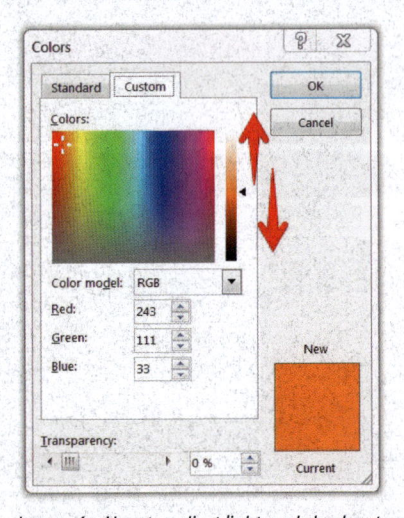

Image 6 - How to adjust light and shadow tones in PowerPoint

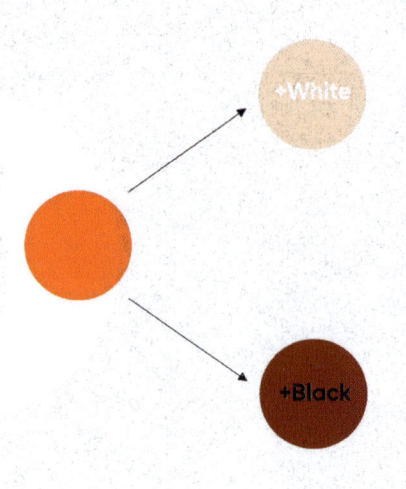

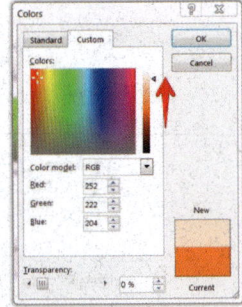

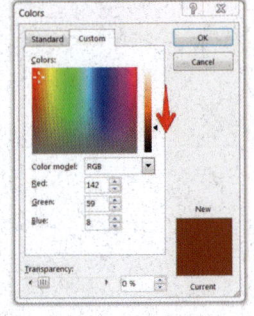

Image 7 - Effects of applying light and shadow tones in PowerPoint

Light and shadow tones are fundamental tools for creating contrast. One of the most common errors in presentations is text that cannot be read because it gets lost in the background color. For a text to be read, you need it to contrast with the background on which it is displayed. Dark characters stand out against light backgrounds and vice versa.

The tones of light stand out on dark backgrounds

The tones of shadow on bright backgrounds

The tones of shadow on bright backgrounds

Image 8 - The contrast between colors

16.3. SATURATION

Saturation is the intensity of the color shade. A very saturated tint has a vivid color, while a desaturated tint will tend to gray.

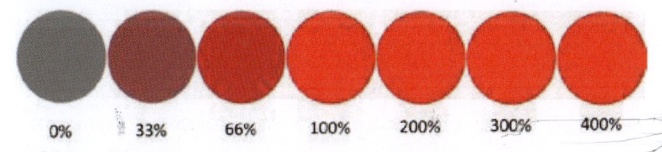

Image 23 - Example of saturation/desaturation effect on a color

In PowerPoint you can easily desaturate images from the relevant color panel. You will find preset saturation options to choose from.

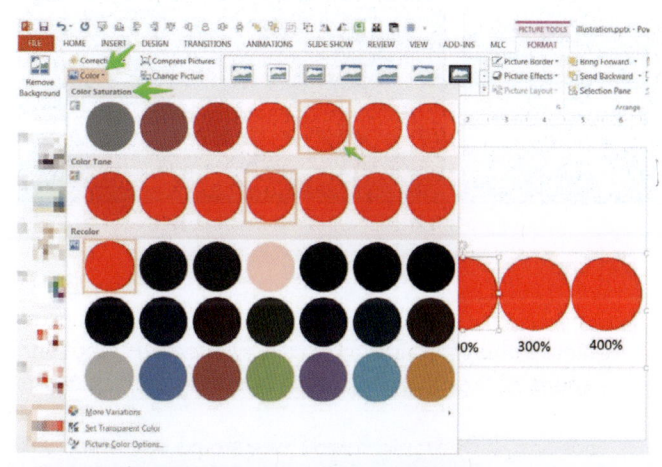

Image 9 - Saturation gradations available in PowerPoint

Saturation is often used on backgrounds to desaturate them and bring out the image in the foreground. This way, it is easy to draw attention to a specific element of the slide and at the same time create space for writing a message.

In the image with the ladybug, for example, by desaturating the background and leaving the ladybug in evidence, we have freed up the space to write a message and make it stand out thanks to a very bright green. Applying light tones to it, the green will clearly stand out against the background.

Image 10 - Use saturation to highlight the message

Note that to get this graphic result you just need to use PowerPoint, you don't need to use more complex software such as Photoshop or other photo editing suites.

How can you create such a slide?

Simple, it's called focus effect.

16.4. FOCUS EFFECT

The focus effect is a simple and powerful graphic tool that allows you to highlight a specific part of an image and create a points of attention path by applying it to slides in progression.

The typical example is when you are presenting software interfaces, thus working with screenshots.

Imagine you have to present Google search results for a defined keyword.

Let's take an example using my name.

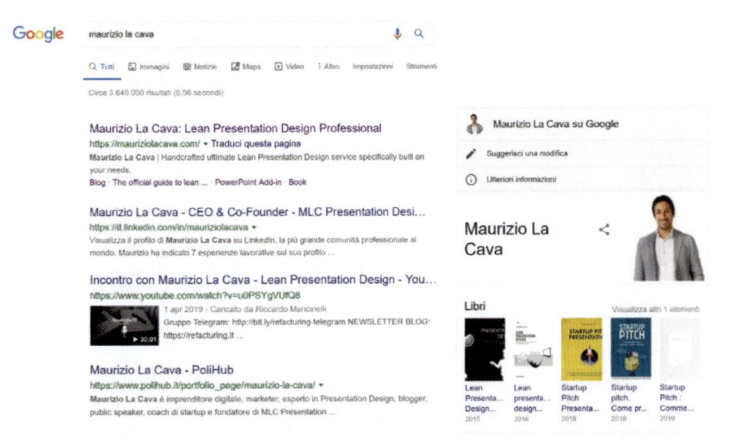

Image 11 - Google search results page

Let's generate a first focus on the results on the left.

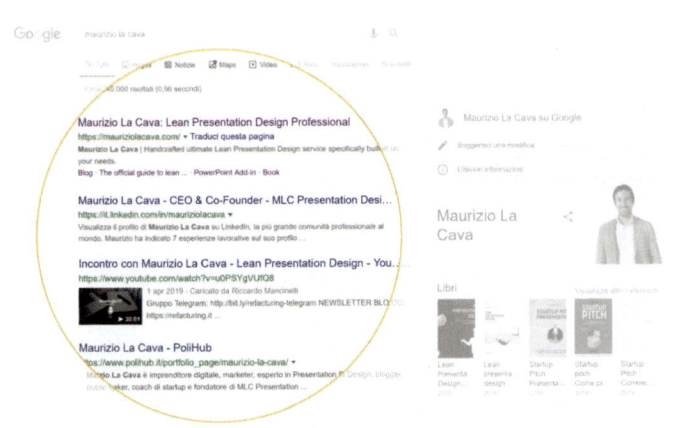

Image 12 - Focus effect on search results

Now let's generate a focus on the author tab.

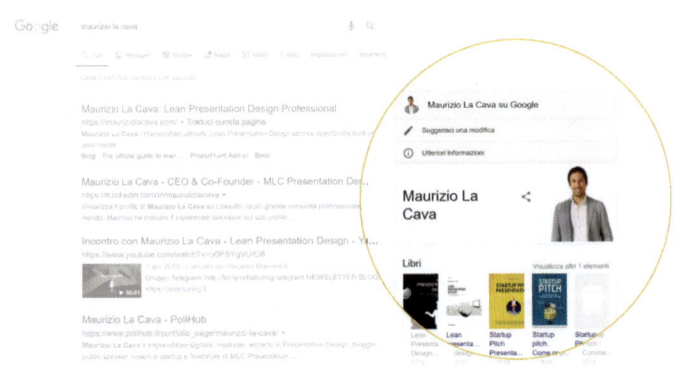

Image 13 – Focus on the author tab

Try to imagine the two slides in sequence.

Without any animation, you will have the impression that the focus moves from one point to another and, if you are good at coordinating, that it is following your speech.

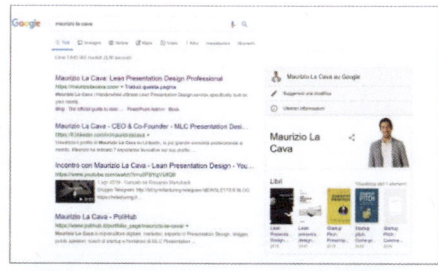

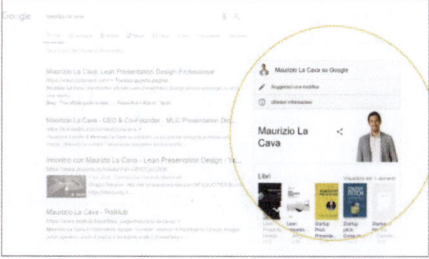

Image 14 - The focus effect becomes dynamic

Therefore, the focus effect is composed of a part of the image that is saturated and a part that is desaturated (in light grey).

This implies that in the desaturated part you could also add some help text.

What do I mean?

I'll show you right away, look at the next example.

Image 15 - Use desaturated areas to add help text

Useful, isn't it?
Imagine it at work while you're presenting!
The focus effect allows you to dynamically guide people's attention through your slides without using animations.

You could also export your PowerPoint to PDF, and the effect would still work.

But how do you create this effect in PowerPoint?
It's very simple, I'll explain.

The focus effect is created by superimposing two images: one of a desaturated background and the other superimposed and trimmed in shape and proportion.

Take, for example, this very cute squirrel.

Image 16 - The Squirrel jump

Duplicate the image (CTRL + D for English versions of PowerPoint).

Image 17 - Duplicating the image of the squirrel

Overlay them perfectly using PowerPoint's alignment functions (it works because the first image is centered on the slide).

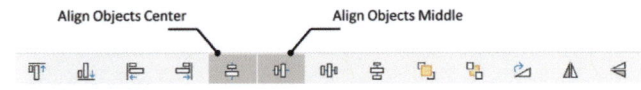

Image 18 - PowerPoint alignment functions

You will only see the upper image.

Image 19 - Upper image perfectly superimposed on the other

Crop the upper image in a 1:1 ratio and in a circular format (an oval in a 1:1 ratio will become the focus circle).

Place the crop circle by taking it from the thin white border between the black crop handles (pay attention, because everyone misses this step).

Image 20 - Place the clipping on the squirrel

Now, all you have to do is confirm the clipping and desaturate the background photo.

Image 21 - Desaturate the background photo, and the overlapping photo will stand out

This way, the overlapping photo will stand out giving life to the focus effect.

16.5. TEMPERATURE

The colors of the wheel can be divided between warm and cold colors:

- Warm colors – red, orange and yellow

- Cold colors – purple, green and blue

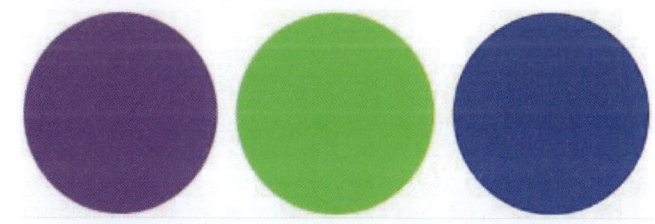

Using the temperature can influence the mood of the audience. Colors like red and orange make us think of something warm - think of a fire, lights, the sun, etc. Colors such as blue and green make us think of something cold - mountains, skiing, snow, etc.

Humans naturally associate warm and cold colors with specific sensations. In fact, red is a passionate color that recalls the sphere of love, while blue is a color that recalls the sphere of loneliness, tranquility, etc.

You can use these associations to convey the message in a deeper way and with greater resonance on the audience.

Image 22 - Example of the application of red as a warm color to emotionally define the message

If this is the cover of a new chapter of a business plan, the audience will expect that the tax section will be particularly difficult and will expect important problems. Red in this case recalls danger, attention.

16.6. THE MEANING OF COLORS

As you've probably already heard, the colors have been studied from a psychological point of view for years. It has now been proven and consolidated that each color has a specific meaning. Here's an analysis of the main colors:

RED

Red is the color of fire and blood, so it is often associated with danger, strength, energy, power and determination as well as passion, desire and love.

Red is an emotionally very intense color; it is associated with danger, it is known to have a direct impact on metabolism, to be able to increase breathing speed and to increase blood pressure. Red has a great visibility and that is why road signs use it in stops, prohibitions and traffic lights, and it is also used in fire-fighting equipment. Red is also often used in national flags because it symbolizes strength.

In presentations, red makes it possible to highlight text and images by making them stand out from the background. Use it as a color to give importance and priority to content. Red also generates an impelling sense of urgency, so it can also be used to force the interlocutor to make a quick decision; think, for example, of the button to purchase a good on a website whose promotion is about to expire. In this case, the red button would rush the potential buyer by reinforcing the message that the promotion is about to expire. In the world of advertising, red is often used to evoke erotic feelings (red lips, red nails, red light districts, etc.). For example, try to search for the word "tango" in Google Images - you will see that in most couples the woman dresses in red.

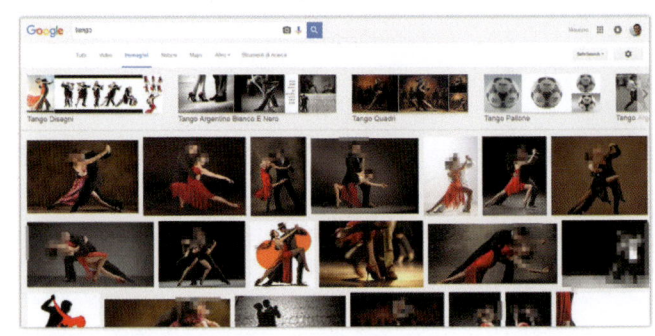

Image 23 - Looking for "Tango" on Google images

Red also goes well with energy drinks, for its meaning that recalls energy themes.

Image 24 - Red Bull & Burn - red dominant color

Variations of red can then be used to recall specific meanings:

- Light red: sexuality, eroticism, passion and love
- Dark red: blood, power, vigor, anger, courage, malice
- Pink: femininity, love, friendship
- Brown: stability and masculinity

YELLOW

Yellow is the color of the sun, of the sunrise. It is often associated with a joyful beginning, with happiness, with intellect. Yellow, like the sun, has a warming effect, spreads joy, stimulates mental activity and produces energy for muscle activity. Yellow is often associated with food.

The bright, vibrant yellow color attracts people's attention, which is why taxis are yellow. If too much is used, yellow can easily cause discomfort; children cry more in yellow rooms.

Yellow stands out more than any other color against black, which is why it is used in combination for warning signs. Use yellow in your presentations to evoke pleasant, cheerful, happy situations. You could use it, for example, to promote products related to entertainment or children.

Yellow is widely used to attract attention - so use it wisely in your designing. It is not recommended to use yellow to promote valuable objects to an adult audience, as it would make them think about childhood and they would not buy a yellow BMW, dress or watch. Yellow is an unstable color that recalls spontaneity, so it is to be avoided if you want to recall a safe and stable situation.

Finally, pay attention to the background on which yellow is applied, because it is almost completely lost on light backgrounds and especially on white backgrounds.

Yellow variations may have different meanings:

- Light yellow: decay, disease, squalor
- Bright yellow: intelligence, freshness and joy

ORANGE

Orange is a secondary color that is obtained by mixing yellow and red. Its meaning is also inherited from the primary colors from which it is obtained. Orange combines the energy of red with the happiness of yellow. It represents joy, dawn, enthusiasm, creativity, attraction, success, encouragement and stimulation.

Orange is a very warm color, which is why it gives the perception of warmth. However, orange is less aggressive than red. Orange can enhance the flow of air to the brain and produce an invigorating effect by stimulating mental activity; it is a youthful color and represents, among other things, harvest and sunset.

In presentations you can use it to promote healthy food products and toys. However, attention should be paid to tonality as, as illustrated below, it can have many facets:

- Dark orange: deception, fraud, falsehood, mistrust
- Reddish orange: desire, passion, sensuality, pleasure, domination, aggression
- Gold: prestige, lighting, wealth, quality

GREEN

Green is the color of nature. It symbolizes harmony, freshness, fertility and growth. Green is a reassuring color, which is why it is used in operating theatres. Green has healing powers; it is the most restful color for the human eye; it is said that it can even improve sight.

Green evokes stability and resistance, even if sometimes it is the color that symbolizes the lack of experience. Green indicates hope for a promising future. Green is significantly opposed to red and means safety; think of the green of the railway level crossing (green = safe, you can pass).

In presentations, use green to evoke safety, for example when promoting healing or natural products.

- Dark green: ambition, money, finance, financial markets
- Water green: healing and protection
- Olive green: traditionally the color of peace

BLUE

The color of the sea and the sky, often associated with depth, stability and safety. It symbolizes trust, loyalty, confidence, intelligence, destiny, truth and paradise.

Blue has positive effects on the mind and body; it slows down the metabolism and calms the mind. Blue is associated with tranquility and calm.

In presentations you can use blue to promote a cleaning or purification service. Blue can be used, for example, for airlines, airports, air conditioners, travel, water parks, shipping companies. Blue is a cold color, it is connected to awareness, interiority and intellect. Blue suggests precision, for example, in the promotion of high-tech products.

Blue, unlike pink, is a masculine color. Blue makes your appetite go away, so it is not recommended to use it to promote food or cooking. When used in conjunction with warmer colors such as yellow or red, blue can generate a strong visual impact and a striking design.

- Light blue: means health, healing, peace of mind, understanding
- Dark blue: represents knowledge, power, integrity, seriousness, precision, experience, stability, firmness.

PURPLE

Purple combines the stability of blue with the energy and strength of red. Purple is a regal color, symbolizing power, nobility, luxury and ambition.

Purple expresses wealth and extravagance, but also wisdom, dignity, independence, creativity, mystery and magic. Purple is a magical color that represents the spell, the dream that becomes reality. The person who prefers purple is often a very empathetic person.

For these reasons, purple is a color loved by children even if it is found very little in nature. Purple is also the color of creativity, so it can be used in presentations to convey design services, web design but also personal consulting services or life coaching, because it recalls the sphere of empathy.

- Clear purple: romance and nostalgia
- Dark purple: darkness, obscurity, sadness, frustration

WHITE

White is the color of light, often associated with innocence, purity and virginity. White is the color of perfection and cleanliness. White is by definition the opposite of black, even in its meaning, and for this reason it often takes on positive connotations. In the advertising world, white represents cleanliness and freshness, just like snow.

White is used a lot to convey efficiency and simplicity (think of the Apple world). White is a perfect color for voluntary organizations. Angels, for example, are traditionally imagined wearing white. White is reminiscent of medical gowns, dairy products and dietary products.

In presentations it is a very important color, because it allows you to create contrasts and above all allows you to create space and give breath to the content.

BLACK

Black is associated with power, elegance, formality, death and mystery. Black is a mysterious color associated with darkness, the unknown and thus fear.

In opposition to white, therefore, it carries negative meanings (blacklist, black mood, black death). Black denotes strength and authority; it is also considered the most formal color of all, elegant and prestigious (a black car, a black dress, etc.). Black is a deep color that lends itself well to play a predominant role in the backgrounds of presentations.

It is widely used in presentations for large events. In fact, when the audience is very large and the presentation is held in a theater or in a conference center, the screen will be very large and the room typically dark. The typical mistake is to use slides with a light background that, by making the screen very bright, dazzle the audience. For this reason, in large events we recommend the use of slides with a black background that does not dazzle the audience and allow the relevant content to stand out.

However, you must be very careful to contrast well the background color with clear content, so that they stand out and can be clearly seen. Black combined with orange or red results in a very powerful color combination. I also like the combination with green or blue.

Now that you have deepened your knowledge of color psychology, I invite you to sharpen your eyes - you will discover the rationale behind the choice of colors for what surrounds us every day.

Image 25 – Colors and brands (Huffington post)

16.7. THE SEMANTIC RESONANCE EFFECT

When choosing colors, always take the opportunity to take advantage of the concept of semantic resonance of color, that is, choose colors related to the theme you are talking about. If you are talking about an organic product of controlled origin, you could use green as the dominant color.

Image 26 - Green slide that recalls the organic theme

If you are talking about an energy drink you could use red, as seen above.

This also affects the choice of colors of the contents of a slide; if you are showing data on Facebook, perhaps related to the results of an advertising campaign, you could use the blue color of Facebook.

CASE STUDY:

THE RIGHT COLOR MAKES DATA EASIER TO READ - HARVARD BUSINESS REVIEW BY SHARON LIN AND JEFFREY HEER

What's the color of money? Of love? Of the ocean? In the United States, most people answer that green is the color of money, love is red, and the ocean is blue. Many concepts evoke a correlated color; this may be due to physical form, common metaphors or cultural beliefs. When colors are matched with concepts that evoke them, we define this color choices as semantically resonant.

Artists and designers regularly use semantically resonant color choices in their work, and in our research with Julie Fortuna, Chinmay Kulkarni and Maureen Stone we found that they can significantly affect data visualization.

Let's consider the (fictitious) fruit sales data represented by the following two graphs:

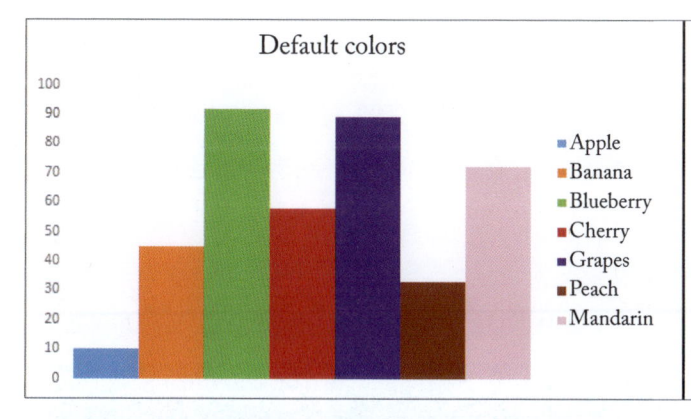

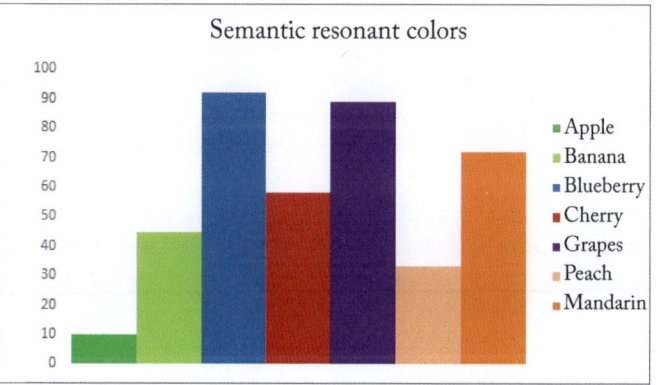

The only difference between the two graphs is the color assignment. The first graph uses colors from a standard color palette; the second graph uses colors from a standard color palette. The graph on the right shows colors assigned with semantic resonance (in this case, the assignment was made automatically by assigning an algorithm that analyzes colors in congruent images on Google Images using searches for each category).

Now, try answering the following data questions by comparing the two charts: Which fruit had the highest sales: blueberries or mandarins? Which chart is easier to read?

If you think the second chart is easier to read, you're not the only one! To measure the incidence of semantic color resonance in chart analysis, we did an experiment based on people's speed in completing a data comparison exercise like the one you just did.

On average, people were a second quicker per comparison by reading data represented by semantically resonant colors (second graph).

It may seem irrelevant, but it is a 10% time saving. Time savings like this can be added up in the case of a data analyst who works all day with an innumerable amount of data.

What's going on? Let's see together different ways in which the semantic resonance of colors could actually help in reading the data. The first mode: semantic resonance colors between them allow you to take advantage of existing relationships easier and faster to remember. Colors that do not generate resonance between them can cause semantic interference: colors and concepts interfere with each other (as in the case of the famous Stroop test; the text in which you are asked to read the name of a color printed but colored with a different color - see following figure)

Image 27 - Stroop test

Second mode: since the concept-color relationship is improved by the semantic resonance effect, looking at the data will allow you not to have to repeatedly look at the legend to remember which concept the different columns of the graph correspond to.

To make effective color choices, you need to consider several factors. Two of the factors are: colors must be visibly different from each other so that the reader can distinguish them more easily - this is called "discrimination". You also must consider how color will look to colorblind people - about eight percent of the male population of the United States!

Do you think colors would be recognizable if they were printed in black and white?

An easy way to combine semantically resonant colors is to use colors from an existing color palette carefully designed for data visualization software and associating colors with data.

However, it should be noted that color associations can change from culture to culture. For example, in the USA and in many Eastern cultures, luck is associated with green (the cloverleaf), while red can be considered a dangerous color. In China, on the other hand, luck is traditionally symbolized by red (e.g. Chinese lanterns).

There are a few other factors to consider, when using semantic resonance colors:

Type of data:
So far, we have discussed data representing specific categories. Other types of data may be numerical or increasingly ordered (e.g. low, medium, high). In these cases, a sequential or divergent color scheme (system in which a color becomes lighter or darker as the data grows/decreases) could be more appropriate.

Similar color associations:
Some concepts can be linked to similar colors. For example, magazines and newspapers can both be represented in grey. One could consider assigning two different shades of gray to the two concepts, but then it would be even more difficult to remember which gradation refers to which concept. In this case it could be decided to identify one of the two concepts with a different color, but which guarantees "discrimination".

The strength of concept-color association:
Some concepts are simply more "colorable" than others. For example, people generally agree on the colors of categories such as "gold", "silver", "money". However, what is the color of "social security", "national defense", or "income security"? In general, using colors in semantic resonance for categories that are more "colorable" tends to greatly improve the performance of data usage.

In conclusion

Colors in semantic resonance reinforce the perception of a vast set of categories. Similar performance improvements can also occur with other forms of data visualization such as maps, scatter graphs and line graphs.

So, when you design presentations or view analyses, carefully choose colors and ask yourself if they actually resonate with the concepts they convey.

16.8. READY-TO-USE COLOR COMBINATIONS

When working on a presentation, the choice of colors is one of the very first choices to face. You don't need a wide spectrum of colors - you just need three or four - but you must be sure that they look attractive and pleasantly combined with each other. In reality, the choice of color in presentations is increasingly turning into a desperate search for colors that "are liked" conducted solely on the basis of personal and subjective preferences. Have you ever spent time changing colors to understand which colors make a message or an image or a shape stand out? How many times have you simply opted for red to make a message stand out just by circling it or pointing it with an arrow?

Although you may be satisfied with the choice, if the colors you have chosen do not combine correctly with each other, the result will be visually disrupted and communication will be affected.

In general, there are colors that can be matched and others that you should never match. Knowing all the color combinations would be impossible even for an experienced designer but fortunately there are simple rules that allow you to orient yourself precisely and make choices very quickly.

Basically, I'm telling you that I don't choose colors, but I calculate them from a given color.

How do I do that?

Using the color combinations technique.

Imagine working with a brand whose main color is dark blue R: 0, G: 57, B: 89 and wanting to obtain colors that, in harmony with the main one, allow you to design the presentation in a consistent manner.

Starting from a given color and moving on the color wheel you can calculate harmonious color combinations.

Among the color combinations, there are three that are particularly useful for any situation: monochromatic, similar, and complementary.

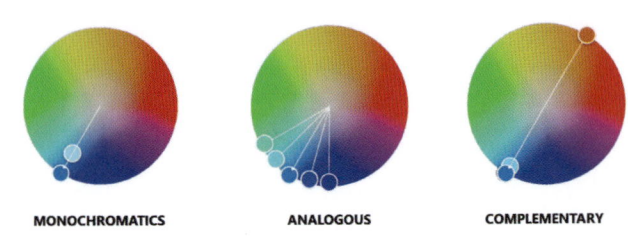

Image 28 - Main color combinations

Basically, if you compose a color palette with colors linked together by means of one of these three schemes, you will never be wrong!

How do I get colors based on the three combinations?

The most popular tool on the web, available free of charge, is certainly Adobe Color (http://color.adobe.com).

Image 29 - https://color.adobe.com

Adobe color provides different color combinations - but we will focus on using the three just mentioned.

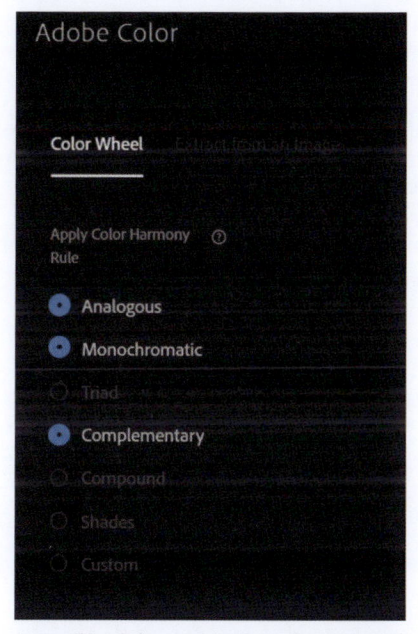

Image 30 - Color combination selection panel

You will notice that by selecting one of the color rules, the color wheel will show different color palettes. For each color palette you will have:

1. RGB color code (R= red, G= Green, B=blue)
2. Hexadecimal color identification code (HEX)

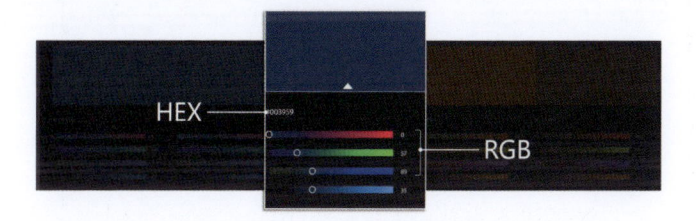

Image 31 - Color selection panel in Adobe Color

This information will help you to uniquely identify the color shades obtained. The five colors from the choice of one of the color rules represent the palette of colors allowed in your presentation for all elements. So, any text, shape, background, table or other object must use colors from this palette.

16.9. IMPORTING COLORS INTO POWERPOINT

To correctly import the colors, you just got into PowerPoint you will need to change the color palette of the template through the design panel. Then open the Design menu, expand the options for customizing the template and enter the submenu: colors.

Inside you will find a long series of readymade color palettes made available by Microsoft. Select the last option at the bottom to introduce a custom color palette.

Image 32 - Customize the look of your current design

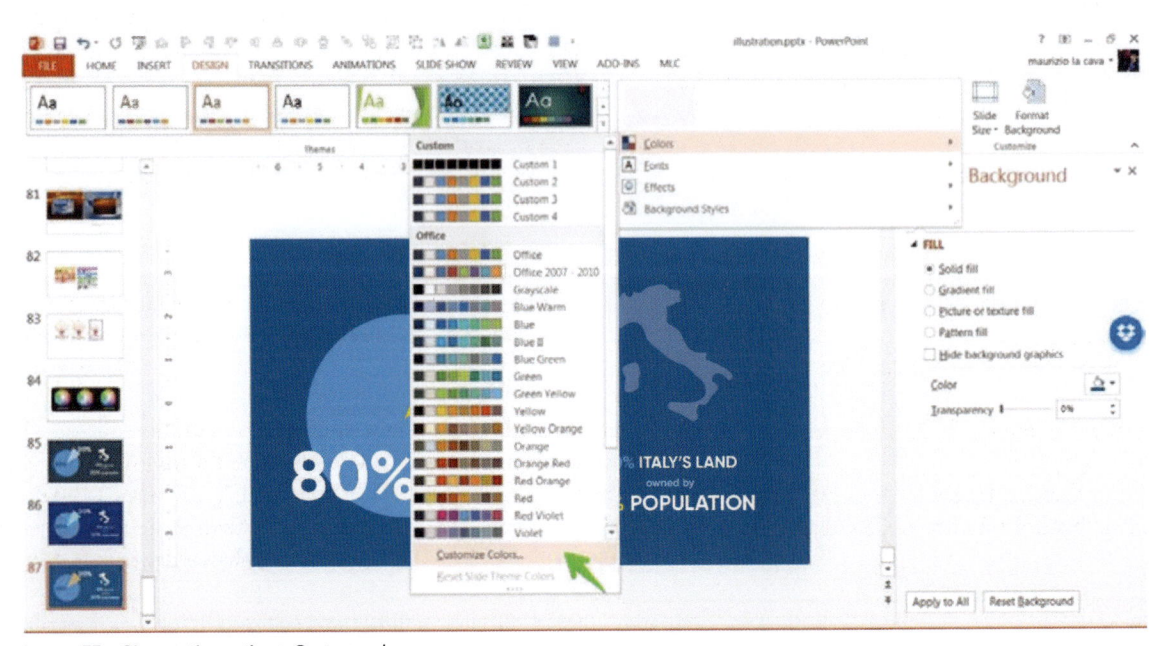

Image 33 - Choose the option > Custom colors

In this panel you can enter the colors one by one by seeing on the right screen on which object will act the change within the presentation.

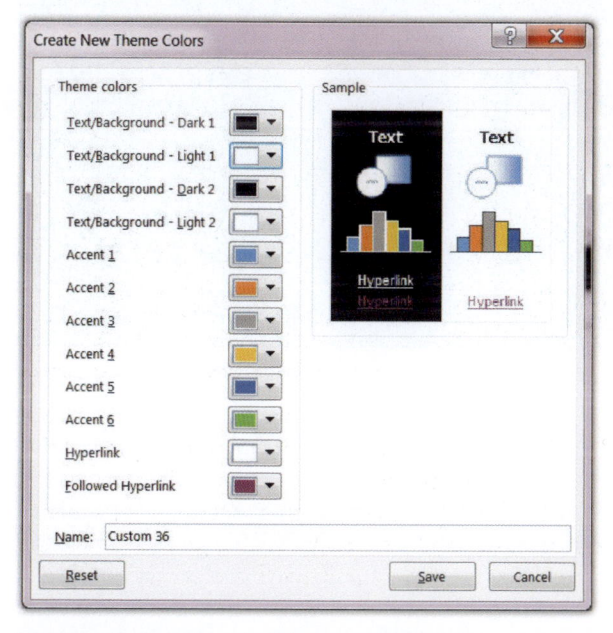

Image 34 - Presentation color palette control panel

Here's how it works:

- **Accent 1:**

default color for lines and shapes; every time you draw a line/form in PowerPoint it will have this color by default

- **Accent 2-5:**

the five colors of your color palette. Enter here one by one the colors obtained from Adobe Color reporting the values of the RGB code

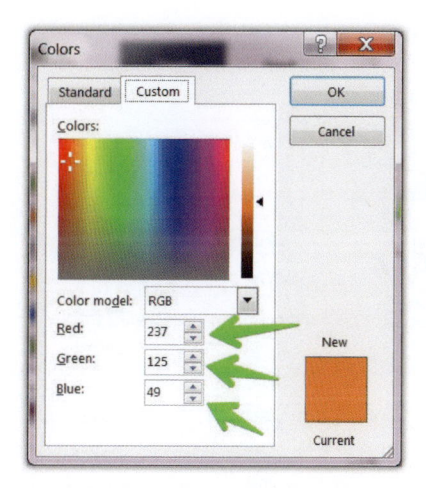

Image 35 - Enter RGB to uniquely identify a color

- **Accents 2-6** colors will take the last five places of the theme color menu

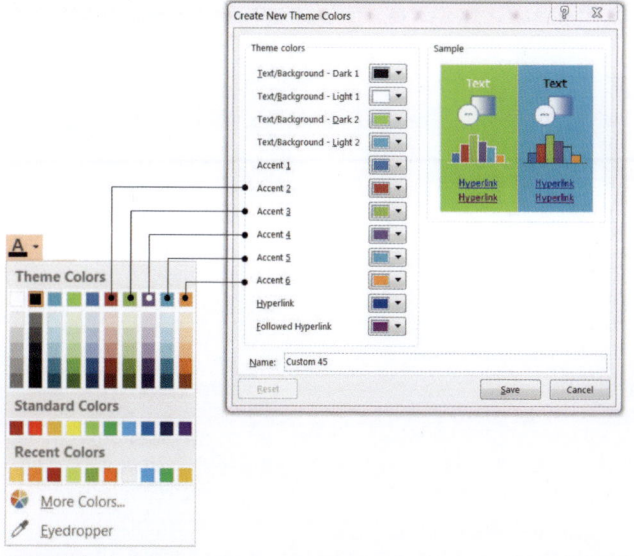

Image 36 - Accents

- **Hyperlink/Followed Hyperlink:**
colors of hyperlinks and hyperlinks that have been clicked at least once in the presentation

- **Text/Background - Dark 1 and Light 1:**
the colors of all your texts. These colors appear in the first two columns of the theme color menu. If you choose black and white, you will get to scale a full combination of grays that vary with a 10% increment from white to black. The greys will be placed in the two columns below black and white

- **Text/Background - Dark 2 and Light 2:**
The colors of the backgrounds that you will have to carefully combine with the colors of the texts so as to always create contrast and make the text readable. These two colors take third and fourth place in the theme's color palette

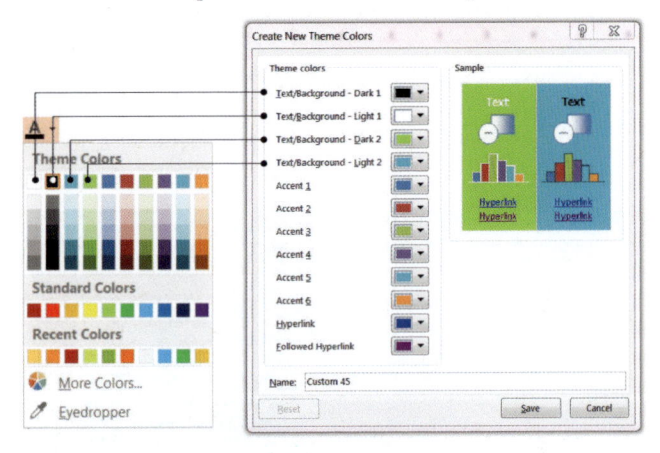

Image 37 - Colors of texts and backgrounds

The Dark 1/2 and Light 1/2 colors are closely related and allow, if combined correctly, to quickly change the background of the presentation ensuring the readability of the contents. The typical example is the case of a presentation used for meetings with a few people (therefore on a white background), which must be projected during a large event in which it is convenient to use a black background that does not dazzle the audience. It would be impossible to change the background and the texts of every single slide. The solution is to change the style of the background, the rest will be taken care of by PowerPoint; let's see how it is done:

1. Open a new presentation and choose the basic style, the first slide will be with a white background and black text

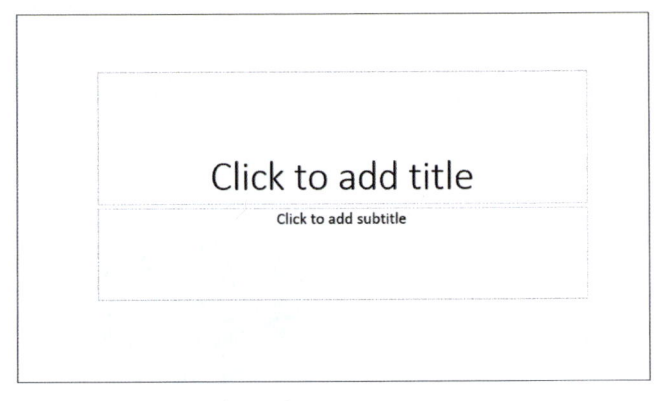

Image 38 – White and black style

2. Now change the background style from Design > Variants > Background Styles and choose a dark background from those available, such as black

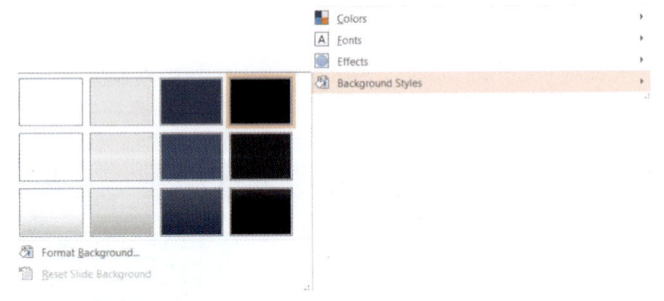

Image 39 - Reverse the color of backgrounds and texts

3. You will notice that the text automatically changes color to white to be more visible

Image 40 - Dark background and light text

I recommend that you take the time to setup the color palette at the beginning of your work on a presentation. When you've finished configuring all the color combinations, rename the palette (I usually name it after the client I'm working on) and close the editing panel so that it is always available in PowerPoint whenever you need to reuse it.

Image 41 - Assign a name to the color combination

16.10. A PRACTICAL CASE STUDY:
COLOR COMBINATIONS

Here are some examples of the application of the three rules on the same slide. You will see how the graphic rendering of one varies with the variation of the applications of the different color combinations. The slide communicates the principle of Pareto:

"20% of the Italian population owns 80% of the total land"

Monochrome
Simple, elegant and very professional combination. This is one of my favorite color combinations because it keeps you away from the risk of introducing noise related to wrong color choices. This combination is perfect for those who are approaching this world for the first time; low risk and guaranteed performance.

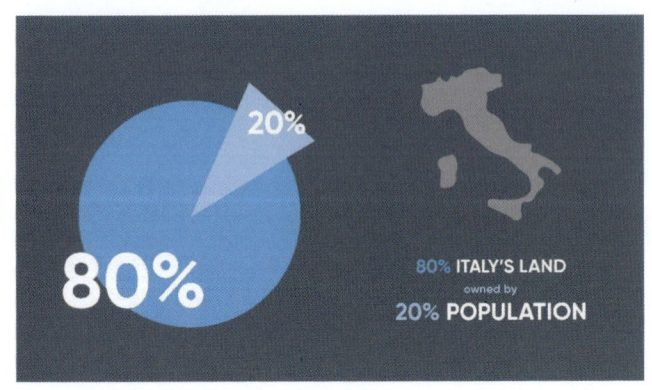

Image 42 - Monochrome color combination

Analogues
Combination that allows access to a wide range of colors, although very close on the color wheel. Give your presentation a harmonious and lively look. In this case, the background has been made in a darker color so that it is visually overshadowed. See how the contrast with the texts brings out the words, are easily readable and capture the attention of the audience at a glance.

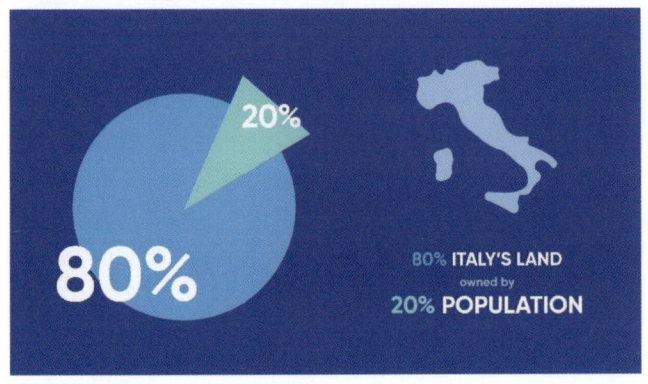

Image 43 - Analog color combination

Complementary
Complementary colors have opposite positions on the color wheel. They are so different that they almost seem to collide when used together, yet they work perfectly. This combination is perfect for creating strong contrasts.

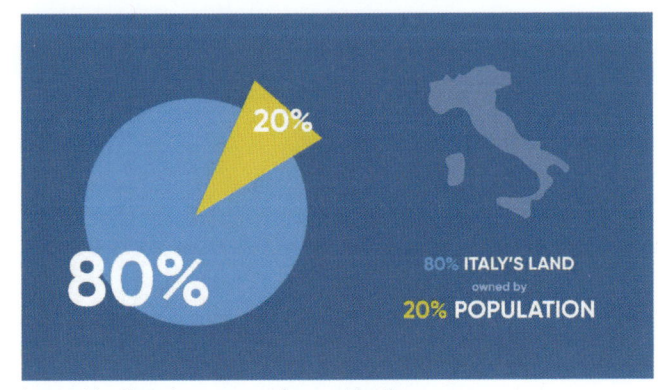

Image 44 - Complementary color combinations

16.11. IN SUMMARY

Color creates harmony within the presentation, connects objects semantically and improves the usability of content for the audience.

Colors can be combined in a variety of ways, but there are color combinations that, if used correctly, allow you to quickly create a palette of colors that work well together.

The technique of color combinations allows you to quickly achieve an effective result and is therefore perfectly part of the set of techniques a Lean Presenter must know.

Give color to your presentations, and let your audience experience your content in the best possible way.

17

CHAPTER

**NEURO
PRESENTATION DESIGN**

« OBEY
THE PRINCIPLES
WITHOUT BEING BIND
BY THEM »

BRUCE LEE

The last step in the Lean process of approaching presentations is to join the dots and trace the path that will guide your audience through the content.

I used a metaphor, but that's exactly how it works in presentations.

So far, you have created and visualized all your contents, respecting a communicative structure that played the role of guideline to order them, now it is time to design every detail of the experience that you want your audience to live through your content.

In short, as you will have understood by now, there are different ways and means of saying the same things.

There is no absolute truth, no single solution that allows you to create the best presentation.

The best solution depends on the context.

17.1. LEARN TO ANALYZE THE CONTEXT

Imagine creating slides to support your live presentation. On the day of the event, you will be in front of the audience and the slides will be behind you to support you.

Image 1 – Live presentation dynamics

First, if you were that presenter in the picture, I'd have to compliment you!

You would have chosen the right side to position yourself for the presentation.

Why?

For the simple fact that you have positioned yourself according to the reading direction of your audience.

Think about it for a moment - in which direction do people read?

In the western part of the world we are used to reading from left to right.

So, if you, as speaker, are positioned to the left (for the audience) of the screen, it means that people will look at you before looking at the slides, then they will continue to the right, they will see the screen and then they will come back to the left to start again.

If you were on the other side of the screen, people would naturally be led to first read the slides and then eventually look at you, triggering a behavior that would strain them and could easily compromise the effectiveness of your presentation.

OK, so you'll be the first thing the audience will see, your slides will follow.

During a presentation, your audience's eyes will first be on you and then quickly pass over the slides.

I wrote quickly because it must be fast.

Image 2 - Focus on the presenter and quick look at the slides

If the slides caught more attention than necessary, they could distract people from what you're saying.

When does this behavior occur?

When people don't find, at a glance, the information that matches what you're saying.

An example is the confusing slide that we previously analyzed; I'll show it in the next picture for your convenience.

The Italian style

· Food (like pizza, pasta, risotto, etc.)
· Design (Renzo Piano)
· Fashion (Gucci, Prada, ...)
· Beautiful panorama (Sicily, Sardinia)
· Friendly people
· Cappucino

Image 3 - Example of confusing slide

Confusion can have two causes:

1. There is too much text content on the slide that forces people to read
2. The content is presented in a disorganized way and forces people to look for information that does not stand out clearly

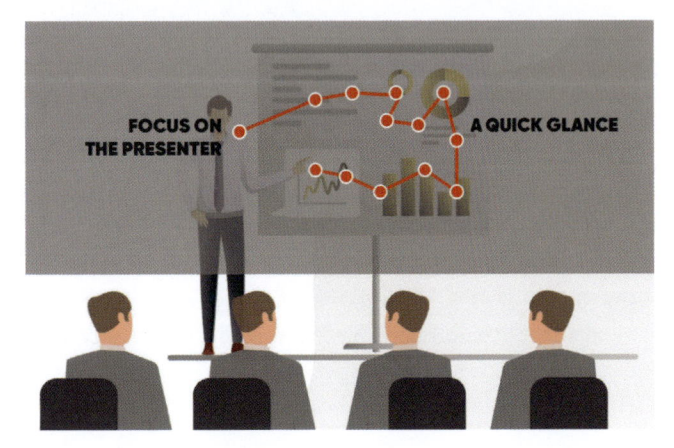

Image 4 - Slide steals attention from the speaker when not optimized

Content must always be organized on slides, and this is not debatable.

However, there are exceptions regarding the amount of text content.

In which case is it convenient to produce text-rich slides?

For example, if the presentation is shared with people so they can read it and it is not presented.

Therefore, the quantity and order of the contents influence the experience of the audience on your slides. Both vary according to the context, as long as there is always a clear reading order.

17.2. READING PATTERNS

Have you ever wondered how people's behavior varies according to the order of the content on the slides?

If you could predict the influence of your slide content on the audience's view, you would be able to design real visual experiences by displaying your content.

Do you understand the strength of this concept?

I'm telling you that by varying the way you arrange your ideas to be displayed on the slide, you will be able to control people's eyes.

How do you do that in practice?

There are some famous reading patterns in literature that describe the behavior of the eyes in some specific situations.

Three of them are of particular interest for presentations:
1. Gutenberg Pattern
2. Z-Pattern
3. F-Pattern

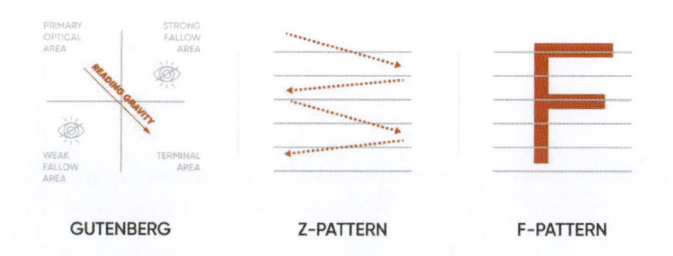

Image 5 - Reading patterns relevant to presentations

Each of them has something to teach us and guides us in a given context.

Let's see them together.

17.2.1 Gutenberg Pattern
Gutenberg's pattern identifies 4 quadrants on which we can analyze a slide.

Image 6 - The 4 quadrants of the Gutenberg pattern

The top left and bottom right quadrants receive more attention than the other two, which are considered as blind quadrants.

People will start reading from the top left quadrant and, for this reason, that is the entry point on the slide.

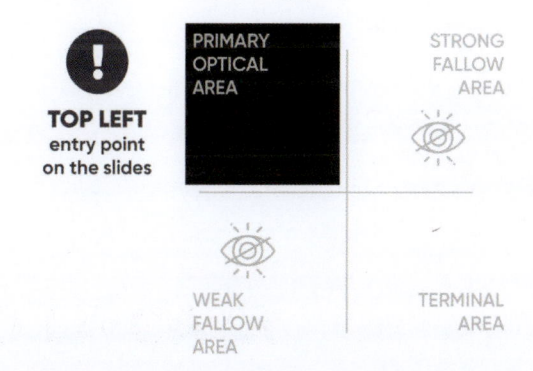

Image 7 - The top left quadrant is the entry point on the slide

Through a series of horizontal and vertical movements, the eyes will converge towards the last quadrant at the bottom right, also known as the terminal area, or the exit quadrant of the eyes.

The movements can be summarized as a diagonal that connects the first and last quadrant.

This diagonal represents the reading gravity effect.

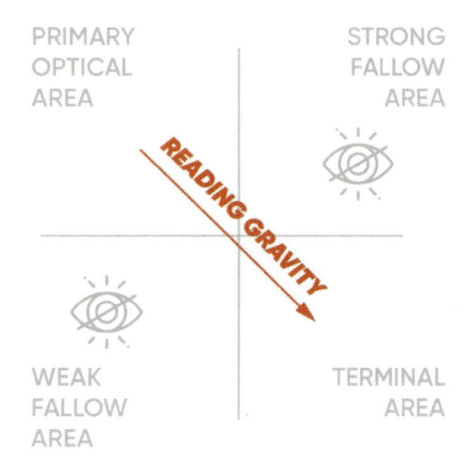

Image 8 - Reading gravity effect

Does this feel all very abstract to you?

Let's give an example right away.

Imagine redrawing the confusing slide on Italianity shown in figure 3 so that it can be presented (and not read).

We must work in order to obtain a very essential slide in terms of content.

I propose you this design, what do you think?

Image 9 - Redesign of the slide in image 3

Simple and clean, right?

In your opinion, what will be the reading path of the audience on this slide?

Let's try to apply the Gutenberg pattern to answer this question.

Image 10 - Probable reading path according to the Gutenberg pattern

So, the eyes enter from the top left and then fall to the bottom right.

What happens then?

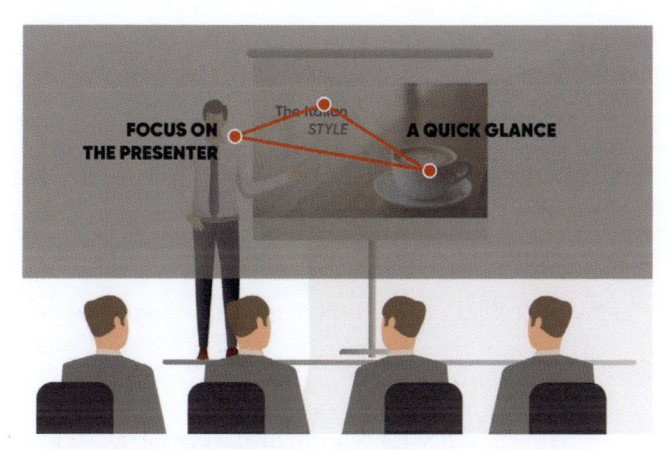

Image 11 - The eyes end reading the slide and return to the speaker

The eyes, now at the end area, will leave the slide to go back to the left, because that's how we usually read.

On the left, they will meet the speaker again.

We can therefore say that this slide is working well, in synergy with the speaker.

This is a good example of the Gutenberg pattern applied to the resolution of a confusing slide.

17.2.2. Z-Pattern

The Z pattern represents the typical behavior of the reader who processes a long text giving importance to each line that he reads.

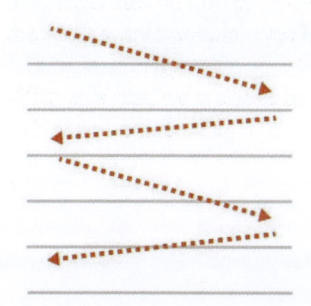

Image 12 - Zigzag reading direction

Starting at the top left, we read the entire line to the end and then we go back to the beginning to process the next line.

From this zigzag comes the name of the pattern.

In particular, we speak of a "back to the start" effect to describe the movement from right to left, like a typewriter that returns to the beginning ready to write the following line.

The typical example of the application of this pattern is the complete reading of texts.

Imagine having to redraw the slide in image 3, but this time, for an audience that has to read it. You can apply the Z pattern and come, for example, to a redesign of the type shown in the following image.

Image 13 - Redesign of the slide in image 3

In this case I used much more text than in the previous one, precisely because I want the slide to be self-explanatory and that people can understand it by reading it.

Applying the Z-Pattern, we can expect a zigzag path.

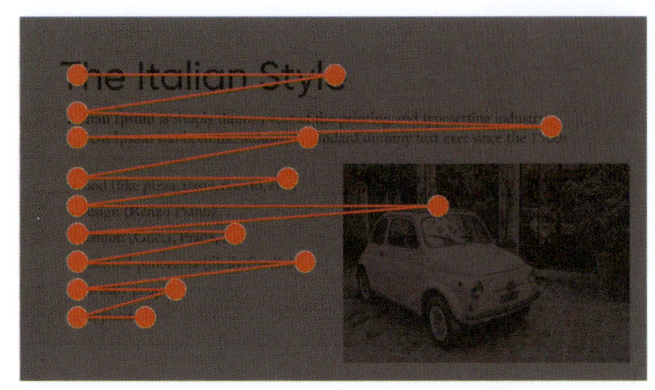

Image 14 - Probable reading path according to the Z-Pattern

In summary, I expect people to read the content of the slide line by line.

17.2.3. F-Pattern

The F pattern is a bit different from the others.

Discovered by Jackob Nielsen in 2006 [1], this pattern describes user behavior on web content.

The name comes precisely from the shape of the heat maps that resulted from Nielsen's studies.

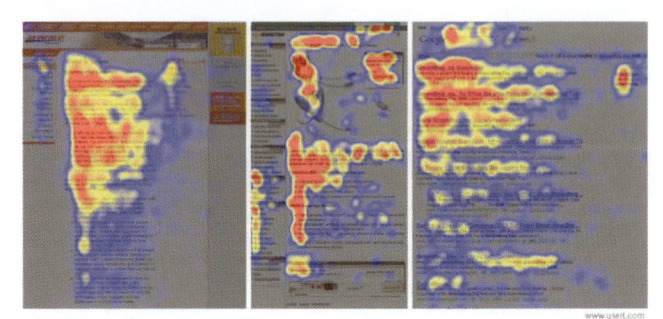

Image 15 – F-Pattern

Unlike the other two, we use this pattern only for the lessons it gives us, not for its shape.

What do I mean by that?

The F pattern teaches us that people pay more attention to the top left of the page.

Does it sound new?

Not at all!

The Gutenberg pattern underlines the importance of the top left part of the slide.

The F-Pattern also teaches us that humans prefer to read horizontally rather than vertically.

We've seen this with the Z-Pattern, and it will help you design the next layouts.

Finally, it teaches us that people like to skim content, that is to say, read by jumping from part to part of the content.

What does that mean?

Think about when you do a Google search and you get 10 websites back on the front page. You don't read line by line, but you jump from one side of the page to the other to find the result that interests you as quickly as possible.

Image 16 - The teachings of the F-Pattern

These three concepts will guide the way you design your layouts for your audience.

---

[1] https://www.nngroup.com

17.3. READING PATTERNS DO NOT WORK

Maybe I've exaggerated in the title, it's not that the reading patterns don't work, it's just that they don't always work.

What do I mean?

Retrieve your last presentation and try to apply the reading patterns to your slides.

Which pattern, among the ones analyzed together, best represents the visual path planned for your audience?

If you have difficulty applying them, don't worry, you are not the only one.

Reading patterns only work when the content reading hierarchy does not violate them.

To explain this concept, I built a small eye-tracking experiment, let's see it together.

What is it about?

I showed slides to people and monitored the areas of greatest interest for their eyes.

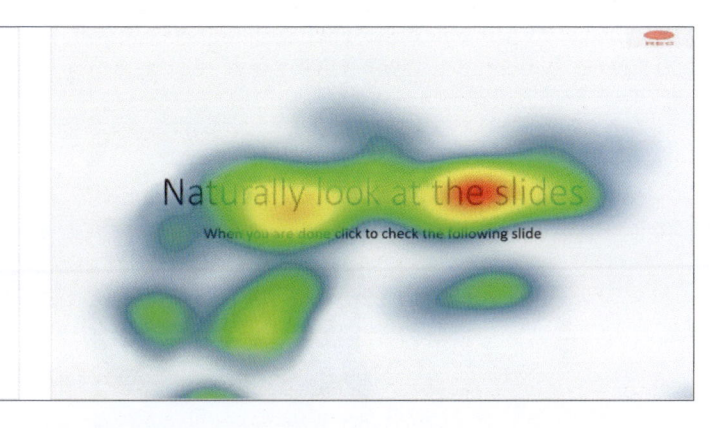

Image 17 – Eye-tracking experiment, setup slide

Red areas are the hottest areas of what we call "heat maps", the areas where people' eyes have lingered longest.

With this test, we are able to understand how people behave in front of a slide.

What happens, in your opinion, if we test the confusing slide on Italian style?

Image 18 - Heat map for the Italian style slide

Since the slide is confusing, the effect it generates can only be confusing!

It is difficult to identify a clear reading pattern on this slide. Did you notice the small and light grey title at the top of the slide?
It doesn't stand out at all!

Let's try to turn it into a big red writing, what will happen then?

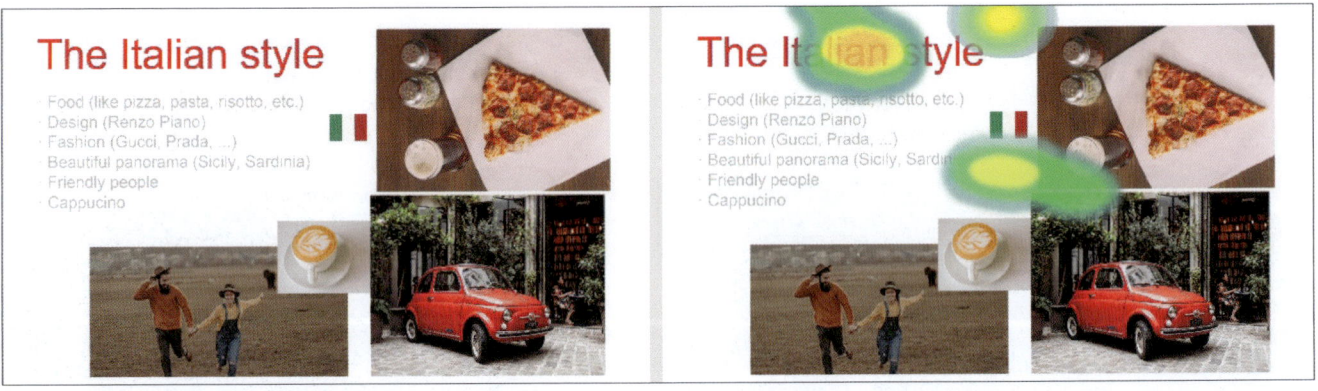

Image 19 - Title change test to draw attention

Clearly, it attracts attention.
Now, let us try to create a real hierarchy of content reading. To do this, let's analyze together the bullet point list of the slide.

Remember, slides should be analyzed in their content, because only after you really understand their meaning you will be able to imagine a design that can convey the message.

If you read well enough, you will realize that there are texts in brackets that detail those outside.
What does that mean?

That the writing in parentheses is less important than the other ones.
For this reason, we could let the public see the important parts first and the less important parts afterwards.

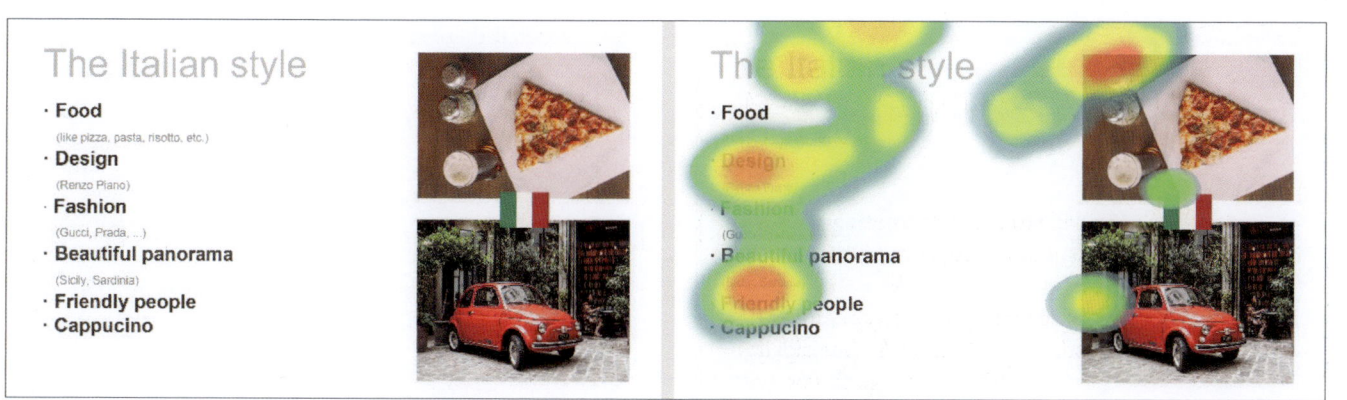

Image 20 - Content hierarchy affects reading experience

What's going on?

As you can see, people now read vertically, from top to bottom, scrolling through the list of keywords highlighted for them.

Only those who stop to read everything will have access to the details, the others will capture the keywords at a glance. So, although the F-Pattern showed us that people are,

preferably, horizontal readers, with a simple hierarchy of contents we were able to influence the reading pattern by giving it a vertical effect.

This redesign could work well in cases where you have to present the slide, but you can't delete text.

What if I could completely redesign it in a not-self-standing way?

Image 21 - Not-self-standing redesign

Do you remember this design?
See how you can identify the Gutenberg pattern.

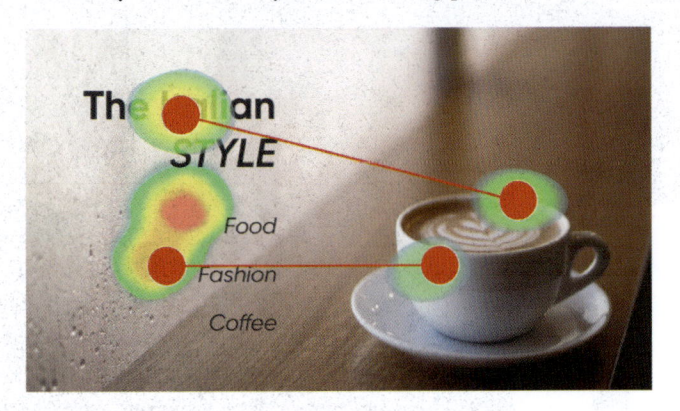

So, what do all these tests teach us?

Reading patterns work until you push the reading hierarchy through your content design.

I don't mind if you break the standard patterns, as long as you do it consciously.

Use patterns, when possible, as a starting point, but design your hierarchies according to the effect you want to achieve.

17.4. IN SUMMARY

Reading patterns describe the behavior of people's visual path on your presentations.

Unfortunately, reading patterns are not always reliable and often the cause of their failure is the way you design your slides.

Learn about reading patterns to take advantage of them when possible and to consciously violate them and design effective user experiences at every opportunity.

18
CHAPTER

DESIGN THE EXPERIENCE

« PEOPLE IGNORE DESIGN THAT IGNORES PEOPLE »

FRANK CHIMERO

The **LEAN PROCESS** for **PRESENTATIONS**

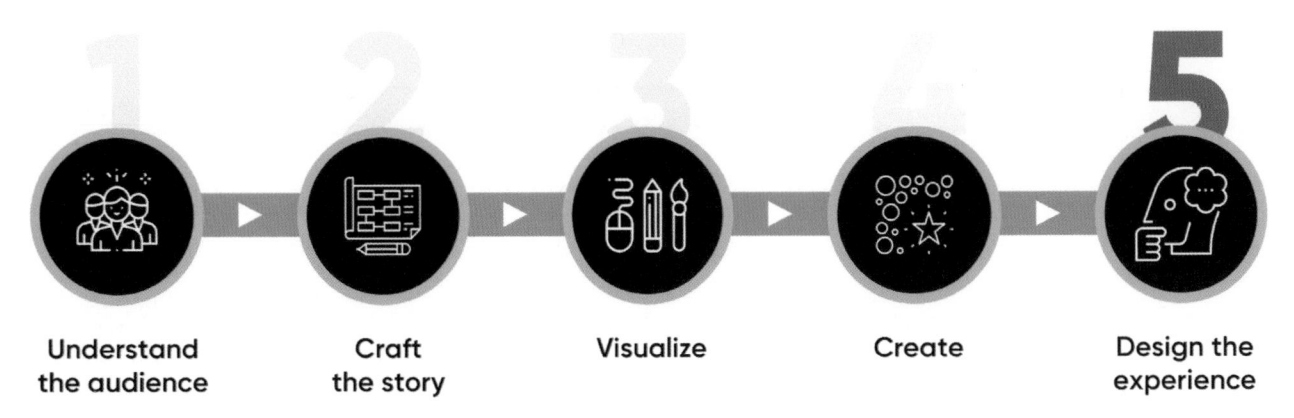

1. Understand the audience
2. Craft the story
3. Visualize
4. Create
5. Design the experience

Image 1 - Lean process for presentations - Design the experience

There is an abyssal difference between redrawing a slide to make it nicer and redrawing it to make it more effective.

We've already discussed it in depth, and now it's time to learn how to design an effective experience for your slides.

When you design a presentation, design and meaning must go hand in hand - no design can be effective if you don't fully understand the message you want to convey.

In design, there are 4 basic principles that govern the relationship between meaning and graphics.

These principles lay the foundations for the technical analysis of presentations and will therefore allow you to objectively make any of your slides effective.

Let's see them together.

18.1. PROXIMITY

Imagine seeing the previous bullet point list, drawn in this disorganized way.

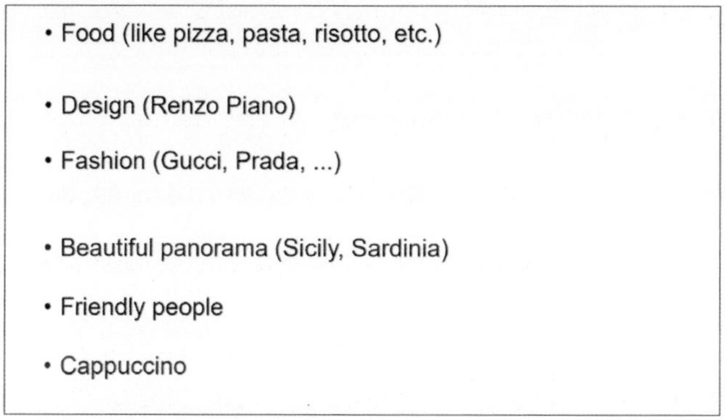

- Food (like pizza, pasta, risotto, etc.)

- Design (Renzo Piano)

- Fashion (Gucci, Prada, ...)

- Beautiful panorama (Sicily, Sardinia)

- Friendly people

- Cappuccino

Image 2 - Lots of disconnected elements

How many items do you count?
I count six.
What if, on the other hand, I proposed the slide in this way?

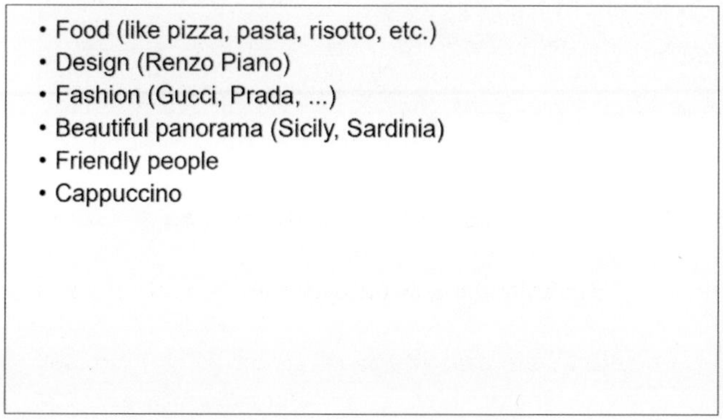

- Food (like pizza, pasta, risotto, etc.)
- Design (Renzo Piano)
- Fashion (Gucci, Prada, ...)
- Beautiful panorama (Sicily, Sardinia)
- Friendly people
- Cappuccino

Image 3 - Grouped items

Your answer would probably be that you now see a single group of objects.

For the proximity principle, when we see two neighboring objects, we assume that they are connected in meaning.

So, one of the tricks to apply to a slide like the one in the figure is to bring together related objects by reorganizing the contents of the slide.

Before proceeding, however, let me introduce you to the next principle.

18.2. ALIGNMENT

We're used to the idea that alignments are just a matter of slide order.
I'd like to see your expression at the sight of the image I'm about to show you.

Image 4 - Misaligned content on the slide creates confusion

What a mess!

In fact, alignments should not be respected just to keep order on the slides, but because aligned objects are perceived as correlated in the meaning they convey.

Imagine that each object on the slide projects invisible alignment lines (image below).

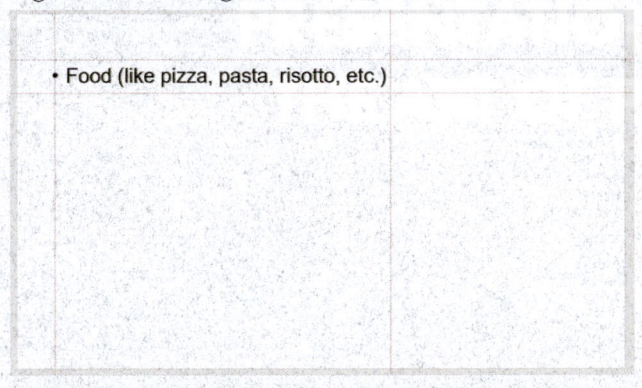

Image 5 - Each object projects invisible alignment lines onto the slide

Any other object placed on its alignment lines, will be expected to be related in meaning with the first.

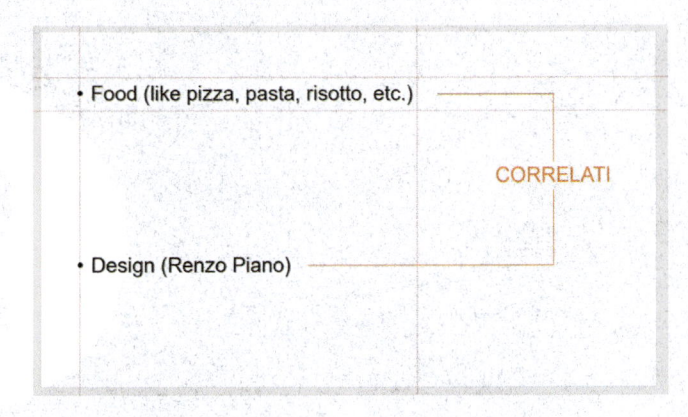

Image 6 - Aligned objects are perceived as related in meaning

So, as the slide designer, you must make sure that the related objects are also aligned with each other.

By combining the principle of alignment with the principle of proximity, seen in the previous paragraph, it is possible to redraw the bullet point list obtaining the result in the following figure.

Image 7 - Bullet point list redesign through application of the principles of alignment and proximity

Looking at the slide, you'll see 3 groups of objects aligned with each other.

What are you communicating?

You are telling the audience that there are 3 groups of objects connected to each other (proximity) to support a main message (alignment). That is, there is one message, supported by 3 groups of 2 elements each.

Let's go on.

18.3. CONTRAST

Contrast is a key principle of design, allowing visual hierarchies of content to be created.

Going back to the previous example, we could clarify one keyword for each of the three groups.

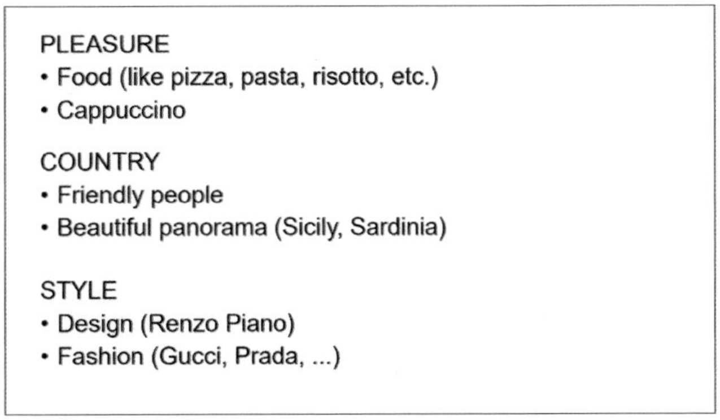

> **PLEASURE**
> - Food (like pizza, pasta, risotto, etc.)
> - Cappuccino
>
> **COUNTRY**
> - Friendly people
> - Beautiful panorama (Sicily, Sardinia)
>
> **STYLE**
> - Design (Renzo Piano)
> - Fashion (Gucci, Prada, ...)

Image 8 - Each keyword represents the meaning of a small group of two elements

I capitalized them so that they would stand out from the bullet point lists.

Do you think they really stand out?

Not so much.

As they are some sort of headlines and therefore on a priority reading level compared to the lists, they should be read first and therefore more visible.

We must then increase the contrast of the key words.

How?

Contrast can be made in various ways, depending on the context.

The simplest example is the application of bold to the 3 keywords.

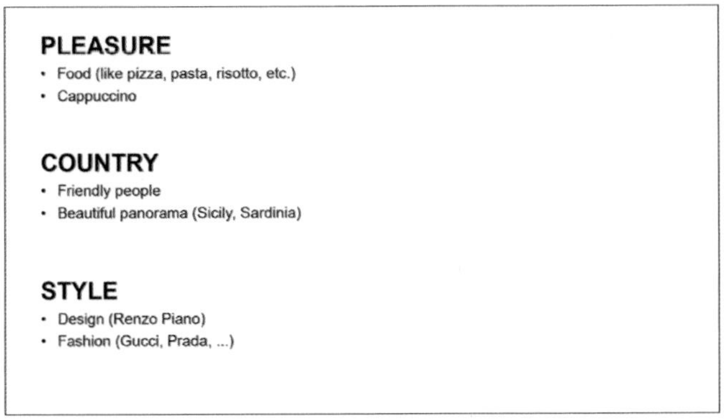

> **PLEASURE**
> - Food (like pizza, pasta, risotto, etc.)
> - Cappuccino
>
> **COUNTRY**
> - Friendly people
> - Beautiful panorama (Sicily, Sardinia)
>
> **STYLE**
> - Design (Renzo Piano)
> - Fashion (Gucci, Prada, ...)

Image 9 - Bold creates contrast

See how readability improves, now that there's a hierarchy? If you notice, however, I have not only applied bold, but I have also reduced the font size of bullet points.
Why?

To create more contrast.

In fact, you always think that to create contrast you must add some effect, bold, highlight or underline, but in fact it is the difference between the elements that sets them in contrast between them.

Since we work with a Lean mentality and therefore an essential one, I always invite you to think first about how to remove, reduce or simplify and only then to what to add on the slide.

Less is more.

For example, I could have colored the bullet point lists in a light grey, which contrasts less with the background than with the black of the titles, further increasing the contrasts and defining the reading hierarchy even better.

Image 10 - Use a lighter color to reduce the contrast of the bullet point

Again, I could have colored boxes and used them as a background for keywords

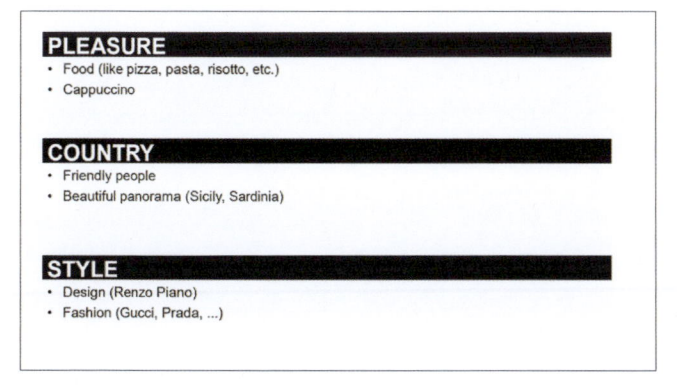

Image 11 – Contrasting boxes

But you must be careful about the color.

In fact, there is often a tendency to believe that coloring something red always gives it visual priority.

It's not at all true that red is the color that increases the contrasts in every occasion - as I told you, it depends on the context.

Which color always contrasts best by definition?

Its complementary.

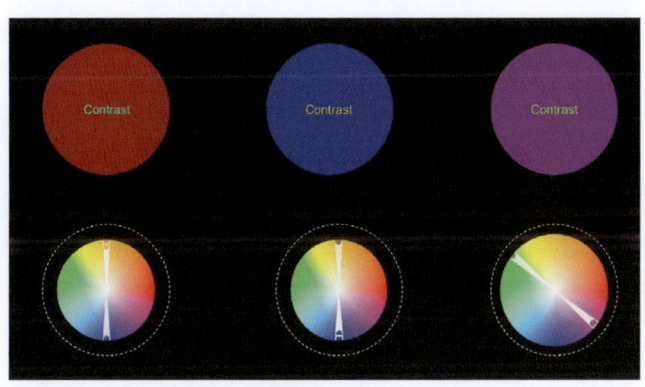

Image 12 - Example of complementary colors

So, if the boxes were purple, the keywords should be yellow.

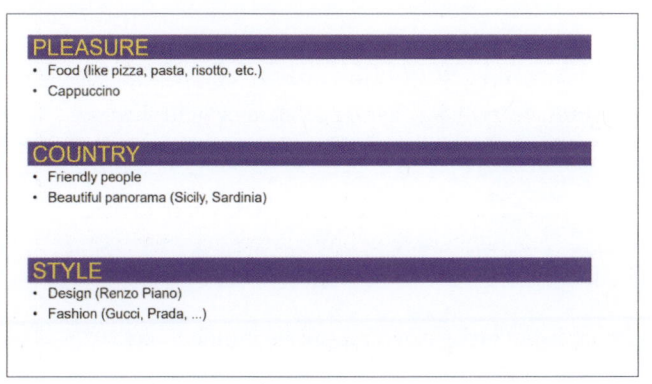

Image 13 - Complementary colors maximize contrast

After all, it's no coincidence if the call to action search on a yellow turns blue, as in the case of booking.com:

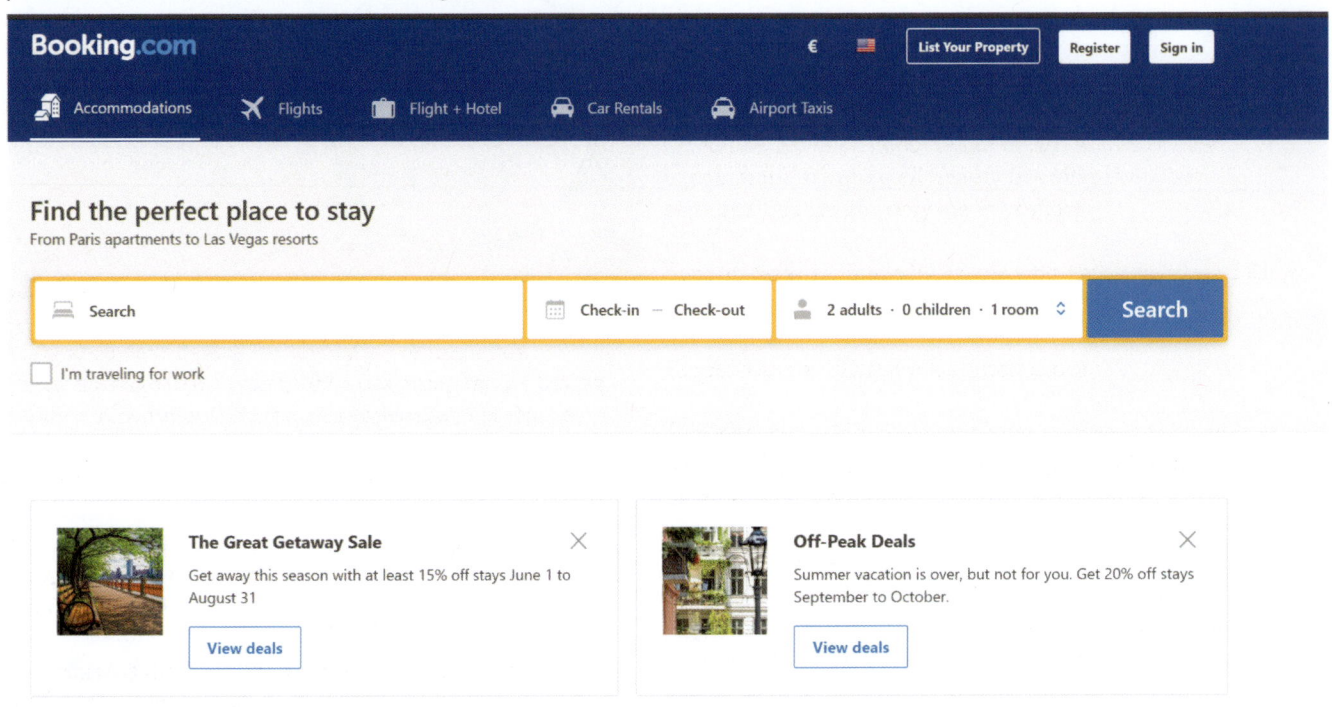

Image 14 - Blue on yellow call to action (complementary)

Or the call to action on a page with a blue header turns yellow.

Image 15 - Yellow call to action on blue background (complementary)

There are various ways to create contrast.

Contrast on slides creates order and priority of content and allows you to directly guide people's eyes.

Let's proceed with one last important fundamental principle.

18.4. REPETITION

Now that you know the first 3 principles, I want to ask you for an opinion on the slide in the following image.

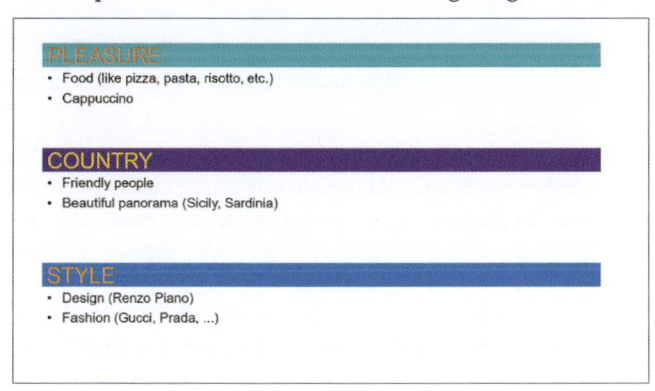

Image 16 - What's wrong with this slide?

What do you think, does it convince you?

Instinctively, certainly not!

Yet, what is actually not working in this slide?

Let's try to analyze it together.

The principle of proximity is correctly applied, the principle of alignment is also correct and, if you notice, even the contrasts are correct because the colors are complementary and in fact the readability is good.

But this slide doesn't work, and you don't like it.

The problem lies in the failure to apply the fourth fundamental principle of design: the principle of repetition.

When similar characteristics are repeated, the human eye tends to correlate objects and we expect that there will be a correlation of meaning.

At this moment, the technical analysis of the slide reveals an inconsistency in the application of the principles, since the principle of repetition is signaling to us that the three titles are not correlated with each other, which clashes with the principle of alignment, which instead sees them correlated.

Your brain no longer knows what to expect, and you experience that feeling of discomfort that makes you realize that the slide does not work but, not knowing how to analyze it, you'll just say that you do not like it.

Actually, that instinct you have is not simply telling you that you don't like it, it is showing you the way to correct and restore the effectiveness of the slide.

In fact, thanks to the technical analysis, you can immediately understand what the problem is and how to intervene.

In this case, you just need to apply the principle of repetition, levelling out the colors and restoring the hierarchical structure of the content.

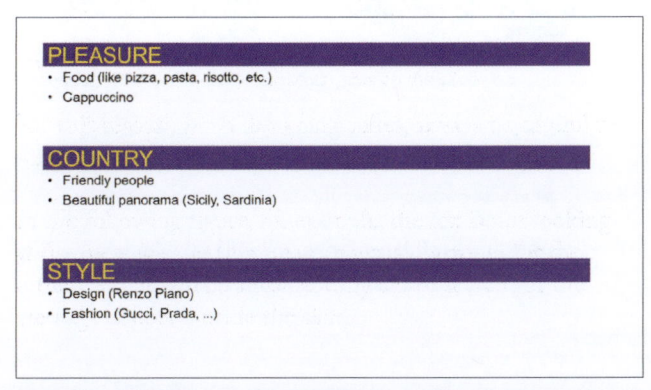

Image 17 - Applied the principle of repetition, the slide works correctly

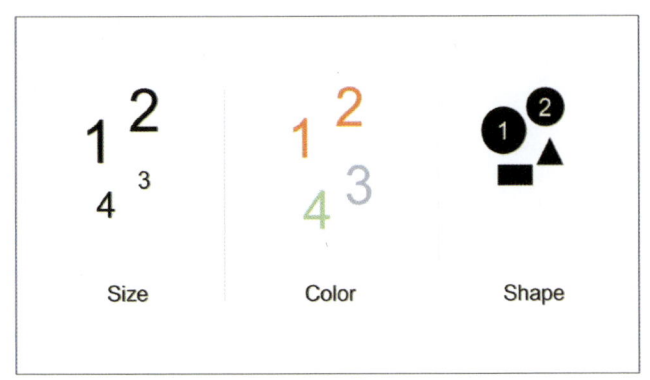

Image 18 - 3 techniques to create repetition

Are you curious to see a technical analysis at work on a real slide?

Here it is.

What message does the slide want to convey in the following figure?

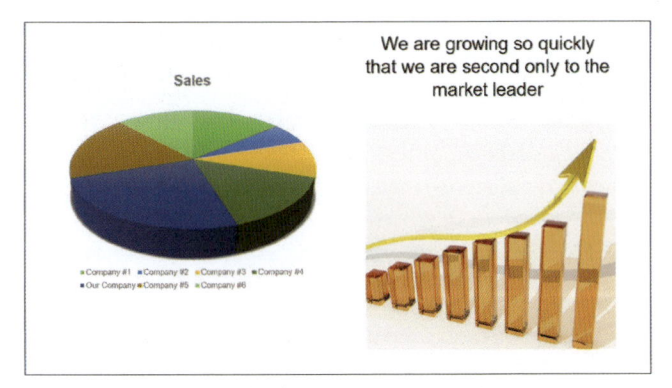

Image 19 - Slide with complex layout that needs redesign

The slide is not rich in text, but it will still take you a moment before you can extract the meaning.

What do you think of this, instead?

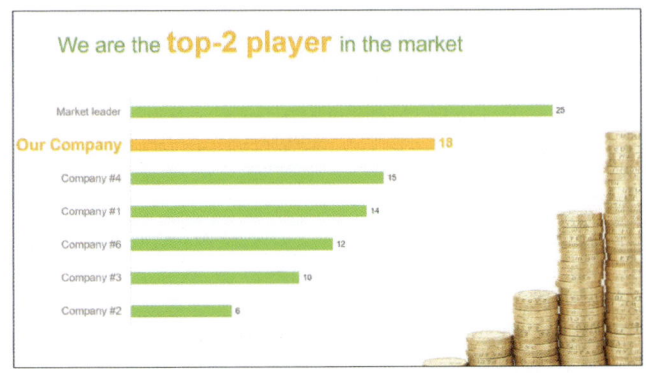

Image 20 - Redesign of the slide in image 18

As you can see, I have reorganized the content by eliminating the superfluous and, above all, I have taken advantage of contrast and repetition to color in orange and thus connect the bar of our company with the fact that we are second in the market.

Image 21 - The principle of repetition at work

This is a radical change in the way of creating presentations, because you will no longer find yourself looking for the solution that works best for you, by trial and error, but you will analyze the slides in a technical way and you will be able to identify the errors to be corrected to make them objectively effective.

No more trying and evaluating slides by instinct, you'll be much faster at designing effective slides.

18.5. CONTROL PEOPLE'S EYES

The four basic principles of design allow you to create visual hierarchies for content and thus guide people's eyes.

There are other techniques that allow you to have a direct impact on your audience's visual path.

18.5.1. Look where others look

Have you ever looked in the direction of someone else's gaze? Humans naturally tend to follow the gaze of others with their eyes.

When you talk to friends and want to draw attention to something, you will naturally look in the direction of the point of attention.

A typical example is the presenter who comments on slides during a meeting by looking at them on his laptop, placed on the table, rather than on the projector.

There are circumstances in which the presenter is so focused on the speech, that he indicates the slides on the pc, forgetting that the screen is facing him and therefore others can't see it.

Therefore, we have a situation where the speaker speaks alone to his computer and the lost audience tries to interpret the speaker's gestures.

Gaze, if properly managed, can help you to guide the audience through complex slides, such as particularly detailed tables or diagrams.

In fact, while you're there, you could turn around, look at yourself and point out the point on which you want the audience's attention.

Remember never to turn your back on the audience and only speak if you are looking at people.

There's nothing worse than seeing a speaker who walks to the screen and talks while showing his back to the audience.

Presenting is like having a dialogue with people, it wouldn't be natural to talk to a person while you are walking away, giving them your back.

James Breeze, Eye Tracking & Consumer Experience Innovator, used eye-tracking software to measure the impact of a child's look in an advertisement [1].

The result of the test showed, through heat maps, that with his eyes the child naturally attracted the attention of the audience to the text.

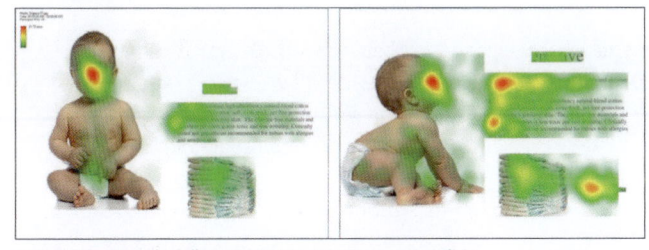

Image 22 - People follow the subjects' gaze on the slide

For this reason, when designing slides, always be careful to weigh the influence of the gaze of the subjects you show.

In the following figure, for example, the fox is not looking at the message and this creates a visual dystonia for the audience that will be automatically led to search for the message almost outside the slide.

---

[1] https://www.linkedin.com/pulse/20140813103409-1146575-here-s-looking-at-you/

Image 23 - The fox's gaze diverts attention from the key message

In the next image, however, the fox is just pointing to the message. You will realize the magnetic effect that the fox generates on the text just by looking at it.

Image 24 - The fox's gaze focuses attention on the text

Note that you do not necessarily have to see the eyes, what matters is the direction of the gaze, as in some examples made by my students during the Lean Presentation Design course.

Image 25 - The direction of the gaze influences the visual path of the observer

18.5.2. Directional objects

How many times have you indicated an object on a slide with an arrow, an arrow connector or even a triangle?

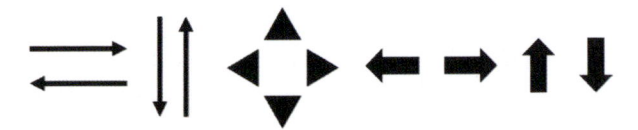

Image 26 - Directional objects

I also suppose you may have drawn an activity process:

Image 27 – Process example

or even a timeline to represent a project roadmap.

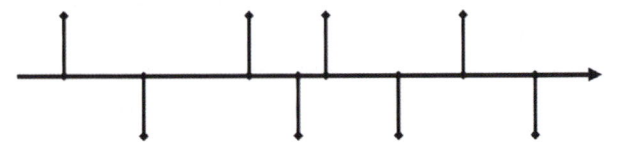

Image 28 – Timeline example

As you can see, these are all objects that give a direction to the slide by guiding people's gaze from one side to the other. I advise you to always develop your content in accordance with the dynamics that directional objects create, exploiting them to your advantage to bring people's eyes straight to the heart of your message.

18.6. THE GOLDEN RULE OF GRAPHIC DESIGN

One of the problems you will most often face is the placement of objects in your slides.

Where will you place each object according to the message you want to send, what is the best position, are there preferential positions within each slide?

It's time to tell you that strategic positions actually exist, and now I'll explain where they are.

In graphics there is a famous grid that divides the slide into 9 equal parts by 4 intersection lines.

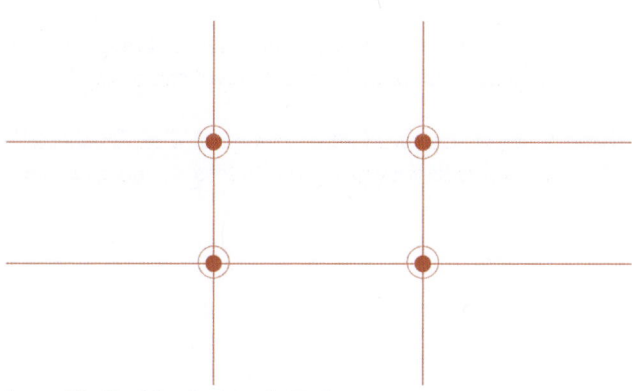

Image 30 – The 4 focal points of attention

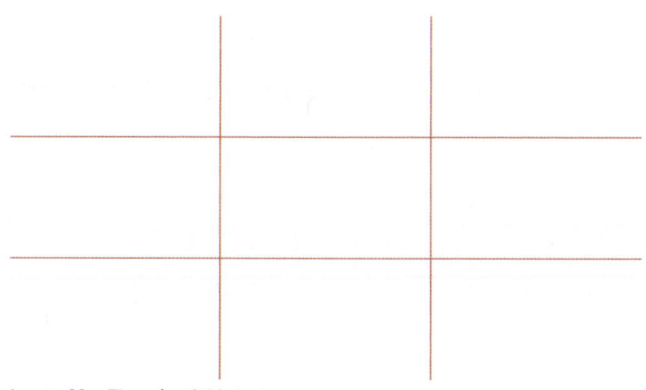

Image 29 – The rule of thirds

This grid is defined as the rule of thirds.

The rule of thirds has been guiding the graphic composition for more than 200 years, that is, since it was first mentioned by John Thomas Smith in 1797 [2].

The 4 points of intersection that are generated in the center of the slide are called power points and represent the points of greatest attention of people on a visual.

If you're wondering where you've already seen this grid, you'll most likely have seen it on your smartphone when taking a photo.

Image 31 – The rule of thirds is everywhere

---

2 Remarks on rural scenery: with twenty etchings of cottages, from nature: and some observations and precepts relative to the picturesque, Smith, John Thomas, 1766-1833; Downes, J. (Joseph), d. 1830

In fact, the rule of thirds belongs to the world of cinema and photography, but we borrow it to create effective slides.

Think about it for a moment - any professional photo never presents the subject in the center but is always moved to one side or the other, usually centered on the power points.

Image 32 - The frog is located on the power points, not in the middle of the slide

This allows you to organize your content on slides and make the most of power points. I'll show you some slides I use during my training.

They are very essential slides, but well-structured in accordance with the thirds rule.

Image 33 - Examples of application of the rule of thirds

The rule of thirds goes beyond the simple use of power points - it also guides you through the graphic composition of the entire slide.

In the next image, look at how the horizon is placed on a line of strength and the sun on the top right power point.

Image 34 - Graphic composition of a photo on the rule of thirds

This magical effect of the rule of thirds is linked to the fact that the grid is very similar to that of the golden section and the contents organized in golden section are naturally perceived as beautiful and well-proportioned.

To work in accordance, roughly, with the golden section, there is a proportion that you must always respect, namely 2/3 and 1/3.

The 2/3 of the slide are usually used for the most important part of the content, while the rest goes into the remaining third.

The next image shows the structure of the sunset photo of the previous figure.

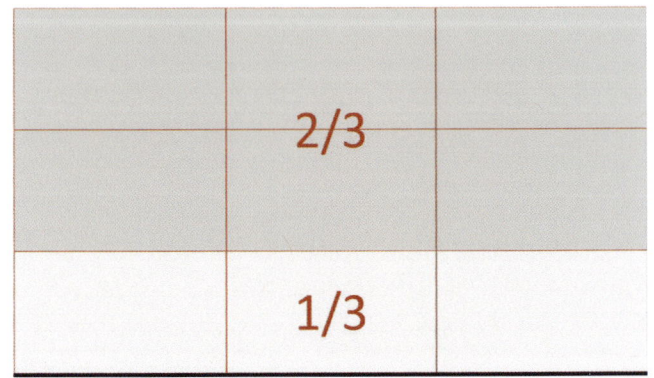

Image 35 - Structural composition of the slide in image 32

At this point, you just have to have fun with all the possible combinations that you can adopt to solve any layout.

If, for example, you had to solve a bullet point list of 3 or 6 bullet points, using the rule of thirds you could imagine a series of virtually ready to use layouts.

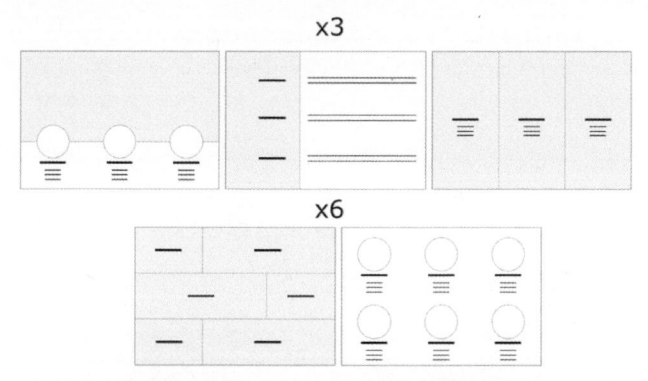

Image 36 – Possible resolution layouts of bullet point slides

The darker black bars indicate the first reading level (titles, subtitles), while the lighter black bars indicate the second reading level (descriptions and paragraphs).

In the circles I would insert icons, and in the grey background parts I would insert high quality images.

The rule of thirds is a powerful tool that guides you through every structural aspect of designing your slide layout.

18.7. A PRACTICAL CASE STUDY:

THE DEFEAT OF THE BULLET POINT LIST

I've explained a lot of graphic design rules to you, I know.

If you feel like there is a lot of meat on the stove, I confirm that you're right, but you don't have to worry because the best way to learn is to put everything into practice as soon as possible - and that's exactly what we're going to do.

Imagine starting from a slide brief in these conditions.

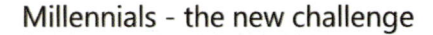

Image 37 - Slide with bullet point list of briefs to fix

If you find yourself in front of such a slide, you are in good company with all those who face presentations daily, it's normal.

Welcome to the gang!

The first thing to do is to understand the structure in order to define the necessary reading levels (technical analysis of the slide).

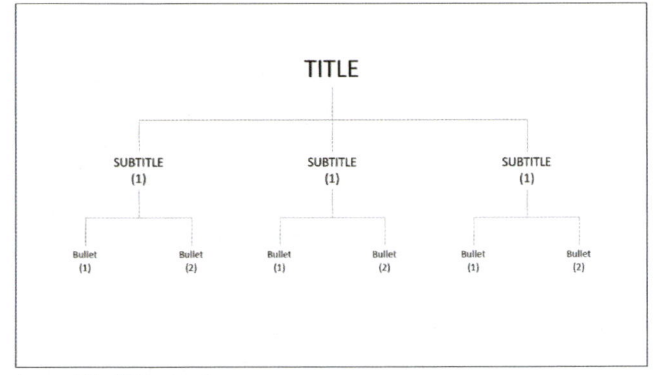

Image 38 – Slide structure

In this case, the slide has three reading levels:

1. Title
2. Subtitles
3. Bullet points

Apply the rule of thirds to the slide to outline the cage in which to place the contents.

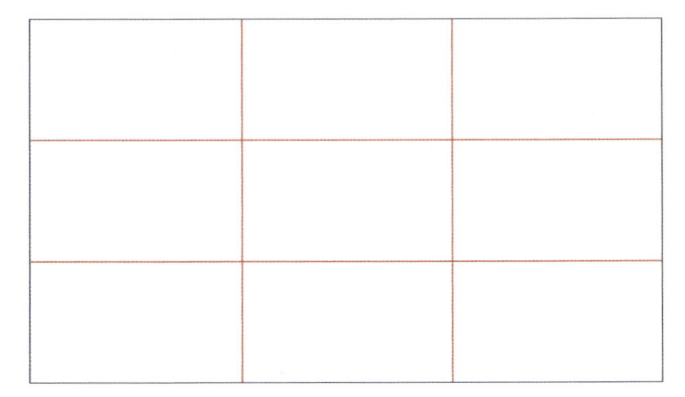

Image 39 – Rule of thirds

Imagine how to arrange the content respecting the 1/3 and 2/3 ratio. In the 2/3 of the slide insert an image to divide the slide and recall the main theme - Millennials at work.

Image 40 - High quality image insertion

The title of the slide (first reading level) must be positioned in the upper center and must overlap the image. In order to create the overlap and make the title readable you can use the technique of the transparent box, as discussed in another chapter.

Image 41 - Transparent box to create contrast for the title

Now you can proceed with the insertion of the title.

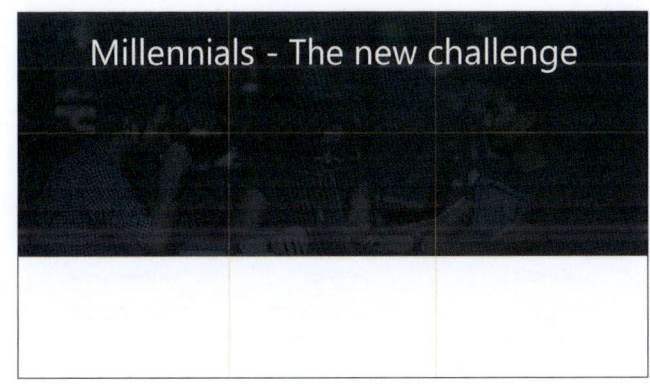

Image 42 - I enter the title in a color that contrasts with the background

Now, think about the second reading level.

How would you distribute it?

At this point, I would say that we could distribute it horizontally, from left to right.

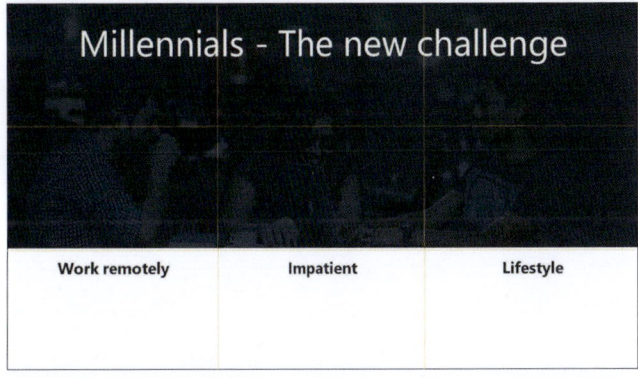

Image 43 - Inserting subtitles

If you notice, I changed the titles to enhance the meaning by reducing the words. It's not always the case that the way the message is explained is always the best.

So, every time you analyze a slide, you study the text and find the best way to express concepts with the least number of objects possible (in this case, words).

Now you can get the spaces to insert the icons.

Image 44 - Spaces for inserting icons

By now, you should know where to find the icons.

Find 3 vectorial icons that represent the points of the second reading level. In this case, I downloaded the icons from Flaticon.com (see chapter - 15 Vector Graphics - Icons)

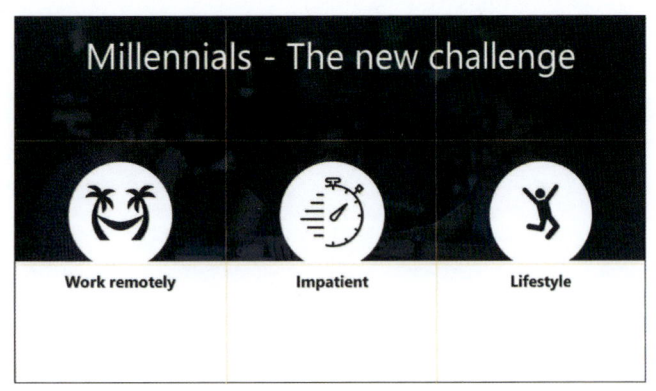

Image 45 - Insertion of vectorial icons

Finally, you can distribute the text related to the last reading level.

Image 46 - Introduction of the third reading level

In distributing the texts between the second and third reading levels I applied the proximity principle by placing the bullet point lists closer to each other (because they are part of the third reading level) and by creating a greater spacing from the second reading level (see red arrows in the next image).

The texts of the third reading level have a central alignment because they are aligned with the titles of the second level and the icons above, according to the principle of alignment.

Image 47 - Spacing created in accordance with the proximity principle

To improve readability at a glance and promote skim reading we can highlight the keywords in the texts of the third reading level and thus avoid the effort of having to read each block.

To do this, according to the principle of contrast, I use the complementary color to the dark green I am using (see chapter 16 - Give color to your presentation).

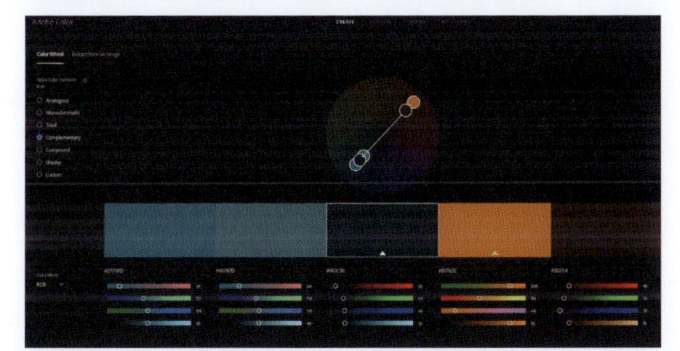

Image 48 - Calculation of the complementary color (color.adobe.com)

Image 50 - Application of the repetition principle to the title

Have you seen how the application of the 4 fundamental principles of design, combined with the thirds rule have guided us in the realization of an effective layout?

Have you already tried to compare it with the original one?

Let's do it together in the next image.

Image 49 - Highlighting of key words in the second reading level

To associate the words in orange directly to Millennials you can, eventually, use the principle of repetition by coloring the word Millennials of the title with the same orange.

Image 51 – Before and after

I'd say the difference is huge.
The message I want to pass you, however, besides the graphics, is the method by which I came to the redesign of this layout.

I followed some logical steps applying clear principles without ever letting myself go to attempts guided by my creativity.

This allowed me to quickly, without any doubt, create an effective layout in a logical and uncreative way.

In short, this is what makes Lean Presentation Design an approach applicable to all contexts and by anyone, without the need to be a designer or particularly creative person.

18.8. IN SUMMARY

The layout design is based on the application of 4 basic design principles: proximity, alignment, contrast, repetition.

These 4 principles, together with the design cage called thirds rule, allow you to define the perimeter of all the graphic choices you will have to make in order to arrive at the most effective layout in the shortest time possible.

Lean Presentation Design is the first innovative approach to presentations that explains how to create effective slides in a logical and non-creative way, configuring itself, therefore, as a methodology that can be used by anyone who produces presentations, without the need to be a designer.

MLC POWERPOINT ADDIN

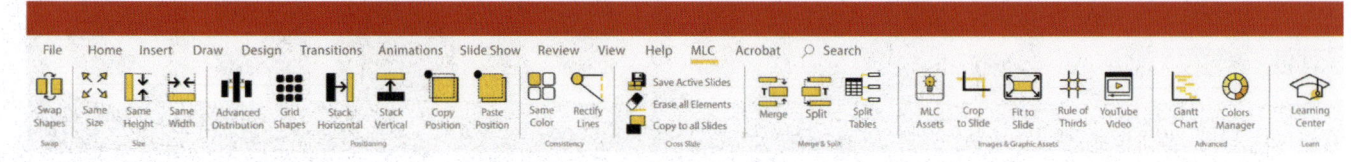

Introducing MLC PowerPoint Addin: a **Super Smart** set of exclusive functionalities developed by presentation maker professionals to **skyrocket your productivity**.
What is MLC PowerPoint addin? It is a proven tool to:

Speed up your **recurrent tasks** in PowerPoint

Craft **beautiful designs**

Achieve **incredible accuracy** levels

Bring harmony between objects on your slides

Get **faster team results**

Join a **vibrant** exclusive **community**

WHAT WILL YOU GET WITH MLC POWERFUL FUNCTIONALITIES

SWAP SHAPES
Swap shape positions in one click. No more wasted time recovering alignments

SAME SIZE
Make all shapes the size of the first one selected. Resizing made easy!

GRID SHAPES
Distribute shapes in a grid. It takes care of alignments and distributions for you!

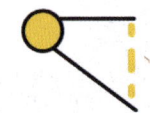

RECTIFY LINES
Quickly rectify your line shapes. No more crooked lines!

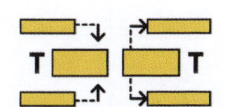

MERGE / SPLIT TEXT WITH SHAPES
Merge or Split text box with shapes

COPY TO ALL SLIDES
Replicate selected item to all slides. Stop copy-pasting slide by slide!

ADVANCED DISTRIBUTION
Send away or Bring near items based on the position of a selected item. Stop caring about distributions

STACK SHAPES
Stack shapes one to the others removing the spaces between

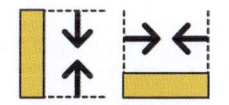

SAME HEIGHT / WIDTH
Make all items the same height/width in one click. Stop resizing manually!

SAVE ACTIVE SLIDES
Export only selected slides into a new PowerPoint file

MAKE SAME COLOR
Make all shapes the color of the first selected shape without spending time checking for the right RGB

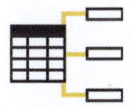

SPLIT TABLES
Split tables into shapes and make beautiful table slides

GANTT CHART
Generate and maintain Gantt charts in a few simple guided steps

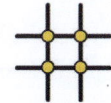

RULE OF THIRDS
Solve complex layouts in a very short time creating slides that communicate effectively

MLC ASSETS
Ready to use, high quality assets for your presentations (images, icons, etc.)

YOUTUBE VIDEO
Insert a video from Youtube with just a URL

CROP TO SLIDE
Cut the parts of the picture that are outside the slide

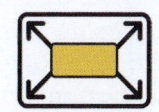

FIT TO SLIDE
Adapt the dimensions of the picture to the slide

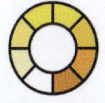

COLORS MANAGER
Check the colors used in the presentation and change them all at once

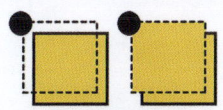

COPY/PASTE POSITION
Copy the position of the object and paste it to any other objet on any other slide

GET YOUR FREE

HOW TO GET YOUR BONUSES

GO TO AMAZON

WRITE A REVIEW

SEND THE SCREENSHOT
INFO@MAURIZIOLACAVA.COM

BONUSES

1 **LEAN PRESENTATION STRATEGY CANVAS**

By following a specific communication structure, this tool will help you to strengthen your presentation and control every aspect of it, persuade the audience and sell your idea.

2 **PRESENTATION ASSESSMENT CANVAS**

Every presentation is based on 3 fundamental pillars: Communication Flow, Visual Contents and Public Speaking. The PAC enables you to track strengths and weaknesses of each pillar in order to identify the fixes and reinforce your presentation.

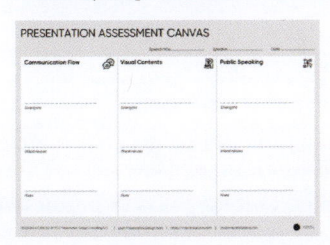

3 **2 WEEKS OF FREE TRIAL OF MLC PPT ADDIN**

Try out the proven tool to speed up your recurrent tasks in PowerPoint and get faster team results while maintaining incredible accuracy level.

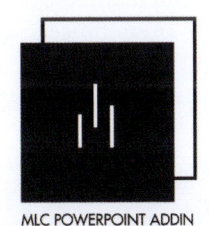

4 **HOW TO SELL YOUR IDEA WITH A PRESENTATION (GUIDE)**

In this guide you will find useful tips of how to construct your presentation in the best way to undoubtedly build the credibility of your audience, keeping their attention and making your messages pass through.

BIBLIOGRAPHY

- Andrew V. Abela, The Presentation: A Story About Communicating Successfully With Very Few Slides, 2010
- Andrew V. Abela, Advanced Presentations by Design: Creating Communication that Drives Action, 2013
- Andrew V. Abela, Encyclopedia of Slide Layouts: Inspiration for Visual Communication, 2014
- Branson R., DotCom Secrets: The Underground Playbook for Growing Your Company Online, Morgan James Publishing, 2015
- Branson R., Expert Secrets: The Underground Playbook for Creating a Mass Movement of People Who Will Pay for Your Advice, Morgan James Publishing, 2017
- Cialdini R., The Psychology of Persuasion, 2003
- Coughter P., The art of the pitch, Palgrave Macmillan, 2012
- Damasio A., Descartes' Error: Emotion, Reason, and the Human Brain, Penguin Books, 2005
- Dr. Abela A., The Presentation, CreateSpace Independent Publishing, 2010
- Duarte N. Slideology - The Art and Science of Creating Great Presentations, 2008
- Duarte N. Reasonate - Present visual storied that transform the audiences, Wiley, 2010
- Fitzpatrick R., The mom test, CreateSpace Independent Publishing, 2013
- Gaskings R., Sweating Bullets, 2012, Vinland Books
- Kawasaki G., The art of start, Penguin Group USA Inc., 2004
- Kawasaki G., Reality check, Penguin Group USA Inc., 2011
- La Cava M., Startup pitch. Come presentare un'idea e convincere gli investitori a finanziarla, 2018
- Patel N., Puri R., The Complete guide to understanding consumer psychology
- Paul D. MacLean, Evoluzione del cervello e comportamento umano, Einaudi, 1984
- Pirotta L., Strategie e tattiche di neuromarketing per aziende e professionisti, Flaccovio Editore, 2019
- Roam D., The Back of the Napkin (Expanded Edition): Solving Problems and Selling Ideas with Pictures, Portfolio; Expanded edition, 2013
- Rosenzweig P., The Halo Effect, 2014
- Saletti A., Neuromarketing e scienze cognitive per vendere di più sul web, Flaccovio Editore, 2019
- Sinek S., How great leaders inspire everyone to take action, Green Penguin, 2009
- Reynolds G., Presentation Zen: Simple Ideas on Presentation Design and Delivery (2nd Edition) (Voices That Matter), 2011
- Reynolds G., Presentation Zen Design A simple visual approach to presenting in today's world (Graphic Design & Visual Communication Courses)
- Reynolds G., The Naked Presenter: Delivering Powerful Presentations With or Without Slides (Voices That Matter), 2010
- V.A. Kral; Paul D. MacLean, A Triune concept of the brain and behaviour, Univ. of Toronto Press, 1973
- Walker Jeff, Launch: An Internet Millionaire's Secret Formula To Sell Almost Anything Online, Build A Business You Love,
- And Live The Life Of Your Dreams, Morgan James Publishing, 2014

SITOGRAPHY

- http://mag.ispo.com/2015/01/90-percent-of-all-purchasing-decisions-are-made-subconsciously/?lang=en
- Chris Anderson: Il segreto di un grande intervento TED | TED Talk
- R. Cialdini on the importance of reciprocity: https://www.youtube.com/watch?v=tkyGOAWoYxA
- https://www.influenceatwork.com/principles-of-persuasion/
- How To Begin Your Presentation with Simon Sinek | https://www.youtube.com/watch?v=e80BbX05D7Y
- https://www.zeroseven.com.au/Blog/2018/March/Design-for-the-Brain
- https://www.apple.com/macbook-air/
- https://www.uber.com/es/en/
- https://www.sequoiacap.com/article/how-to-present-to-investors/
- https://www.ted.com/talks/jorge_soto_the_future_of_early_cancer_detection
- https://extremepresentation.com
- https://www.linkedin.com/pulse/20140813103409-1146575-here-s-looking-at-you/

UNIVERSITY PAPERS AND ARTICLES

• Bechara A., Damasio H., Damasio A., Emotion, decision making and the orbitofrontal cortex, Department of Neurology, Division of behavioral Neurology and Cognitive Neuroscience, University of Iowa College of Medicine, Iowa City, USA, 2000

• Conger J. A., The Necessary Art of Persuasion, Harvard Business Review, 1998

• Garner R., What's in a Name? Persuasion Perhaps, Sam Houston State University, Journal of Consumer Psychology, 2005

• Garner Randy, Name similarity and persuasion, Sam Houston State University

• Elsbach K, How to pitch a brilliant idea, University of California, Davis, 2003

• Hellman T., Financial projections for startups, University of Oxford, 2014

• Jason A. Colquitt, Brent A. Scott, and Jeffery A. LePine, Trust, Trustworthiness, and Trust propensity: A Meta-Analytic Test of Their Unique Relationships With Risk Taking and Job Performance, University of Florida, 2006

• Natasha D.Tidwell, Paul W. Eastwick, Eli J. Finkel, Perceived, not actual, similarity predicts initial attraction in a live romantic context: Evidence from the speed-dating paradigm, Texas A&M University and Northwestern University, 2012

• Peterson R., The neuroscience of investing: fMRI of the reward system, Brain Research Bulletin, 2005

• Robert Fantz, Visual Preference Paradigm, 1961, Case Western Reserve University

• Smith, John Thomas, Remarks on rural scenery: with twenty etchings of cottages, from nature: and some observations and precepts relative to the picturesque, 1766-1833; Downes, J. (Joseph), d. 1830

• The picture superiority effect in recognition memory: A developmental study using the response signal procedure, Margaret Anne Defeyter, Riccardo Russo, Pamela Louise Graham

Printed in Great Britain
by Amazon